Praise for *Scaling Machine Learning with Spark*

If there is one book the Spark community has been craving for the last decade, it's this. Writing about the combination of Spark and AI requires broad knowledge, a deep technical skillset, and the ability to break down complex concepts so they're easy to understand. Adi delivers all of this and more while covering big data, AI, and everything in between.

—*Andy Petrella, founder at Kensu and author of*
Fundamentals of Data Observability *(O'Reilly)*

Scaling Machine Learning with Spark is a wealth of knowledge for data and ML practitioners, providing a holistic and creative approach to building end-to-end scalable machine learning solutions. The author's expertise and knowledge, combined with a focus on collaboration and understanding, makes this book a must-read for anyone in the industry.

—*Noah Gift, Duke executive in residence*

Adi's book is without any doubt a good reference and resource to have beside you when working with Spark and distributed ML. You will learn best practices she has to share along with her experience working in the industry for many years. Worth the investment and time reading it.

—*Laura Uzcategui, machine learning engineer at TalentBait*

This book is an amazing synthesis of knowledge and experience. I consider it essential reading for both novice and veteran machine learning engineers. Readers will deepen their understanding of general principles for machine learning in distributed systems while simultaneously engaging with the technical details required to integrate and scale the most widely used tools of the trade including Spark, PyTorch, Tensorflow.

—*Matthew Housley, CTO and coauthor of* Fundamentals of
Data Engineering *(O'Reilly)*

Adi's done a wonderful job at creating a very readable, practical, and insanely detailed deep dive into machine learning with Spark.

—*Joe Reis, coauthor of* Fundamentals of Data Engineering
(O'Reilly) and "recovering data scientist"

Scaling Machine Learning
with Spark
Distributed ML with MLlib,
TensorFlow, and PyTorch

Adi Polak

Beijing · Boston · Farnham · Sebastopol · Tokyo

Scaling Machine Learning with Spark

by Adi Polak

Copyright © 2023 Adi Polak. All rights reserved.

Published by O'Reilly Media, Inc., 1005 Gravenstein Highway North, Sebastopol, CA 95472.

O'Reilly books may be purchased for educational, business, or sales promotional use. Online editions are also available for most titles (*https://oreilly.com*). For more information, contact our corporate/institutional sales department: 800-998-9938 or *corporate@oreilly.com*.

Acquisitions Editor: Nicole Butterfield
Development Editor: Jill Leonard
Production Editor: Jonathon Owen
Copyeditor: Rachel Head
Proofreader: Piper Editorial Consulting, LLC

Indexer: Potomac Indexing, LLC
Interior Designer: David Futato
Cover Designer: Karen Montgomery
Illustrator: Kate Dullea

March 2023:   First Edition

Revision History for the First Edition
2023-03-02:   First Release

See *http://oreilly.com/catalog/errata.csp?isbn=9781098106829* for release details.

978-1-098-10682-9

[LSI]

Table of Contents

Preface

Welcome to *Scaling Machine Learning with Spark: Distributed ML with MLlib, Tensor-Flow, and PyTorch*. This book aims to guide you in your journey as you learn more about machine learning (ML) systems. Apache Spark is currently the most popular framework for large-scale data processing. It has numerous APIs implemented in Python, Java, and Scala and is used by many powerhouse companies, including Netflix, Microsoft, and Apple. PyTorch and TensorFlow are among the most popular frameworks for machine learning. Combining these tools, which are already in use in many organizations today, allows you to take full advantage of their strengths.

Before we get started, though, perhaps you are wondering why I decided to write this book. Good question. There are two reasons. The first is to support the machine learning ecosystem and community by sharing the knowledge, experience, and expertise I have accumulated over the last decade working as a machine learning algorithm researcher, designing and implementing algorithms to run on large-scale data. I have spent most of my career working as a data infrastructure engineer, building infrastructure for large-scale analytics with all sorts of formatting, types, schemas, etc., and integrating knowledge collected from customers, community members, and colleagues who have shared their experience while brainstorming and developing solutions. Our industry can use such knowledge to propel itself forward at a faster rate, by leveraging the expertise of others. While not all of this book's content will be applicable to everyone, much of it will open up new approaches for a wide array of practitioners.

This brings me to my second reason for writing this book: I want to provide a holistic approach to building end-to-end scalable machine learning solutions that extends beyond the traditional approach. Today, many solutions are customized to the specific requirements of the organization and specific business goals. This will most likely continue to be the industry norm for many years to come. In this book, I aim to challenge the status quo and inspire more creative solutions while explaining the pros and cons of multiple approaches and tools, enabling you to leverage whichever tools are used in your organization and get the best of all worlds. My overall goal is to make it simpler for data and machine learning practitioners to collaborate and understand each other better.

Who Should Read This Book?

This book is designed for machine learning practitioners with previous industry experience who want to learn about Apache Spark's MLlib and increase their understanding of the overall system and flow. It will be particularly relevant to data scientists and machine learning engineers, but MLOps engineers, software engineers, and anyone interested in learning about or building distributed machine learning models and building pipelines with MLlib, distributed PyTorch, and TensorFlow will also find value. Technologists who understand high-level concepts of working with machine learning and want to dip their feet into the technical side as well should also find the book interesting and accessible.

Do You Need Distributed Machine Learning?

As with every good thing, it depends. If you have small datasets that fit into your machine's memory, the answer is no. If at some point you will need to scale out your code and make sure you can train a model on a larger dataset that does not fit into a single machine's memory, then yes.

It is often better to use the same tools across the software development lifecycle, from the local development environment to staging and production. Take into consideration, though, that this also introduces other complexities involved in managing a distributed system, which typically will be handled by a different team in your organization. It's a good idea to have a common language to collaborate with your colleagues.

Also, one of the greatest challenges people who create machine learning models face today is moving them from local development all the way to production. Many of us sin with spaghetti code that should be reproducible but often is not and is hard to maintain and collaborate on. I will touch upon that topic as part of the discussion of managing the lifecycle of experiments.

Navigating This Book

This book is designed to build from foundational information in the first few chapters, covering the machine learning workflow using Apache Spark and PySpark and managing the machine learning experiment lifecycle with MLflow, to bridging into a dedicated machine learning platform in Chapters 7, 8, and 9. The book concludes with a look at deployment patterns, inference, and monitoring of models in production. Here's a breakdown of what you will find in each chapter:

Chapter 1, "Distributed Machine Learning Terminology and Concepts"

This chapter provides a high-level introduction to machine learning and covers terminology and concepts related to distributed computing and network topologies. I will walk you through various concepts and terms, so you have a strong foundation for the next chapters.

Chapter 2, "Introduction to Spark and PySpark"

The goal of this chapter is to bring you up to speed on Spark and its Python library, PySpark. We'll discuss terminology, software abstractions, and more.

Chapter 3, "Managing the Machine Learning Experiment Lifecycle with MLflow"

This chapter introduces MLflow, a platform that facilitates managing the machine learning lifecycle. We'll discuss what a machine learning experiment is and why managing its lifecycle is important, and we'll examine the various components of MLflow that make this possible.

Chapter 4, "Data Ingestion, Preprocessing, and Descriptive Statistics"

Next, we will dive into working with data. In this chapter, I will discuss how to use Spark to ingest your data, perform basic preprocessing (using image files as an example), and get a feel for the data. I'll also cover how to avoid the so-called small file problem with image files by leveraging the PySpark API.

Chapter 5, "Feature Engineering"

Once you've performed the steps in the previous chapter, you're ready to engineer the features you will use to train your machine learning model. This chapter explains in detail what feature engineering is, covering various types, and showcases how to leverage Spark's functionality for extracting features. We'll also look at how and when to use `applyInPandas` and `pandas_udf` to optimize performance.

Chapter 6, "Training Models with Spark MLlib"

This chapter walks you through working with MLlib to train a model, evaluate and build a pipeline to reproduce the model, and finally persist it to disk.

Chapter 7, "Bridging Spark and Deep Learning Frameworks"

This chapter breaks down how to build a data system to combine the power of Spark with deep learning frameworks. It discusses bridging Spark and deep learning clusters and provides an introduction to Petastorm, Horovod, and the Spark initiative Project Hydrogen.

Chapter 8, "TensorFlow Distributed Machine Learning Approach"

Here, I'll lead you through a step-by-step example of working with distributed TensorFlow—specifically `tf.keras`—while leveraging the preprocessing you've done with Spark. You will also learn about the various TensorFlow patterns for scaling machine learning and the component architectures that support it.

Chapter 9, "PyTorch Distributed Machine Learning Approach"
> This chapter covers the PyTorch approach to scaling machine learning, including its internal architecture. We will walk through a step-by-step example of working with distributed PyTorch while leveraging the preprocessing you did with Spark in previous chapters.

Chapter 10, "Deployment Patterns for Machine Learning Models"
> In this chapter, I present the various deployment patterns available to us, including batch and streaming inference with Spark and MLflow, and provide examples of using the pyfunc functionality in MLflow that allows us to deploy just about any machine learning model. This chapter also covers monitoring and implementing a production machine learning system in phases.

What Is Not Covered

There are many ways to go about distributed machine learning. Some involve running multiple experiments in parallel, with multiple hyperparameters, on data that has been loaded into memory. You might be able to load the dataset into a single machine's memory, or it may be so large that it has to be partitioned across multiple machines. We will briefly discuss grid search, a technique for finding the optimal values for a set of hyperparameters, but this book will only extend that far.

This book does *not* cover the following topics:

An introduction to machine learning algorithms
> There are many wonderful books that go into depth on the various machine learning algorithms and their uses, and this book won't repeat them.

Deploying models to mobile or embedded devices
> This often requires working with TinyML and dedicated algorithms to shrink the size of the final model (which may initially be created from a large dataset).

TinyML
> TinyML is focused on building relatively small machine learning models that can run on resource-constrained devices. To learn about this topic, check out *TinyML* (*https://oreil.ly/tinyML*) by Peter Warden and Daniel Situnayake (O'Reilly).

Online learning
> Online learning is used when the data is generated as a function of time or when the machine learning algorithm needs to adapt dynamically to new patterns in the data. It's also used when training over the entire dataset is computationally infeasible, requiring out-of-core algorithms. This is a fundamentally different way of approaching machine learning with specialized applications, and it is not covered in this book.

Parallel experiments

> While the tools discussed in this book, such as PyTorch and TensorFlow, enable us to conduct parallel experiments, this book will focus solely on parallel data training, where the logic stays the same, and each machine processes a different chunk of the data.

This is not an exhaustive list—since all roads lead to distribution in one way or another, I might have forgotten to mention some topics here, or new ones may have gained traction in the industry since the time of writing. As mentioned previously, my aim is to share my perspective, given my accumulated experience and knowledge in the field of machine learning, and to equip others with a holistic approach to use in their own endeavors; it is my intention to cover as many of the key points as possible to provide a foundation, and I encourage you to explore further to deepen your understanding of the topics discussed here.

The Environment and Tools

Now that you understand the topics that will (and won't) be covered, it's time to set up your tutorial environment. You'll be using various platforms and libraries together to develop a machine learning pipeline as you work through the exercises in this book.

The Tools

This section briefly introduces the tools that we will use to build the solutions discussed in this book. If you aren't familiar with them, you may want to review their documentation before getting started. To implement the code samples provided in the book on your own machine, you will need to have the following tools installed locally:

Apache Spark

> A general-purpose, large-scale analytics engine for data processing.

PySpark

> An interface for Apache Spark in Python.

PyTorch

> A machine learning framework developed by Facebook, based on the Torch library, used for computer vision and natural language processing applications. We will use its distributed training capabilities.

TensorFlow

> A platform for machine learning pipelines developed by Google. We will use its distributed training capabilities.

MLflow

An open source platform for managing the machine learning lifecycle. We will use it to manage the experiments in this book.

Petastorm

A library that enables distributed training and evaluation of deep learning models using datasets in Apache Parquet format. Petastorm supports machine learning frameworks such as TensorFlow and PyTorch. We will use it to bridge between Spark and a deep learning cluster.

Horovod

A distributed training framework for TensorFlow, Keras, PyTorch, and Apache MXNet. This project aims to support developers in scaling a single-GPU training script to train across many GPUs in parallel. We will use it both to optimize workloads over multiple GPUs and to coordinate the distributed systems of a Spark cluster and a deep learning cluster, which requires a dedicated distributed system scheduler to manage the cluster resources and enable them to work together using the same hardware.

NumPy

A Python library for scientific computing that enables efficient performance of various types of operations on arrays (mathematical, logical, shape manipulation, sorting, selecting, I/O, and more). We will use it for various statistical and mathematical operations that can be done on a single machine.

PIL

The Python Imaging Library, also known as Pillow (*https://oreil.ly/V2V2j*). We will use this for working with images.

In today's ecosystem, new tools in the space of machine learning and distributed data are emerging every day. History has taught us that some of them will stick around and others won't. Keep an eye out for the tools that are already used in your workplace, and try to exhaust their capabilities before jumping into introducing new ones.

The Datasets

In this book's examples, we will leverage existing datasets where practical and produce dedicated datasets when necessary to better convey the message. The datasets listed here, all available on Kaggle (*https://www.kaggle.com*), are used throughout the book and are included in the accompanying GitHub repository (*https://oreil.ly/smls-git*):

Caltech 256 dataset

Caltech 256 (*https://oreil.ly/Ns9uy*) is an extension of the Caltech 101 dataset (*https://oreil.ly/1jgcC*), which contains pictures of objects in 101 categories. The Caltech 256 dataset contains 30,607 images of objects spanning 257 categories.

The categories are extremely diverse, ranging from tennis shoes to zebras, and there are images with and without backgrounds and in horizontal and vertical orientations. Most categories have about 100 images, but some have as many as 800.

CO_2 Emission by Vehicles dataset
The CO_2 Emission by Vehicles dataset (*https://oreil.ly/akVrk*) is based on seven years' worth of data about vehicular CO_2 emissions from the Government of Canada's Open Data website. There are 7,385 rows and 12 columns (make, model, transmission, etc., as well as CO_2 emissions and various fuel consumption measures).

Zoo Animal Classification dataset
For learning about the statistics functions available in the MLlib library, we will use the Zoo Animal Classification dataset (*https://oreil.ly/lPqbv*). It consists of 101 animals, with 16 Boolean-valued attributes used to describe them. The animals can be classified into seven types: Mammal, Bird, Reptile, Fish, Amphibian, Bug, and Invertebrate. I chose it because it's fun and relatively simple to grasp.

If you're working through the tutorials on your local machine, I recommend using the sample datasets provided in the book's GitHub repo.

Conventions Used in This Book

The following typographical conventions are used in this book:

Italic
Indicates new terms, URLs, file and directory names, and file extensions.

`Constant width`
Used for command-line input/output and code examples, as well as for code elements that appear in the text, including variable and function names, classes, and modules.

`Constant width italic`
Shows text to be replaced with user-supplied values in code examples and commands.

`Constant width bold`
Shows commands or other text that should be typed literally by the user.

This element signifies a tip or suggestion.

This element signifies a general note.

This element indicates a warning or caution.

Using Code Examples

Supplemental material (code examples, exercises, etc.) is available for download at *https://oreil.ly/smls-git*.

This book is here to help you get your job done. In general, if example code is offered with this book, you may use it in your programs and documentation. You do not need to contact us for permission unless you're reproducing a significant portion of the code. For example, writing a program that uses several chunks of code from this book does not require permission. Selling or distributing a CD-ROM of examples from O'Reilly books does require permission. Answering a question by citing this book and quoting example code does not require permission. Incorporating a significant amount of example code from this book into your product's documentation does require permission.

We appreciate, but do not require, attribution. An attribution usually includes the title, author, publisher, and ISBN. For example: "*Scaling Machine Learning with Spark*, by Adi Polak. Copyright 2023 by Adi Polak, 978-1-098-10682-9."

If you feel your use of code examples falls outside fair use or the permission given above, feel free to contact us at *permissions@oreilly.com*.

O'Reilly Online Learning

For more than 40 years, *O'Reilly Media* has provided technology and business training, knowledge, and insight to help companies succeed.

Our unique network of experts and innovators share their knowledge and expertise through books, articles, and our online learning platform. O'Reilly's online learning platform gives you on-demand access to live training courses, in-depth learning paths, interactive coding environments, and a vast collection of text and video from O'Reilly and 200+ other publishers. For more information, visit *https://oreilly.com*.

How to Contact Us

Please address comments and questions concerning this book to the publisher:

O'Reilly Media, Inc.
1005 Gravenstein Highway North
Sebastopol, CA 95472
800-998-9938 (in the United States or Canada)
707-829-0515 (international or local)
707-829-0104 (fax)

We have a web page for this book, where we list errata, examples, and any additional information. You can access this page at *https://oreil.ly/sml-spark*.

Email *bookquestions@oreilly.com* to comment or ask technical questions about this book.

For news and information about our books and courses, visit *https://oreilly.com*.

Find us on LinkedIn: *https://linkedin.com/company/oreilly-media*.

Follow us on Twitter: *https://twitter.com/oreillymedia*.

Watch us on YouTube: *https://youtube.com/oreillymedia*.

Acknowledgments

The book wouldn't exist without the support of the Spark, data engineering, and machine learning communities. It truly takes a village to bring a technical book to life, so thank you so much for your help!

Thanks to all the early readers and reviewers for all your help and advice: Holden Karau, Amitai Stern, Andy Petrella, Joe Reis, Laura Uzcátegui, Noah Gift, Kyle Gallatin, Parviz Deyhim, Sean Owen, Chitra Agastya, Kyle Hamilton, Terry McCann, Joseph Kambourakis, Marc Ramirez Invernon, Bartosz Konieczny, Beegee Alop, and many others.

Any remaining mistakes are the author's fault, sometimes against the advice of the reviewers.

Last, I would like to express my gratitude to my life partner for putting up with my long nights, early mornings, holidays, and weekends writing.

## CHAPTER 1

Distributed Machine Learning Terminology and Concepts

Remember when data scientists ran their machine learning algorithms on datasets that fit in a laptop's memory? Or generated their own data? It wasn't because of a lack of data in the world; we had already entered the Zettabyte Era. For many, the data was there, but it was locked in the production systems that created, captured, copied, and processed data at a massive scale. Data scientists knew that gaining access to it would allow them to produce better, more profound machine learning models. But this wasn't the only problem—what about computation? In many cases, data scientists didn't have access to sufficient computation power or tools to support running machine learning algorithms on large datasets. Because of this, they had to sample their data and work with CSV or text files.

When the public cloud revolution occurred around 2016–2017, we could finally get hold of that desired computation capacity. All we needed was a credit card in one hand and a computer mouse in the other. One click of a button and boom, hundreds of machines were available to us! But we still lacked the proper open source tools to process huge amounts of data. There was a need for distributed compute and for automated tools with a healthy ecosystem.

The growth in *digitalization*, where businesses use digital technologies to change their business model and create new revenue streams and value-producing opportunities, increased data scientists' frustration. Digitalization led to larger amounts of data being available, but data scientists couldn't work with that data fast enough because

---

1 Depending on how you define it, this era of computer science history began in either 2012 or 2016—the amount of digital data estimated to exist in the world exceeded 1 zettabyte in 2012, and Cisco Systems announced that global IP traffic hit 1.2 zettabytes in 2016.

they didn't have the tools. The tedious process of waiting for days to try out one machine learning algorithm or to get a sample of production data blocked many from reaching their full potential. The need to improve and automate grew.

Small companies saw how larger ones had demonstrated a positive impact on their business by providing automated, personalized solutions to their customers, improving sentiment and boosting revenue. From a fantasy, machine learning became a hot commodity. Companies understood that to take advantage of it they would need more tools, and dedicated teams to build those tools in house, which in turn increased the demand for engineers to build reliable, scalable, accelerated, and high-performance tools to support machine learning workloads.

Netflix, the world-leading internet television network that streams hundreds of millions of hours of content daily, has stated that it uses machine learning pervasively, across all aspects of the business. This includes recommending personalized content for customers, optimizing the movie and show production processes in the Netflix studios, optimizing video and audio encoding, and improving advertising spending and ad creativity to reach new potential customers.

Machine learning has found applications in a broad array of industries, however, not just in technology-focused businesses. Data scientists and analytics teams at the multinational oil and gas company Shell plc leverage machine learning over large-scale datasets to support the business with insights regarding product opportunities and process optimizations and to test the effectiveness of different courses of action. One example is their inventory prediction model, which runs over 10,000 simulations (*https://oreil.ly/pgrJZ*) across all parts and facilities, predicting demand and improving stocking. Shell also uses machine learning to power a recommendation engine for its customer loyalty program, Go+, which offers personalized offers and rewards to individual customers. This approach provides Shell with an enhanced engagement model that helps retain customers by catering to their specific needs.

Other industries use machine learning for fraud detection, recommendation systems, patient diagnosis, and more. Take a look at Figure 1-1 to get an idea of how you may be able to drive innovation using machine learning in your industry.

As these examples suggest, the ability to use large datasets to create solutions with proven business impact has been eye-opening for many companies looking to grow their business and improve revenue.

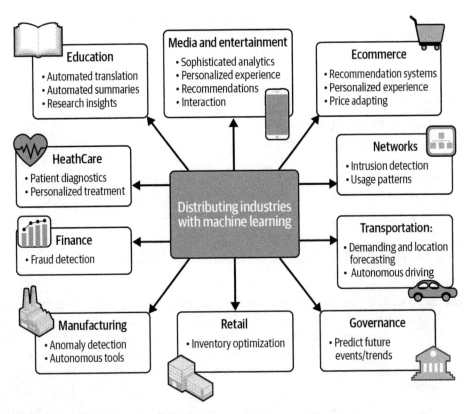

Figure 1-1. Some of the many uses of machine learning across industries

The computer science and engineering research communities have helped greatly in enabling scalable machine learning. In recent years, academic researchers have conducted hundreds if not thousands of studies on using machine learning, distributed computation, and databases and building smarter, more efficient algorithms to support distributed machine learning. As a result, general-purpose distributed platforms have emerged, such as the immensely popular Apache Spark. Apache Spark provides a scalable, general-purpose engine for analytics and machine learning workloads. At the same time, the teams behind various machine learning libraries built to support workloads on a single machine are tirelessly adding backend support for executing in a distributed setting. To list a few examples, additional capabilities to support distributed machine learning have been added to Google's TensorFlow, which simplifies deep neural network workloads, and Facebook's PyTorch, used for computer vision and natural language processing.

Throughout this book, we'll focus on using Apache Spark, and I will show you how to bridge from it into distributed machine learning with TensorFlow and PyTorch. The book concludes with a discussion of machine learning deployment patterns in

Chapter 10. To get you started, this chapter provides an introduction to the fundamental concepts, terminology, and building blocks of distributed machine learning. We will cover the basics of the following:

- The machine learning workflow
- Spark MLlib
- Distributed computing
- Distributed systems

Familiar with those concepts? We'll shift to an introduction to Spark and PySpark in Chapter 2 and managing the machine learning lifecycle in Chapter 3.

Excited? Let's dive in!

The Stages of the Machine Learning Workflow

Many applications today are driven by machine learning, using machine learning models to answer questions such as: How can my application automatically adapt itself to the customer's needs? How can I automate this tedious process to enable my employees to do more with their time? How can I make sense of my pile of data without spending the whole year going over it? However, as data practitioners, we have just one question to answer: How can we enable the process to answer those questions?

The short answer is machine learning. A more comprehensive response is the machine learning workflow.

The machine learning workflow comprises a set of stages that help us reach the goal of having a machine learning model running in production solving a business problem. What is a machine learning model? Good question! A machine learning model is the output of a machine learning algorithm. From now on, we will refer to it simply as a model. The automation of this workflow is referred to as the machine learning pipeline. To improve the accuracy of the model, the workflow is iterative. This allows us to exercise complete control over the model—including automation, monitoring, and deployment—and its output.

The machine learning workflows consist of multiple stages, some of which can be skipped and some of which may be repeated:

1. *Collect and load/ingest data.* The first stage is to collect the data required for the process and load it into the environment where you will execute your machine learning experiment.

2. *Explore and validate the data.* Next, explore the data you have collected and evaluate its quality. This stage often involves statistical testing of how well the

training data represents real-world events, its distribution, and the variety in the dataset. This is also referred to as *exploratory data analysis* (EDA).

3. *Clean/preprocess the data.* After stage 2, you might reach the conclusion that the data is *noisy*. A noisy dataset is one with columns that do not contribute to the training at all—for example, rows with null values, or long string values. They require more processing power but don't improve model accuracy. In this stage, data scientists will run statistical tests on the data to validate the correlation between features and analyze which features provide value as is, which require more preprocessing or engineering, and which are redundant.

4. *Extract features/perform feature engineering.* The previous stage outputs the data columns as features. These are the descriptors of the data, used as the inputs to the machine learning model. Features in machine learning are often external to the original data, meaning we need to enrich the existing data with data from other sources. That requires us to develop the code to compute and produce these features and enrich the dataset with them before training the model. There are many ways to do this, and it often requires domain expertise. Alternatively, the features may already be present in another dataset, in which case all we need to do is merge the two datasets into one before training the model.

5. *Split the data into a training set and a validation set.* The training set is used for training the machine learning model, and the validation set is for evaluating the performance of the model on unseen data.

6. *Train and tune the model.* Feed the training data to the machine learning algorithm, and adjust the parameters to improve performance. Validate the outcome using the dedicated validation dataset. The validation process takes place in the development environment, either locally on your machine or in a development/experimentation environment in the cloud. The outcome of this stage is the model.

7. *Evaluate the model with test data.* This is the last testing stage before the model is pushed to production. In this stage, you again measure the model's performance on previously unseen data, this time testing it in a production-like setting. After this stage, you might want to go back and revisit stage 6.

8. *Deploy the model.* During this stage, data scientists together with machine learning and production engineers package the model and deploy it to production with all its requirements.

9. *Monitor the model.* In production, the model must constantly be monitored for drift (different types of drift are discussed in Chapter 10). It is crucial to continually evaluate the model's value to the business and know when to replace it.

Each of these stages is repeatable on its own, and it may be that given a specific result you will want to complete the whole process again. For example, in the case of model drift, the data and the model are not representative of the business problem, and you will need to start the process over from the beginning.

Each stage is unique and highly dependent on the data, the system requirements, your knowledge, the algorithms in use, the existing infrastructure, and the desired outcome.

Stages 3 to 6 are often considered the experimental phase of machine learning. You will want to iterate repeatedly and produce multiple versions of the data and the model until you find the best version of the model.

To learn more about machine learning workflows and automating them using pipelines with TensorFlow and TensorBoard, read *Building Machine Learning Pipelines* (*https://oreil.ly/building-ml*) by Hannes Hapke and Catherine Nelson (O'Reilly).

Tools and Technologies in the Machine Learning Pipeline

Figure 1-2 shows an overview of the machine learning pipeline and some of the tools that may be used in each stage.

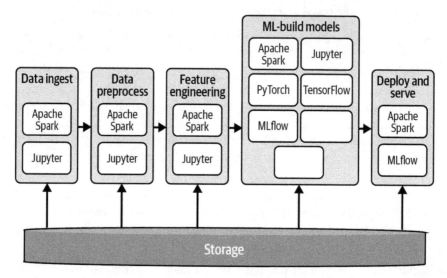

Figure 1-2. A high-level view of the machine learning pipeline and tools used in each stage

We'll use various tools and platforms in the tutorials in this book to complete the different stages (you can, of course, decide to replace any of these tools with a different tool of your choice). For experimenting with data ingestion, preprocessing, and feature engineering, we will use Jupyter, which provides a UI and a backend server. We'll write the code in a notebook in the UI, and the backend will package it and send it over to the Spark engine.

In the model-building stage (corresponding to stages 6 and 7 in the machine learning workflow described earlier), we train, validate, and tune the model. We will use multiple servers and backends in this stage, including Jupyter, PyTorch, TensorFlow, Horovod, Petastorm, and MLflow, to orchestrate operations, cache the data, and transition the workflow from a Spark cluster to a deep learning cluster.

Finally, to deploy and serve our models, we will use Spark and MLflow. We'll load the model from the MLflow storage server and serve it with Spark or as a REST API with a Python function.

 In most organizations, developing an end-to-end machine learning pipeline requires a dedicated team whose members have various sets of skills, as well as an integrated development environment (IDE) like PyCharm that provides rich developer tools and code autocompletion, dedicated scripts for continuous integration/ continuous deployment (CI/CD), and much more. For the educational purposes of this book, we'll stick to Jupyter notebooks.

Different Ways to Scale

You're probably wondering how to execute the machine learning workflow given a large dataset. For that, there are two terms you should know: *machine learning at scale* and *distributed machine learning*. With distributed machine learning, we make use of a multinode machine learning system to execute the workflow. With machine learning at scale, we operationalize serving the model so it can scale to meet the demands of the applications that consume it.

There are two practical, complementary ways to scale computation capacity:

Scaling vertically (aka scaling up)
  This involves adding dedicated hardware with greater processing capacity on the existing machine(s). For example, you might add a programmable GPU to speed up computation on a single node/machine.

Scaling horizontally (aka scaling out)
  This involves adding more nodes/machines and creating a distributed topology of nodes that compute workloads in a shared manner.

While machine learning at scale can be accomplished with either method of scaling, distributed machine learning training with Spark is fundamentally based on scaling out using distributed system topologies. Perhaps you're thinking, "I can train and infer with a more powerful GPU/TPU processor and scale vertically." While it's often the case that we have access to a GPU during training, when serving the model in production and using it for inference, we often don't. We will discuss this issue in more detail in Chapter 10, where you will learn about deploying and monitoring machine learning models in production.

Distributed Computing Models

Distributed computing is the use of *distributed systems*, where multiple machines work together as a single unit, to solve a computational problem. A program that runs inside such a system is called a *distributed program*, and the process of writing such a program is known as *distributed programming*. That's what we'll be doing in this book. Our goal is to find the best way to divide a problem into separate tasks that multiple machines can solve in parallel through message communication. There are different distributed computing models for machine learning, and we can categorize these into two groups: *general-purpose* models that we can tweak to support distributed machine learning applications, and *dedicated* computing models specifically designed for running machine learning algorithms.

General-Purpose Models

General-purpose distributed computing models allow users to write a custom data processing flow using a defined abstraction. Apache Spark is a general-purpose distributed computing engine that, at its heart, implements the MapReduce programming model and has more recently been extended to support the barrier model. You'll learn about both of those in this section, as well as some other distributed computing models (MPI [Message Passing Interface] and shared memory) that are available with TensorFlow and PyTorch.

MapReduce

The MapReduce programming model was inspired by the functional programming paradigm (*https://oreil.ly/YrPPz*). Google introduced the MapReduce algorithm in 2004, in a research paper discussing how its search engine processes large-scale data. As developers or data science practitioners, we specify a *map* function that processes a key/value pair to generate a set of intermediate key/value pairs and a *reduce* function that merges all the intermediate values associated with the same intermediate key. This approach is an extension of the split-apply-combine strategy for data analysis. In practice, every task is split into multiple map and reduce functions. Data is partitioned and distributed over various nodes/machines, and each chunk of data is processed on a dedicated node. Many solutions aim to preserve data locality as much as possible, where the partitioned data is local to the node processing it. A logic function is applied to the data on that node, then a shuffle operation of moving the data over the network is performed to combine the data from the different nodes, and a reduce operation is performed on the combined output from the mappers.

If necessary, another split-apply-combine round can then be performed on the output of the reducer. Examples of open source solutions that implement these concepts in one way or another include Apache Spark, Hadoop MapReduce, and Apache Flink. We'll talk about the MapReduce model in more detail throughout the book.

MPI

Another interesting general-purpose distributed computing model is the Message Passing Interface (MPI) programming model. This is the most flexible model available today, and it was designed for high-performance, scalable, and portable distributed computing. MPI is a message passing interface that models a parallel program running on a distributed-memory system. It standardizes the communication between a set of processors by defining the data types that can be sent between the processors. Each processor has a unique identifier, and each *communicator* is a set of processors ordered in a specific topology. MPI is a low-level standard that can be implemented in hardware, compilers, wrappers, etc. Different versions of it have been implemented commercially by HP, Intel, Microsoft, and others.

MPI provides functions like `MPI_Bcast`, which broadcasts a message to all processors in the communicator, sharing the data; `MPI_Alltoall`, which sends all data to all nodes; and `MPI_Reduce` and `MPI_Allreduce`, which are similar to MapReduce and Apache Spark's `reduce` functions. You can think of the interface as a set of building blocks for distributed frameworks that provides functionality for distributed machine learning.

The downside of MPI lies in its low-level permissiveness. It can be pretty labor-intensive and error-prone to execute and implement complex operations with MPI; it requires explicitly managing data type distribution, sending and receiving functionality, and fault tolerance and generally demands the developer to think about distributed arrays, data frames, hash tables, trees, etc. MPI is often used for deep learning workloads. Horovod's core functions are based on MPI concepts, such as `size`, `rank`, `local_rank`, `allreduce`, `allgather`, and `broadcast`. For distributed computing, TensorFlow provides support for MPI as part of its communication protocol.

Barrier

A barrier is a synchronization method that is commonly used in parallel computing and is implemented in distributed computing frameworks like Apache Spark. A task or job is split into dependent stages or subtasks that need to be completed before processing can continue in the next stage. A barrier makes a group of machines stop at a certain point and wait for the rest of the machines to finish their computation before they can move on together to the next stage of the computation logic. Barrier models can be implemented in hardware and software, and stages can take many shapes, from directed acyclic graphs (DAGs) to trees or sequential operations.

Although it is a general-purpose distributed computing model, the barrier model enables diverse distributed machine learning algorithms. For example, in deep learning, each layer in the stacked artificial neural network is a stage, and each stage's computation depends on the output of the previous stage. Barrier models enable the management of many layers of training in this case.

Shared memory

Shared memory models have a long history: they originated in operating systems like POSIX and Windows, where processes running on the same machine needed to communicate over a shared address space. Distributed shared memory models try to meet the same need when multiple nodes/users are communicating over the network in a distributed environment and require access to the same data from various machines. Today, there is no one partitioned global address space but an in-memory or fast database that provides strong consistency.

Strong consistency in a distributed shared memory environment means that all access to the data by all processes and nodes is consistent. Ensuring this is not an easy task. One of TensorFlow's distributed strategies implements a shared memory model; you will learn all about it and its pros and cons in Chapter 8.

Dedicated Distributed Computing Models

Dedicated distributed computing models are models that were developed to support a specific need in the machine learning development cycle. Often, they leverage the general-purpose models as building blocks to construct a more user-friendly framework that data science practitioners can use out of the box. You can make use of them with TensorFlow and PyTorch.

One example of a dedicated distributed computing model for machine learning workloads is a *parameter server*. TensorFlow implements this as part of its distribution strategy for training models. Parameter servers leverage the shared memory approach: you have a dedicated group of servers guaranteeing strong consistency of the data that serves the workers with consistent information. The parameters are the weights and precomputed features the machine learning algorithm requires during its training and retraining lifecycle. In some cases, the parameters can fit into one machine's memory, but in real-life use cases where there are billions of parameters, having a cluster of parameter servers is a requirement. We will look at this in more detail when we discuss the different TensorFlow distributed computing strategies in Chapter 8.

With research and industry investing heavily in distributed machine learning, it's only a matter of time until more models are developed. It's always a good practice to keep an eye out for new developments. Hopefully, by the end of this book, you will have all the tools and information you need to make an educated decision about which of the various distributed computing models to use and how to leverage it to meet your business's technological needs.

Now that you are familiar with these concepts, let's take a look at the bigger picture of distributed machine learning architecture and where each of these concepts comes into play.

Introduction to Distributed Systems Architecture

We'll begin with a brief discussion of network topologies. *Topologies* are how we organize computers to form distributed systems. We can divide them into two types: *physical* topologies that describe how the computers are arranged and connected, and *logical* topologies that describe the way data flows in the system and how the computers exchange information over the network. Multinode computer topologies are typically scaled physically by adding more computers (aka nodes).

Engineers often discuss topologies in the final architecture conversation. The architectural requirements stem from the project's goals, the data, the system's behavior, and the existing software tools that are in use. For data scientists, the main goal is to define the distributed model training methods and how the models will be deployed and served.

In some cases, you might identify a gap where the available software tools are not addressing the project's needs well enough or are too complex to integrate into your solution, and you'll need to source or develop new tools. This is an advanced scenario that we won't be addressing in this book.

The nodes that form the topology of a distributed system are connected through a network in a specific architectural pattern designed to improve the load-handling capability and optimize speed and resource use. The architectural choices that are made in the design phase will impact each node's role in the topology, how they communicate, and the overall system's resilience to failure.

As well as understanding the physical topology of a distributed system, you should be aware of the differences between centralized and decentralized systems, how the machines interact, the modes of communication that are supported, and how the system handles security and failures. You can think of these as building blocks as you design your system.

Centralized Versus Decentralized Systems

In a *centralized* system, all the nodes depend on a single node to make decisions. Such a system benefits from greater control over decisions yet is more prone to failures as the decision-making node becomes a single point of failure that can bring the whole system down.

In a *decentralized* system topology, the nodes are independent and make their own decisions. Each node stores and operates on its own data, so there is no single point of failure. This means the system is more tolerant of faults; however, it also means that the decisions made by the individual nodes need to be coordinated and reconciled.

Decentralized systems can benefit from a multicloud/hybrid cloud architecture, where machine nodes reside in different regions and with different cloud providers. An example is a network of connected Internet of Things (IoT) devices: each device is independent but shares data over the network with other devices and/or the cloud, depending on its internet connectivity. The topology you choose will affect the communication methods the devices can use and their possible roles within the network. When it comes to training models, a decentralized approach means that every model is being trained on its own. We'll talk more about the implications of this design decision later in this chapter, when we look at ensemble methods.

Interaction Models

The architecture of the interaction model defines how the nodes in a system communicate over the network, what their roles are in the system, and what responsibilities come along with those roles. We'll look at three possible architectures in this section: client/server, peer-to-peer, and geo-distributed. There are other architectures in use and in development that are not covered here, but these are the ones you are most likely to encounter.

Client/server

In the client/server interaction model, there is a clear definition of responsibilities. Tasks are divided between clients, which issue requests, and servers, which provide the responses to those requests. The role of a node can change subject to the structure and needs of the system, but this depends on whether the servers are stateless (storing no state) or stateful (storing state that the next operations are based on).

Peer-to-peer

In the peer-to-peer (P2P) interaction model, the workload is partitioned between the nodes, or peers. All nodes have equal privileges and can share information directly without relying on a dedicated central server. Every peer can be both a client and a server. This topology is more permissive and cheaper to implement, as there is no need to bind a machine to a specific responsibility. However, it does have some downsides: each node needs to have a full copy of the data, and because all data is exchanged over the network without a dedicated coordinator, multiple copies can reach the same node.

Geo-distributed

The geo-distributed interaction model is most commonly seen in geo-distributed cloud data centers. It aims to solve challenges related to issues such as data privacy and resource allocation. One concern is that the latency of peer-to-peer communication in the geo-distributed model may be high, depending on the distance between the nodes. Therefore, when developing distributed machine learning workloads based on this interaction model, we need to provide a clear definition of how the nodes communicate and in which cases. An example of when the geo-distributed interaction model is a good choice is to enable federated learning with IoT/edge devices, where data cannot be centralized in one data center. Developing a system to train a model on each device across multiple decentralized nodes and assemble the output to create one cohesive model allows us to benefit from the data insights of all the devices, without exchanging private information.

Communication in a Distributed Setting

How our nodes communicate in a distributed environment has a significant impact on failure mechanisms, security, and throughput. Communication can be synchronous or asynchronous, depending on the needs of the distributed computation model. For example, a parameter server (a dedicated machine learning computing model mentioned earlier in this chapter) can be implemented with asynchronous or synchronous communications, and TensorFlow supports both synchronous and asynchronous training for distributing training with data parallelism.

Distributing machine learning workloads across more than one machine requires partitioning the data and/or the program itself, to divide the workload evenly across all machines. The decision of whether to use asynchronous or synchronous communications between the machines affects compute time and can lead to bottlenecks. For instance, shuffling data over the network can improve accuracy and help reduce overfitting. However, shuffling often involves writing data to the local disk before sending it over the network; this results in more input/output (I/O) operations, increasing the overall computation time and creating a bottleneck on the local disk, as well as a large amount of communication overhead. For such tasks, you need to examine the communication approach you take carefully.

Asynchronous

The underlying mechanism for asynchronous communication is a *queue*. Requests to a given node are placed in a queue to be executed and can eventually return a result or not. This mechanism is useful in systems where information exchange is not dependent on time, as there is no need to receive a response right away. You can think of it like a text message: you send a text to your friend asking about dinner plans for next Saturday, knowing that you will likely eventually get a response, but you don't need it right away. Asynchronous communication allows for a flow of messages in a distributed system without blocking any processes while waiting for a reply; it's generally preferred when possible.

Synchronous

The requirement for synchronous communication arises from the computer science function stack, where functions must be executed in a specific order—meaning that if a node sends a request to another node, it can't continue processing further function logic while waiting for the response. You may use synchronous communication for specific distributed machine learning cases and leverage dedicated hardware like special network cables when necessary (some cloud vendors enable you to configure the network bandwidth). Suppose you want to make dinner plans with your friend for tonight. Your actions will depend on your friend's food preferences and availability and your chosen restaurant's availability. You know that if you decide on a popular restaurant and don't book a table now, there won't be any space left. What do you do? Rather than sending a text, you pick up the phone and call your friend to collect the information synchronously; both of you are now blocked as you talk on the phone. You get the necessary information and continue to the following stage, which is contacting the restaurant.

Now that you have an idea of some of the main architectural considerations in a distributed machine learning topology, let's take a look at a technique that has been gaining in popularity in machine learning applications in recent years: ensemble learning.

Introduction to Ensemble Methods

Ensemble machine learning methods use multiple machine learning algorithms to produce a single model with better performance and less bias and variance than the individual algorithms could achieve on their own. Ensemble methods are often designed around supervised learning and require a clear definition of model aggregation that can be used during prediction time. We'll begin by exploring why these methods are useful, then look at the main types of ensemble methods in machine learning and some specific examples.

---

2 The bandwidth indicates how much data can be transmitted over a network connection in a given amount of time over a wired or wireless connection.

High Versus Low Bias

Bias is a major problem in machine learning, and reducing bias is one of the machine learning engineer's main goals. A model with high bias makes too many assumptions about the results, leading to *overfitting* to the training data. Such a model tends to have difficulty making accurate predictions about new data that doesn't exactly conform to the data it has already seen and will perform badly on test data and in production. Conversely, a model with low bias incorporates fewer assumptions about the data. Taken to an extreme, this can also be problematic as it can result in *underfitting*, where the model fails to learn enough about the data to classify it accurately. Models with high bias tend to have low variance, and vice versa. You can think of variance as the ability of a machine learning algorithm to deal with fluctuations in the data.

Often, bias can also derive from the machine learning algorithm itself. For example, linear regression is a simple algorithm that learns fast but frequently has high bias, especially when used to model the relationship between two variables when no real linear (or close to linear) correlation exists between them. It all depends on the underlying relationship of the features.

Types of Ensemble Methods

In many cases, ensemble methods turn out to be more accurate than single models; by combining the individual predictions of all the component models, they are able to produce more robust results. In ensembles, each model is called a *learner*. We define the relationship between the learners based on the desired goal.

When we want to reduce variance, we often build dependencies between the learners by training them in a sequential manner. For example, we might train one decision tree at a time, with each new tree trained to correct the mistakes of the previous trees in the series. This strategy of building multiple learners with the goal of reducing previous learners' mistakes is known as *boosting*. The ensemble model makes its final predictions by weighting the votes, calculating the majority vote, or calculating an overall sum that acts as the prediction or classification. An example is the gradient-boosted trees classifier (GBTClassifier) implemented in Spark MLlib. This is an ensemble technique to iteratively combine decision trees using a deterministic averaging process; the algorithm's goal is to minimize the information lost in training/mistakes (more on this in Chapter 5). It's important to be aware, however, that the iterative combination of the trees can sometimes lead to overfitting.

To avoid overfitting, we might prefer training the learners independently in parallel and combining their predictions using *bagging* or *stacking*. With the bagging

---

3 If the variance of the model is low, the sampled data will be close to what the model predicted. If the variance is high, the model will perform well on the training data but not on new data.

technique (short for *bootstrap aggregation*), we train each learner (typically all using the same machine learning algorithm) on a different part of the dataset, with the goal of reducing variance and overfitting and improving the accuracy of predictions on previously unseen data. The outcome of this ensemble method is a combined model where each learner makes its prediction independently and the algorithm collects all the votes and produces a final prediction. An example is the `Random Forest Classifier` implemented in Spark MLlib (random forest is an ensemble technique to combine independent decision trees).

Stacking is similar to bagging, in that it involves building a set of independent learners and combining their predictions using an ensemble function that takes the output from all the learners and reduces it into a single score. However, with stacking, the learners are usually of different types, rather than all using the same learning algorithm, which means they make different assumptions and are less likely to make the same kinds of errors. You can use any type of machine learning model as the combiner that aggregates the predictions. A linear model is often used, but it can be nonlinear, taking in the learners' scores together with the given data—for example, a neural network where the base learners are decision trees. This approach is more advanced and can help uncover deeper relationships between the variables.

 Ensemble methods are said to be *homogeneous* when the learners have the same base learning algorithm. Ensembles whose learners have different base learning algorithms are referred to as *heterogeneous* ensembles. Boosting and bagging are considered homogeneous ensemble methods, while stacking is a heterogeneous method.

Distributed Training Topologies

You can leverage cluster topologies to improve training and serving of ensemble models. Let's take a look at a couple of examples.

Centralized ensemble learning

Centralized systems often use a client/server architecture, where client nodes are communicating directly with centralized server nodes. It resembles a star topology in computer networks. In a distributed machine learning deployment approach, this means that all the requests for predictions, classifications, etc., from the distributed models go through the main servers.

Whether there's one server node or several that act as the final decision makers, there is a strict hierarchical logic for aggregation at the server level that happens in a centralized location. This topology is dedicated specifically to a distributed model workload and is not general-purpose. For example, consider the random forest ensemble learning method. `RandomForest` is a bagging algorithm that can be used for classification or regression, depending on the nature of the data, and aims to mitigate overfitting, as described earlier. A random forest consists of a collection of decision trees. When you decide to leverage RandomForest as your algorithm, the program making the queries will interact as a client interacting with the main server nodes. Those server nodes will send the queries to the tree nodes, collect answers (the output of the model) from the trees, aggregate the output based on ensemble logic, and return the answers to the client. The individual trees in the ensemble may be trained on completely different or overlapping datasets.

Decentralized decision trees

Decision trees can be deployed in a decentralized topology as well. You can use this approach when you want to provide answers on edge devices and are constrained by data privacy concerns, internet bandwidth, and strict time requirements for the responses. Decentralized decision trees are useful for Edge AI, where the algorithm is processed and the model is served locally on the device. Each node does not need to be permanently connected to the network, though it can leverage the network to improve the accuracy of its predictions and avoid overfitting. In this case, when an edge node receives a query requesting it to make a prediction, it sends the query to its parent and child nodes, which in turn send the query to their parents and children, and each node calculates and broadcasts its response. Each node will have its own aggregation function and can decide whether or not to use it based on whether its response is available within the specified time constraints. To keep communication overhead to a minimum, you can limit the number of "hops," to define how far a query can travel. This constraint enforces a *node neighborhood*. A node's neighborhood can change based on network and edge device availability.

Centralized, distributed training with parameter servers

In a centralized distributed training topology, the entire workload is processed in one data center. The machines are well connected and communicate over a shared network. The dataset and the training workload are spread out among the client nodes, and the server nodes maintain globally shared parameters. The server nodes act as parameter servers that all the client nodes share access to and consume information from—a global shared memory. They have to have fast access to the information and often leverage in-memory data structures. One family of machine learning algorithms that can leverage this topology is deep learning algorithms. With this approach, the parameters are broadcasted and replicated across all the machines, and each client node separately calculates its own part of the main function. The variables are created on the parameter servers and shared and updated by the client or worker nodes in each step.

Chapter 8 discusses this strategy in detail, with code examples illustrating making use of this topology with TensorFlow.

Centralized, distributed training in a P2P topology

In a peer-to-peer topology, there are no client and server roles. All nodes can communicate with all of the other nodes, and each node has its own copy of the parameters. This is useful for leveraging data parallelism when there are a fixed number of parameters that can fit into the nodes' memory, the logic itself does not change, and the nodes can share their outcomes in a peer-to-peer manner. *Gossip learning* is one example of a method that uses this approach. Each node computes its model based on the dataset available to it and performs independent calls to its peers on the network to share its model with them. The nodes then each combine their current model with their neighbors' models. As with decision trees in a decentralized deployment environment, this topology should be restricted with time constraints, and the maximum number of edges each node will broadcast the information to should be defined. With the P2P topology, you might also want to specify a protocol like MPI to standardize the workload.

The Challenges of Distributed Machine Learning Systems

> Rome was not built in a day, but they were laying bricks every hour.
>
> —John Heywood

Although you're just beginning your journey into distributed machine learning, it's important to be aware of some of the challenges that lie ahead. Working with distributed machine learning is significantly different from developing machine learning workloads that will run on one machine, and ultimately it's your responsibility to build a system that meets the defined requirements. However, experienced practitioners will tell you that *all requirements are negotiable* and *what can fail will fail*. Both of these are true and should be kept in mind as you weigh your efforts throughout the process.

Performance

Improving performance is the fundamental goal of implementing a distributed system. Achieving higher throughput and performing end-to-end machine learning computations faster are critical justifications for distributed machine learning systems. There are many approaches you can take to improve performance, depending on your goal, your data, and the behavior of your system. Let's take a look at some of the things you should consider and some problems you will likely face.

Data parallelism versus model parallelism

In computer science, distributed computing often goes hand in hand with parallel computing. Parallel computing on a single node/computer means using that single node's multiple processors to perform various tasks at the same time. This is also called *task-parallel processing*. In comparison, in the context of distributed computing, parallel computing refers to using numerous nodes to perform tasks, with each node operating in parallel. When discussing distributed computation, parallel computation is a given and won't be mentioned explicitly.

One of the most significant sources of confusion when approaching distributed machine learning is the lack of a clear understanding of what precisely is distributed across the nodes. In the machine learning workflow/lifecycle, you preprocess your data, perform feature engineering to extract relevant features, enrich the data, and finally ingest it into your machine learning algorithm along with a set of *hyperparameters* (parameters whose values are used to control the learning process, also known as the machine learning algorithm's tuning parameters). During the learning process, the values/data ingested are affected by the hyperparameters, so it is recommended that you try out a wide range of hyperparameters to ensure that you identify the best possible model to use in production.

Dealing with a large set of data and a large set of tuning parameters raises the issue of how to manage your resources and the training process efficiently. Generally speaking, there are two approaches to training machine learning algorithms at scale. You can have the same algorithm with the same hyperparameters duplicated across all the nodes, with every machine running the same logic on its own piece of the data. Conversely, you can have each node running a different part of the algorithm, on the same set of data. Figure 1-3 illustrates the difference between these approaches: with *data parallelism*, the data is split into shards or partitions, and those partitions are distributed among the nodes, while with *model parallelism*, the model itself is split into pieces and distributed across machines.

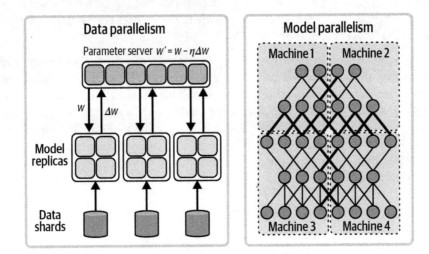

Figure 1-3. Data parallelism and model parallelism

With data parallelism, each node runs the same computation logic, which means that code must also be distributed across the nodes. From node to node, the data input changes, but all the nodes run the same code, as illustrated in Figure 1-4.

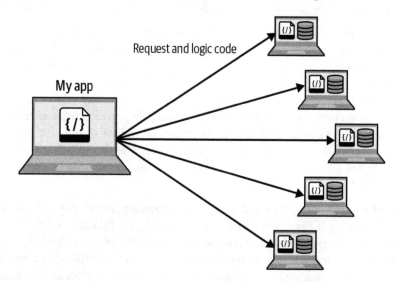

Figure 1-4. Data parallelism: the same logic is distributed to all the machines, and each machine runs the logic with its local data

With model parallelism, multiple nodes each execute different pieces of the machine learning algorithm, and the distributed outputs are then assembled to produce the model itself. This approach is suitable for algorithms that can be parallelized by representing them in a directed acyclic graph, where the vertices represent the computations and the edges represent the data flow.

One challenge in serving an existing model is that sometimes the model itself can't fit into one machine's memory and requires adjustments to be served optimally. Think about the random forest ensemble method. It may be that the whole forest can fit into a single machine's memory, but what if the forest has billions of trees? One option (which requires dedicated tools and hardware) is to divide the model into subsets, placing each one on a different machine, and have the machines communicate in a well-defined manner to serve the model efficiently. This approach is often employed by deep learning frameworks such as PyTorch and TensorFlow.

Combining data parallelism and model parallelism

Combining data and model parallelism is not at all straightforward, due to the nature of the existing open source tools and the complexity of building a dedicated system that will leverage both. However, whereas in the past we had to choose between data parallelism tools such as Apache Spark and model parallelism tools such as PyTorch, today many of these tools support each other, either natively or through extensions like Petastorm, Horovod, and others.

The need to combine both types of parallelism can have a significant effect on how long it takes to produce a new model, serve it, and start using it for prediction. For example, GPT-3 (Generative Pre-trained Transformer 3), a model developed by OpenAI, uses deep learning to produce human-like text. At its maximum capacity of 175 billion parameters, it is estimated that it would take 355 years and cost $4.6 million to train this model with a Tesla v100 GPU. For most companies, even with a far smaller number of parameters, this is an expensive and extremely slow option. Not only that, but it takes multiple tries to find suitable hyperparameters that will yield accurate results. We won't discuss this GPT-3 further in the book, but it is important to know that it exists.

Deep learning

Deep learning algorithms pose a particular challenge for distributed machine learning performance. Deep learning is based on an artificial neural network (ANN) with feature learning, which means that the system discovers the features automatically from the raw data. Training a deep learning model requires forward computation and/or backward propagation. *Forward computation* is the act of feeding the data forward in the neural network (NN) to calculate the outcome. *Backward propagation*, or *backpropagation*, is the act of feeding the "loss" of accuracy backward into the neural network through the layers in order to understand how much of that loss every node is responsible for, and updating the weights of the neural network layers accordingly. To simplify it, you can think of it as feeding inaccuracies back into the model to fix them.

Both forward computation and backpropagation inherently require sequential computation. Each layer or stage must wait for input from the former stage. While we can distribute each stage on its own, the model training as a whole is sequential. As a result, we still need orchestration to enforce a sequence or some form of an automated pipeline during the training. One scheduling algorithm that enables us to run distributed deep learning workloads is gang scheduling. Based on this algorithm, the community introduced *barrier execution mode* in Apache Spark 2.4, which allows us to create groups of machines that work together on a stage and proceed to the next stage only when they have all finished. Barrier execution mode is part of Project Hydrogen, which aims to enable a greater variety of distributed machine learning workloads on the general-purpose Apache Spark framework.

Resource Management

Deciding how to split cluster resources is one of the biggest challenges in a distributed system. When you add in distributed machine learning workloads as well, it gets even more complicated. The reason for that is the need to improve performance by pairing the software with dedicated hardware. And it's not only the GPU versus CPU conversation—today, Intel, NVIDIA, Google, and other companies are producing machines that are built with dedicated hardware chips for AI. These *AI accelerators* are built for high-performance massive parallel computation that goes beyond the traditional threaded algorithms. What's more, many machine learning algorithms are still evolving. This is why Microsoft introduced field-programmable gate array (FPGA) chips to its cloud, as part of Project Catapult to enable fast real-time AI serving of deep learning. FPGAs have a reconfigurable design, which makes it easier to adjust the hardware as needed after software updates.

Resource sharing is also a challenge in a distributed environment, when there are competing workloads. When there is a need for 10 machines but only 5 are available, the software can either use what it has or wait for more machines to become available. This creates a bottleneck and can result in great pain. Think about a scenario where you are running machine learning training in a production environment to save on resources, and your training workloads compete for resources with your product's real-time workloads. You might find yourself in trouble with customers at that point. This is why it's best to have multiple environments for critical workloads and long-term/offline workloads. But what if your model is critical, and training it now on fresh data might allow you to discover an unforeseen real-time trend in the industry (and missing out on this might result in revenue loss)? You might need to maintain two environments for critical workloads, though that can be costly and results in a low return on investment (ROI).

Reconfiguring and resource sharing are only part of the story. Another challenge is automating the decision of when to use GPUs versus CPUs or FPGAs and other hardware options that are available in the market. With the cloud and a sufficient budget, we can get all the hardware we need, but again, we have to think about ROI. What should we do? How can we automate this decision? There is as yet no definitive answer to that question, but the happy news is that more and more software and hardware solutions are introducing support for one another. For example, NVIDIA created RAPIDS, which is a suite of open source libraries layered on top of NVIDIA CUDA processors. CUDA enables GPU acceleration of data science processes. With RAPIDS support for Apache Spark 3.0 accelerating not only data science workloads but also ETL/data preparation, we can potentially build a cluster based on it that will power both data preparation and model training and serving, eliminating the need to automate a switch in resources (although the question of ROI remains).

Fault Tolerance

Fault tolerance is what allows a distributed system to continue operating properly in case of a failure. In distributed machine learning, failures can take two forms:

- Typical failure of a machine that can be detected and mitigated
- Undetected failure of a machine that produced bad output

Let's start with the first one. To better understand the need for a fault-tolerant procedure, ask yourself: If we distribute our workload to a cluster of 1,000 computational nodes, what will happen if one of those nodes crashes? Is there a way to fix it other than just restarting the job from the very beginning?

When one of the stages fails, do we need to recompute everything? The answer is no. Today, many distributed computation frameworks have a built-in procedure for fault tolerance: they achieve it by replicating the data and writing information to disk between stages for faster recovery. Other frameworks leave defining this mechanism up to us. For example, in TensorFlow with synchronous training, if one of the workers fails and we didn't provide a fault tolerance procedure, the whole cluster will fail. This is why, when deciding on the TensorFlow distribution strategy, we need to pay attention to the fault tolerance mechanism. On the other hand, Apache Spark does not expose this decision to us. Rather, it has a built-in hidden mechanism that we cannot tweak from the machine learning API itself. Sticking with the automatic data-parallel workload fault tolerance mechanism in Spark saves us a lot of time by eliminating the need to think through the possible failure cases and solutions.

The second type of failure is specific to distributed machine learning, as it directly impacts the performance of the machine learning algorithm itself. In this case, we can look at it as if we have a Byzantine adversary machine or an intentionally or unintentionally faulty agent. Faulty agents (or adversaries) can harm the machine learning model's performance by exposing erroneous data. It's hard to mitigate such behavior, and the effects are highly dependent on the algorithm we use. Detecting such failures is one reason why it's important to monitor machine learning models, as discussed in Chapter 10.

Privacy

Discussions of privacy in machine learning generally focus on protecting data collected from users/customers or protecting the model and parameters themselves. The model and its parameters can be the company's intellectual property, and it might be important to keep them private (for example, in a financial market system).

One option for enforcing data privacy is avoiding the restrictions of centralizing data. That is, we want to build a model without uploading the members' training data to centralized servers. To do that, we can leverage techniques like *federated learning*. With this approach, we train the algorithm on the edge devices, with each device using its own data. The devices then each exchange a summary of the model they built with other devices or a dedicated server. However, this approach is not foolproof. An adversarial attack can happen during the training itself, with the attacker getting hold of some or all of the data or the results of the training. This can easily occur during federated learning when the attacker takes an active part in the training process through their edge devices.

Let's assume we have found a way to securely centralize the data or train the models without doing this. There is still a chance that a malicious actor can recover information about the data (statistics about a specific population, classification classes, and more) that we used to train the model by interacting with the model itself. As you can probably tell by now, there is no one-size-fits-all solution when it comes to ensuring privacy in machine learning—it requires dedicated technologies and architectures. Although privacy in distributed machine learning is a fascinating topic, it's also a big one, and we won't discuss it further in this book.

Portability

Portability ties back to the general challenges of a distributed system. When we add dedicated computing hardware such as multiple types of GPUs paired with the software we build, it makes moving the workloads from one cluster to another more difficult. In the early days of the cloud, many companies used the "lift and shift" migration strategy, moving their workloads and applications to the cloud without redesigning them. However, in many cases this resulted in higher costs since they didn't take advantage of the environment's features. Specifically, in the cloud, native features were built with optimizations for specific workloads. The same happens with a distributed machine learning approach: the various types of hardware available, the requirements, and the need to improve ROI by reducing development, storage, and compute costs can impact portability.

There are other challenges that are inherent to distributed systems that don't relate directly to machine learning but can still have an impact on machine learning workloads, like trust or zero trust systems, network overhead, ensuring consistency, and more. We won't cover those issues in this book, but you should consider them when designing your product strategy.

Setting Up Your Local Environment

Now that you understand the landscape better, let's set you up for success! Many of the code samples in this book are available for you in the book's GitHub repository (*https://oreil.ly/smls-git*). To gain hands-on experience with them, you should set up a learning environment, which you can run locally on your machine.

You'll want to go through this setup process twice, first for the tutorials in Chapters 2–6 and then for the tutorials in Chapters 7–10.

Chapters 2–6 Tutorials Environment

To follow along with the tutorials in Chapters 2 to 6, make sure you have the latest version of Docker installed on your machine and follow these steps:

1. Run Docker.

2. In a terminal window/command line, run the following command:

```
$ docker run -it -p 8888:8888 adipolak/ml-with-apache-spark
```

This pulls an image of a PySpark Jupyter notebook with Apache Spark 3.1.1, which includes most of the libraries we'll use. You will learn how to add the rest later. After executing this command, you will get a response like this:

```
[I 13:50:03.885 NotebookApp] Serving notebooks from local directory:
/home/jovyan
[I 13:50:03.885 NotebookApp] Jupyter Notebook 6.3.0 is running at:
[I 13:50:03.885 NotebookApp] http://6cb805089793:8888/?token=e14171684af
c305b4702cbda99ae879d3faecf5db6bea37d
[I 13:50:03.885 NotebookApp] or http://127.0.0.1:8888/?token=e14171684af
c305b4702cbda99ae879d3faecf5db6bea37d
[I 13:50:03.885 NotebookApp] Use Control-C to stop this server and shut
down all kernels (twice to skip confirmation).
[C 13:50:03.891 NotebookApp]

    To access the notebook, open this file in a browser:
        file:///home/jovyan/.local/share/jupyter/runtime/nbserver-8-open
            .html
    Or copy and paste one of these URLs:
        http://6cb805089793:8888/?token=e14171684afc305b4702cbda99ae879d
            3faecf5db6bea37d
     or http://127.0.0.1:8888/?token=e14171684afc305b4702cbda99ae879d3fa
            ecf5db6bea37d
^C[I 13:50:27.037 NotebookApp] interrupted
Serving notebooks from local directory: /home/jovyan
0 active kernels
Jupyter Notebook 6.3.0 is running at:
http://6cb805089793:8888/?token=e14171684afc305b4702cbda99ae879d3faecf5d
b6bea37d
 or
http://127.0.0.1:8888/?token=e14171684afc305b4702cbda99ae879d3faecf5db6b
ea37d
```

Getting an error about AMD? Use this command instead:

```
$ docker run -p 8888:8888 \
    adipolak/amd-ml-with-apache-spark
```

3. Copy the last URL with the `token` parameter. It will look something like this, but you will have your own token:

```
http://127.0.0.1:8888/?token=43143a485357351ef522a1840f8c8c141a1be2bcf5f
9b4de
```

Paste it in your browser. This will be your Jupyter tutorial environment.

4. Clone or download the book's repo.

5. Extract (unzip) the files and upload the notebooks and data files into Jupyter using the Upload button (see Figure 1-5).

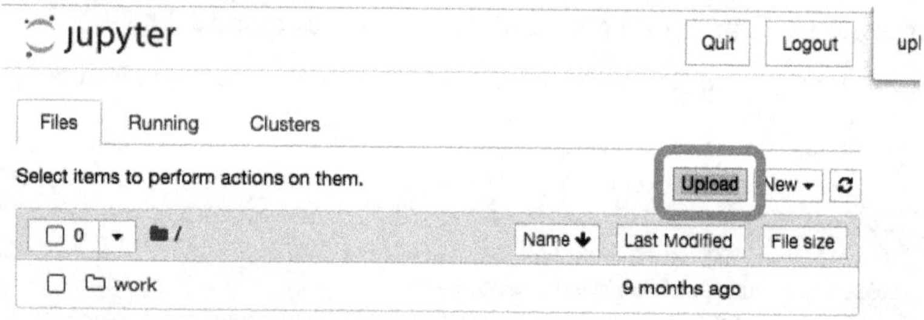

Figure 1-5. Jupyter Upload button

The `pyspark-notebook` Docker image is very simple at this stage: it simply contains Jupyter and PySpark, the main tools used in this book. Figure 1-6 shows how the images in Jupyter Docker Stacks (*https://oreil.ly/SdkSP*) are stacked.

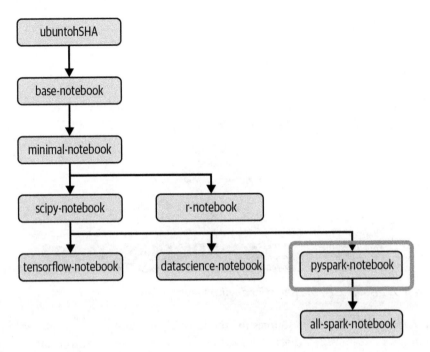

Figure 1-6. Jupyter Docker Stacks images

Chapters 7–10 Tutorials Environment

The tutorials in Chapters 7–10 require PySpark, PyTorch, Petastorm, TensorFlow, and everything related to the build, deploy, and serve parts of the machine learning lifecycle. You can follow the same steps outlined in the previous section to set up an environment for these chapters. In addition, to work with PyTorch, you'll need to install it directly from the Jupyter terminal. Figure 1-7 shows you how to do this using the following conda command on macOS (note that during this process, you may be prompted to answer some questions about the installation):

```
$ conda install pytorch==1.12.1 torchvision==0.13.1 -c pytorch
```

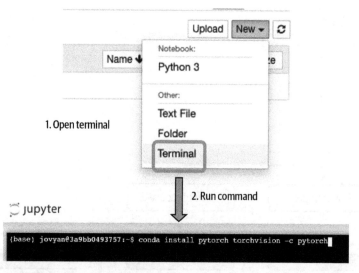

Figure 1-7. Installing PyTorch in your environment

You may need additional resources for the tutorials in these chapters—for example, you might need more RAM for faster execution. To configure that, you can leverage the docker command with the --memory and --memory-swap tags. Make sure to define the amounts according to your machine's capabilities:

```
$ sudo docker run -it --memory="16g" --memory-swap="24g" -p 8888:8888 \
    adipolak/amd-ml-with-apache-spark
```

Summary

In this chapter, we covered the very basics of distributed machine learning, touching lightly on a number of complex topics: machine learning workflows, distributed computing models, network topologies, distributed training and serving, and much more. As you know, Apache Spark supports parallel data processing across clusters or computer processors in real time. The framework is based on the MapReduce paradigm, which has numerous advantages when it comes to processing data, analytics, and machine learning algorithms. However, it also has some limitations, particularly with regard to deep learning workloads (as a result, I'll show you how to bridge from Spark into deep learning frameworks in Chapter 7).

The next chapter provides a quick introduction to PySpark, to get you up to speed or help you brush up on the basics. Chapter 3 will get you started with machine learning lifecycle management using MLflow and show you how to package your experiments so that you can follow along with the tutorials in the rest of the book. You will learn how to utilize PySpark for your machine learning needs in Chapters 4, 5, and 6.

## CHAPTER 2

Introduction to Spark and PySpark

The aim of this chapter is to bring you up to speed on PySpark and Spark, giving you enough information so you're comfortable with the tutorials in the rest of the book. Let's start at the beginning. What exactly is Spark? Originally developed at UC Berkeley in 2009, Apache Spark is an open source analytics engine for big data and machine learning. It gained rapid adoption by enterprises across many industries soon after its release and is deployed at massive scale by powerhouses like Netflix, Yahoo, and eBay to process exabytes of data on clusters of many thousands of nodes. The Spark community has grown rapidly too, encompassing over 1,000 contributors from 250+ organizations.

 For a deep dive into Spark itself, grab a copy of *Spark: The Definitive Guide* (*https://oreil.ly/sparkTDG*), by Bill Chambers and Matei Zaharia (O'Reilly).

To set you up for the remainder of this book, this chapter will cover the following areas:

- Apache Spark's distributed architecture
- Apache Spark basics (software architecture and data structures)
- DataFrame immutability
- PySpark's functional paradigm
- How pandas DataFrames differ from Spark DataFrames
- Scikit-learn versus PySpark for machine learning

Apache Spark Architecture

The Spark architecture consists of the following main components:

Driver program

The driver program (aka Spark driver) is a dedicated process that runs on the driver machine. It is responsible for executing and holding the SparkSession, which encapsulates the SparkContext—this is considered the application's entry point, or the "real program." The SparkContext contains all the basic functions, context delivered at start time, and information about the cluster. The driver also holds the DAG scheduler, task scheduler, block manager, and everything that is needed to turn the code into jobs that the worker and executors can execute on the cluster. The driver program works in synergy with the cluster manager to find the existing machines and allocated resources.

Executor

An executor is a process launched for a particular Spark application on a worker node. Multiple tasks can be assigned to each executor. A JVM process communicates with the cluster manager and receives tasks to execute. Tasks on the same executor can benefit from shared memory, such as the cache, and global parameters, which make the tasks run fast.

A task is the smallest unit of schedulable work in Spark. It runs the code assigned to it, with the data pieces assigned to it.

Worker node

A worker node, as its name indicates, is responsible for executing the work. Multiple executors can run on a single worker node and serve multiple Spark applications.

Cluster manager

Together with the driver program, the cluster manager is responsible for orchestrating the distributed system. It assigns executors to worker nodes, assigns resources, and communicates information about resource availability to the driver program. In addition to Spark's standalone cluster manager, this can be any other cluster manager that can manage machines and network capacity, such as Kubernetes, Apache Mesos, or Hadoop YARN.

Figure 2-1 shows how these various components fit together.

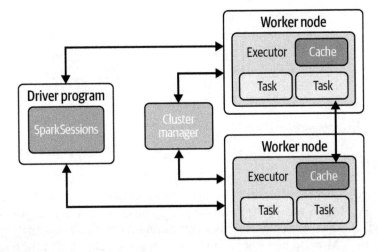

Figure 2-1. Spark's distributed architecture

Each of these components plays a critical part in orchestrating Spark programs at a large scale. A Spark driver can launch multiple jobs within one application, each consisting of multiple tasks. However, it cannot launch more than one application, as Spark resource management takes place on a per-application basis, not a per-job basis. Tasks run on one or more executors and typically process different chunks of the data (see Figure 2-2). Notice that executors are not assigned dedicated storage, although in Figure 2-2 you can see that storage is attached to the executors. In some deployments, like on-prem Hadoop clusters, storage can be local to executors, but often in cloud solutions, this is not the case; in cloud deployments (AWS, Azure, etc.) there is a separation between storage and compute. In general, Spark prefers to schedule tasks that access local data, but assigning tasks and executors to local data is not a requirement.

---

1 Kubernetes (K8s) (*https://kubernetes.io*) is a tool that automates the deployment, scaling, and management of containerized applications.

2 Apache Mesos (*https://mesos.apache.org*) is an open source cluster manager.

3 In Hadoop's distributed processing framework, YARN (*https://oreil.ly/F-3bR*) is the resource management and job scheduling technology.

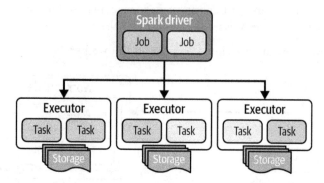

Figure 2-2. Spark launching two jobs

Intro to PySpark

I mentioned earlier that Python is a different kind of language—it is not part of the JVM family. Python is an *interpreted* language, which means that(unlike with the JVM) Python code doesn't go through compilation. You also know that at Spark's core, it runs JVM-based processes and is based on Scala and Java. So how does Spark work with Python? Let's take a look.

At the most basic level, Spark application components communicate through APIs, over a shared network. This means that if I have a task running a JVM process, it can leverage interprocess communication (IPC) to work with Python.

Suppose you've written a PySpark app. How does it work with Spark? Essentially, every time you launch a PySpark job, it creates two processes under the hood: Python and the JVM. Python is the main program where the code is defined, and the JVM is the program responsible for Spark query optimization, computation, distribution of tasks to clusters, etc. Within a PySpark application, the `SparkContext` itself has a parameter called `_gateway`, which is responsible for holding the context to pass the Py4J application to a JVM Spark server.

Wait, what's a Py4J application? Py4J (*https://www.py4j.org*) is a library written in Python and Java that enables Python programs running in a Python interpreter to dynamically access Java objects and collections in a JVM via standard Python methods, as if they resided in the Python interpreter. In other words, it enables the Python code to communicate with the JVM, transparently to the user. Figure 2-3 shows how this works. When the PySpark driver starts, it initiates a Spark JVM application with a Py4J server configured to communicate directly with the Spark JVM. Information is transferred between the PySpark driver and Py4J in a serialized or "pickled" form.

---

4 *Pickling* is a process for converting Python objects into byte streams.

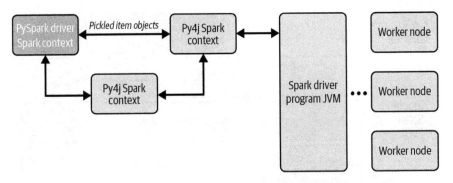

Figure 2-3. Py4J acting as a mediator between the Python application and the Spark JVM

Since Python is an interpreter and the code is not being compiled in advance, there is an executor that holds Python code within each worker node. The executor launches a Python application whenever necessary to execute the logic. Of course, I'm simplifying things here—there are some exceptions and some optimizations that have been added over the years. You should also be aware that PySpark is often less efficient in terms of running time than traditional Scala/Java code.

Apache Spark Basics

In this section, we'll take a brief look at the basics of Spark itself, starting with the software architecture and the key programming abstractions.

Software Architecture

Since Spark was built as a generic engine to enable various distributed computing workloads, its software architecture is built in layers, as you can see in Figure 2-4.

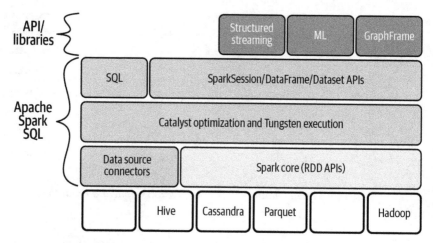

Figure 2-4. Spark software architecture

The bottom layer abstracts away the storage using *resilient distributed dataset* (RDD) APIs and data source connectors. Storage in Spark can be anything with a readable format (more on that in Chapter 4).

The top layer holds the APIs and libraries for us to take advantage of. These APIs, which work directly with Spark's DataFrame or Dataset APIs, abstract away all of the Spark internals. A *DataFrame* in Spark is a distributed collection of data organized in columns, similar to a table in a database. It has a dedicated structure and format, and you can run specific operations on it. It also has a schema, where each column has support for specific data types (*https://oreil.ly/NE8r5*) (numeric, string, binary, Boolean, datetime, interval, etc.). The main difference between Datasets and Data-Frames is that Datasets come with type safety for columns, which means that there is no way for us to mistake a column of type `string`, say, as an `int`. However, we pay the price for that: operating on Datasets is generally slower than operating on a Data-Frame.

Note that the schema is an essential part of a DataFrame. Spark may try to infer the schema of a given dataset from the file format itself—for example, it does this with Parquet files (more on that in Chapter 4). It tries its best to infer the schema from CSV files as well, but it may make mistakes due to specific character encodings (such as UTF formats) or issues like extra spaces/tabs, and occasionally the delimiters are inferred incorrectly.

To read a CSV file into a DataFrame, all you need to do is call the `read` operation with the dedicated format function:

```
df = spark.read.csv("some_file")
```

In this case, PySpark will try to infer the schema from the file.

Following that line with `df.printSchema()` will execute the `read` function and print the schema for you to examine. If you wish, you can also change the delimiter using the `option` function. For example, you could add the following to the previous line to set the delimiter to a comma:

```
.option(delimiter=',')
```

Creating a custom schema

Often, you'll want to control the flow and provide your own custom schema. That enables collaboration and reproducibility of the code itself. It also saves you precious time later on debugging issues.

So how do you do that with PySpark? You will need to create a `StructType` and pass it to the reader during reading as the desired schema. In the `StructType`, add all the column names and types using the dedicated APIs, as illustrated in the following code sample:

```
schema = StructType([
    StructField("Number",IntegerType(),True),
    StructField("City",StringType(),True),
    StructField("Age",DoubleType(),True),
    StructField("Decommissioned",BooleanType(),True)
])

df_with_schema = spark.read.format("csv")
                        .schema(schema)
                        .load("{some_file_path}.csv")
```

Passing `True` to the `StructField` object indicates that the value can be null.

Saving Your Schema

To enable code reusability and modularity, write the schema into a JSON file. This is a cleaner way of writing code; it decouples the schema configuration from the code itself and allows you to quickly load the file later, when needed.

To convert the schema we just wrote to JSON, all you need to do is call `df_with_schema.schema.json`. It will output the following:

```
{
  "type" : "struct",
  "fields" : [ {
    "name" : "Number",
    "type" : "integer",
    "nullable" : true,
    "metadata" : { }
  }, {
    "name" : "City",
    "type" : "string",
```

```
        "nullable" : true,
        "metadata" : { }
    }, {
        "name" : "Age",
        "type" : "float",
        "nullable" : true,
        "metadata" : { }
    }, {
        "name" : "Decommissioned",
        "type" : "bool",
        "nullable" : true,
        "metadata" : { }
    } ]
}
```

Save this output to a file of your choice, as follows:

```
with open(schema.json, 'w') as f:
    # Change the standard output to the file
    sys.stdout = f
    print(df_with_schema.schema.json())
```

You can then load it back using the fromJson function, as shown here:

```
import json
schemaFromJson = StructType.fromJson(json.loads(
                    schema.json))
```

Now that you have an instance of the schema, you can read the DataFrame with this schema as shown previously.

So how do you convert Python data types to Spark data types? Or rather, how does PySpark interpret the types? Table 2-1 provides a guide for some of the most common conversions.

Table 2-1. Basic Python data types and how to initiate them when designing a schema

Value in Python	Spark type
int (1 byte)	DataTypes.ByteType()
int (2 bytes)	DataTypes.ShortType()
int (4 bytes)	DataTypes.IntegerType()
int (8 bytes)	DataTypes.LongType()
float (4 bytes, single precision)	DataTypes.FloatType()
float (8 bytes, double precision)	DataTypes.DoubleType()
str	DataTypes.StringType()
bool	DataTypes.BooleanType()
decimal.Decimal	DataTypes.DecimalType()

Note that while there are many types in Python, when initiating the types for schema definition, there are types that repeat themselves, like int and float. Spark provides different types that int values, for example, may translate into, representing different numbers of bytes in memory (ShortType is 2 bytes, IntegerType is 4 bytes, etc.). This is one of the challenges you'll need to navigate when working with PySpark.

Key Spark data abstractions and APIs

What exactly does an RDD abstract? This is a fantastic question, a full consideration of which would take us deep into the concepts of distributed storage and data source connectors. RDDs are essentially read-only distributed collections of JVM objects. However, Spark hides many complications here: RDDs combine application dependencies, partitions, and iterator[T] => compute functions. A partition is a logical division of the data itself—you can think of it as a chunk of distributed data. The purpose of the RDD is to connect each partition to a logical iterator, given the application dependencies that the executors can iterate on. Partitions are critical because they provide Spark with the ability to split the work easily across executors.

Spark's other core data abstractions are DataFrames and Datasets. A DataFrame is similar to an RDD, but it organizes the data into named columns, like a table in a relational database. Datasets are an extension of the DataFrame API, providing type safety. DataFrames and Datasets both benefit from query optimization provided by the Spark Catalyst engine. This optimization is important, as it makes running Spark faster and cheaper. As a result, whenever possible, it is advisable to leverage the top-layer APIs and avoid using RDDs.

A lot of innovation went into the Catalyst, and it is truly fascinating to dive into this world. However, given that it has little to no impact on machine learning workloads, I will not delve further into it here.

As Figure 2-4 showed, Spark provides many APIs/libraries. Let's take a look at some of the ones that are supported in PySpark:

MLlib
This library is used for running machine learning workloads at scale. Under the hood, there are two libraries, MLlib itself and machine learning (more on these in Chapter 6).

GraphFrames
This library enables running graph operations on data with edges and nodes. It optimizes the representation of vertex and edge types when they are primitive

---

5 Spark also provides the GraphX library; at a high level, their functionality is similar, but GraphFrames is based on DataFrames, while GraphX is based on RDDs. GraphFrames is the one supported in PySpark.

data types (`int`, `double`, etc.), reducing the in-memory footprint by storing them in specialized arrays. While machine learning has a lot to do with graph computation, MLlib and GraphFrames are separate and are used for different purposes. GraphFrames does, however, have interesting algorithms (such as PageRank) that can assist you in enriching your data and performing preprocessing and feature engineering.

Structured Streaming

This API launches a never-ending Spark job that processes microbatch data in a streaming way. There is also an improved engine for lower latency called Continuous Processing. The Spark application itself creates a listener, which waits to collect new data. When a new microbatch of data arrives, Spark SQL handles the processing and updates the final results accordingly.

DataFrames are immutable

It is important to note that DataFrames, Datasets, and RDDs are considered *immutable* storage. Immutability means that an object's state cannot be changed after its creation. When writing PySpark code, we must keep that in mind. Every time we execute an operation on a DataFrame, since it cannot change the original one (immutable), to store the results it creates a new DataFrame. Consider the following code sample, where we read a DataFrame and run a `select` operation on it:

```
train_df = spark.read.csv('training_data.csv', header = True)
train_df.select('bot')
```

Notice that in the first line we assigned the DataFrame to the `train_df` variable. What happens to `train_df` after the `select` operation? Nothing! That's right, absolutely nothing. This is the power of immutability: the object itself does not change. Essentially, `train_df` is now pointing to the location in memory where the DataFrame is represented. The representation itself cannot change. By selecting the bot data, we simply created a new pointer to that subset of the data. Because we didn't assign the new pointer to a variable, essentially the last line of code does nothing. The underlying DataFrame is still the same, and `train_df` still points to the same place in memory that represented the DataFrame.

You should also be aware that Spark uses *lazy execution*. This means it will not start the execution of a process until an operation of type *action* is called. An action can be anything that returns a value that is not part of a DataFrame—for example, getting the count of rows in a DataFrame or performing a write operation. The other type of operation is a *transformation*. Transformation operations create new DataFrames from existing ones. Spark accumulates all the transformations into a DAG and optimizes them but acts on them only when an action requiring them occurs.

So, going back to our example, Spark did not even load the data into memory. It created a graph of operations that has `read` and `select` in it. If, later, there are no action operations on the DataFrame created by the `select`, Spark will prune it and won't execute it at all. Spark's lazy execution and immutable data structures help prevent us from making mistakes and performing unnecessary computations; be mindful of these features.

So what can we do to correct the previous mistake? We can start by simply assigning the DataFrame resulting from the `select` operation into an instance, as shown here:

```
train_df = spark.read.csv('training_data.csv', header = True)
tmp_df = train_df.select('bot')
```

This saves the reference to `tmp_df`. If we later continue to execute on it and have an *action* operation in place, Spark will execute this `select` operation (fetching the results and saving them to the `tmp_df` variable) as part of its operations graph only if an action occurs that requires its result to be returned to the driver program. Otherwise, it will be pruned.

You are probably asking yourself, *Why is immutability important?* Immutability of operations is one of the backbones of *functional programming*, a paradigm that aims to allow us to build applications that are more reliable and maintainable (you'll learn more about functional programming in the next section). Ensuring that an object's state cannot change after it is created makes it possible for the developer to keep track of all the operations that are performed on that object, preserving the chain of events. This, in return, makes the application scalable.

The same concept applies when working with Spark: essentially, every DataFrame is a result of a specific operation which is reproducible and trackable. This is critical and becomes even more challenging in a distributed system. The choice to go with immutability enables us to achieve resilience, even though, to save on memory, Spark does not automatically save every DataFrame that we produce. Take this into account and learn to work with Spark in a way that enables you to reproduce your machine learning experiments (more on that in Chapter 3).

PySpark and Functional Programming

I mentioned functional programming in the previous section, and this was not by accident. Spark borrows many concepts from functional programming in addition to immutability, starting with *anonymous functions*. These are functions that are executed without state yet are not named. The idea originated in mathematics, with lambda calculus, and you will often hear these referred to as *lambda functions*.

You can pass an anonymous function to an RDD to execute on the data. Take a look at the following code snippet:

```
rdd2 = rdd.map(lambda x: (x,1))
```

Here, we call the map function on an RDD instance. Inside that function, we call an anonymous function. For every x—meaning, for every row in the RDD—this function returns a pair (x,1). For example, if our original RDD contained rows with values (1,2,3), the function would return ((1,1),(2,1),(3,1)). This is a transformation operation, and rdd2 holds the graph operations with the requirements to turn every x into (x,1).

The map function in this example leverages the functionality of passing in an independent function to execute on the RDD that is repeatable and independent of state. This capability makes it effortless to parallelize the execution. Think about it: every executor runs the operation on its partition of the data and returns an answer. There is no need to exchange information, which makes this system extremely scalable and resilient. If one node is down, there is no need to recompute everything—just the portion of the data it was responsible for. The final result is the same as if the operation had been executed on a single node.

To take a more advanced example, suppose the client requests that you find the maximum value out of all the values. You can do this by using a reduce operation together with a max operation, as illustrated in the following code snippet:

```
rdd3 = rdd2.reduce((a,b)=> (("max",a._2 max b._2)._2))
```

reduce will calculate the maximum value among all values, starting with local values, by comparing each pair. After each node finds its local maximum, the data will be shuffled (moved) to a dedicated executor which will calculate the final result. In our case, ((1,1),(2,1),(3,1)) will return 3.

Although functional programming has more core principles, Spark doesn't necessarily follow all of them to the fullest extent possible. The main principles are these:

- Immutability
- Disciplined state (minimizing dependence on the state)

Executing PySpark Code

If you want to run PySpark code where your cluster is configured, ensure that you have access to your cluster with the right libraries and that you have the required permissions. For a cloud installation, if you are not an IT professional, it is best to leverage a managed Spark solution or consult your IT department. Executing the code itself is very similar to the JVM process. As discussed previously, the PySpark code will take care of the rest.

For executing locally with a dedicated notebook, follow the instructions in the Quick Start guide in the README file in the book's GitHub repo (*https://oreil.ly/smls-git*). This should be sufficient for following along with the tutorials.

Spark supports shell commands as well, through the PySpark shell (an interactive shell that enables you to try PySpark using the command line). The PySpark shell is responsible for linking the Python API to the Spark core and initializing the Spark Session and SparkContext. It is based on a Scala concept called the REPL, or Read–Eval–Print Loop. For more information, check out the Quick Start guide (*https://oreil.ly/0NB-X*) in the Spark documentation.

pandas DataFrames Versus Spark DataFrames

Spark DataFrames were inspired by pandas (*https://oreil.ly/ADLio*), which also provides an abstraction on top of the data called a DataFrame. pandas is a widely adopted library for data manipulation and analytics. Many developers use it to extrapolate data using Python. Reading a pandas DataFrame is straightforward—here is a code example showing how to do it:

```
import pandas as pd
df = pd.read_csv(....)
```

It may seem easy to confuse the two at the beginning, but there are many key differences between pandas and Spark. Most importantly, pandas was not built for scale; it was built to operate on data that fits into one machine's memory. Consequently, it does not have the distributed Spark architecture we discussed at the beginning of the chapter. It also does not adhere to functional programming principles: pandas DataFrames are mutable.

> The multiple permutations of the data it keeps in memory can cause pandas to fail even when the original dataset fits easily in a single machine's memory.

Table 2-2 provides a quick comparison of some of the key features of Spark and pandas DataFrames.

Table 2-2. Spark DataFrames versus pandas DataFrames

	Spark DataFrame	pandas DataFrame
Operation in parallel	Yes	Not out of the box
Lazy evaluation	Yes	No
Immutable	Yes	No

Although, as you can see, there is no out-of-the-box way to operate in parallel over a pandas DataFrame, that does not mean it is entirely impossible. It simply means that you have to create a solution and consider the possible problems you might encounter (thread locks, race conditions, etc.) and their impact on the end result. Other differences are that Spark supports lazy evaluation, while in pandas, operations take place immediately as soon as the Python code line is executed, and DataFrames in pandas are not immutable. This makes it easy to operate on pandas DataFrames, as you don't need to remember or be aware of the lazy execution approach—when you call a function, it is executed immediately and you can interact with the results right away. However, it also makes it challenging to scale using parallel or distributed computing.

 The Spark community has created an open source library called Koalas that provides a pandas-like API on Spark. It is also known as pandas-on-Spark. While it is not the same as parallelizing pandas, the API does a good job of mimicking the pandas API from a user perspective. This library is part of the official Spark APIs, which also makes it easier to use right away. To learn more about it, search for "pandas API" in the Spark docs. Starting from Spark version 3.2, you can import it directly from PySpark like so:

```
import pyspark.pandas as ps
```

Scikit-Learn Versus MLlib

Scikit-learn (`sklearn`) and Spark MLlib are sometimes confused as well. Scikit-learn is a machine learning library written in Python that leverages well-known Python libraries such as NumPy, SciPy, and matplotlib. While it is known to have fantastic performance when operating on data that fits in RAM, it does it in a nondistributed fashion. Spark adds the overhead of configuring a cluster to operate at a larger scale but provides algorithms that are tuned for parallel/distributed execution.

When should you go with each tool? Here are a few hints:

- It is better to use Spark to process large datasets (GB, TB, or even PB scale), and MLlib to perform machine learning on them.
- It is more efficient to construct your algorithm in Python using scikit-learn together with pandas and other libraries when all of your data fits into the memory of your machine. Additionally, this way, serving your model in production isn't bound to a specific constellation (more on serving models and deployment in Chapter 10).

Scikit-learn uses the notion of datasets, similar to Spark and other Python libraries such as pandas. The datasets are mutable, and scaling out of the box is restricted and requires working in conjunction with other tools. Model deployment can be similar to with Spark (depending on your serving pattern), and models can be saved to disk and reloaded using multiple APIs. Scikit-learn can operate on pandas DataFrames and NumPy arrays too.

Table 2-3 provides a quick comparison of some of the key features of scikit-learn and MLlib. The similarity will become even more evident when you reach Chapter 6, which discusses Spark's machine learning pipelines. This is because the concept of pipelines in Spark was inspired by the scikit-learn project; the Spark community decided to use a similar concept (as it did when designing DataFrames) to ease the learning curve of Spark as much as possible.

Table 2-3. scikit-learn versus Spark MLlib

	Scikit-learn	MLlib
Datasets	Mutable (columns can be updated in place)	Immutable (new columns must be created)
Scalability	Data must fit in a single machine's memory	Distributed (enabling big data analytics)
Model deployment	• Model can be "pickled" to disk and reloaded via a REST API • Is supported by MLflow • Provides many deployment options	• Supports Parquet and Snappy file formats and other open file formats • Is supported by MLflow

Summary

This chapter covered the very basics of Spark, giving you some high-level insights into the architecture and APIs and comparing it to some other popular Python tools. With this background, you should be ready to embark on the journey ahead and gain some hands-on experience with Spark and end-to-end machine learning pipelines. One thing to remember is that machine learning projects are long-term, requiring time, effort, and collaboration. To improve the maintainability of your code, keep it reusable, friendly, and modular.

## CHAPTER 3

Managing the Machine Learning Experiment Lifecycle with MLflow

Machine learning development and data science are often done in collaboration—but building models collaboratively, while experimenting with a large combination of features, standardization techniques, and hyperparameters, is a complex undertaking. Part of the reason for this is simply because it's a complex task to track experiments, reproduce results, package models for deployment, and store and manage those models in a way that ensures they are well documented and provide the desired accuracy.

To facilitate this process, there is a need to evolve the machine learning development workflow so it is more robust, predictable, and standardized. To this end, many organizations have started to build internal machine learning platforms to manage the machine learning lifecycle. However, these platforms often support only a small set of built-in algorithms, dictated by the company's infrastructure and the software that is available, without much openness to supporting new software due to the added complexity. Moreover, these platforms are usually not open source, and users cannot easily leverage new machine learning libraries or share their work with others in the community.

Managing the machine learning experiment lifecycle, sometimes referred to as *MLOps*, is a combination of machine learning, development, and operations. The machine learning part is all about the experiment itself: training, tuning, and finding the optimal model. Development is about developing the pipelines and tools to take the machine learning model from the development/experimental stage into staging and production. And last, operations is about the CI/CD tools and monitoring, managing, and serving the models at scale. Figure 3-1 illustrates the steps of the machine learning model's lifecycle, each of which must be supported by the MLOps teams.

Figure 3-1. The lifecycle of a machine learning model, from development to archiving

Machine learning experiments can be organized in machine learning pipeline code or machine learning modules living in a repository, such as a Git branch. They contain the *code*, the *data*, and the *model* and are an integral part of the machine learning software lifecycle.

Machine Learning Lifecycle Management Requirements

The aim of most machine learning projects is to reach the position where they have covered all the requirements and developed all capabilities needed to tackle the business problem or question at hand. However, defining (let alone meeting) all the requirements of the machine learning lifecycle is often easier said than done. Furthermore, sometimes these requirements can come from external entities. For example, if I am conducting machine learning research for a new drug, it might be that my project and outcomes need to adhere to US Food and Drug Administration (FDA) requirements. To gain FDA approval, data on the drug's effects must have been reviewed, and the drug must have been determined to provide benefits that outweigh its known and potential risks for the intended population. This means, at the very least, that the machine learning experiment needs to be *reproducible*. Of course, this is just one of the requirements. Many of the others come from a software engineering process called the *software development lifecycle* (SDLC). Generally speaking, the SDLC includes seven stages: *planning, analysis, design, development, testing, implementation,* and *maintenance*. We can translate these into machine learning lifecycle stages, focusing on the areas that are relevant to machine learning. That is, taking a closer look at what those stages involve, we can make decisions about how to implement them and adopt concepts that are relevant to machine learning, leveraging existing SDLC tools and methodologies.

On the technical side, we can distill the following set of core requirements:

Reproducibility
> This refers to the ability to run your algorithm repeatedly on different datasets and obtain the same (or similar) results. Analyzing, reporting, auditing, and interpreting data are all aspects of this process, meaning each step in the lifecycle needs to be tracked and saved.

Code version control
> Software developers often use version control for their code, and machine learning developers should too. Maintaining a history of all the different versions of

the code, parameters, and data can help us in collaborating with others and keeping track of all the variations of the experiments we conduct.

Data version control

As mentioned previously, a machine learning experiment consists of code, data, and a model. When conducting such an experiment, it is essential to track and log the code and data that produced a specific model. Just as our code changes, our data changes as well. We might extract new features or perform different kinds of preprocessing on the data itself, resulting in variations of the dataset that we need to log for future use. Tools that enable data version control give us these capabilities. Note that out of the box, MLflow (the tool discussed in this chapter) doesn't provide data version control; however, there are other open source tools that do, such as lakeFS (*https://oreil.ly/AzqiF*), DVC (*https://oreil.ly/HQJCE*), and others.

There are various tools available to manage the machine learning experiment lifecycle that can ensure that these three requirements are met. For this book, I chose MLflow, because it is open source, natively integrated with Apache Spark, and abstracts away complex functionality while allowing flexibility for collaboration and expansion to other tools. In the remainder of this chapter, I will introduce this tool and how it enables us to manage our machine learning experiments.

What Is MLflow?

MLflow is a platform that makes it simpler to manage the entire machine learning lifecycle. It enables you to track your experiments and their results, deploy and manage your models, and package your machine learning code in a reusable, reproducible format. It provides a central model registry that supports versioning and annotating, as well as model serving capabilities. It does that by redefining experimentation logs and module structure.

At a high level, the two main components are the tracking server and the model registry, as shown in Figure 3-2. The others, which we will look at in more detail later, are supporting components of the flow. After the model is registered, the team can build automated jobs and use REST-serving APIs to move it downstream. Notice that the open source platform itself does not support model monitoring and the like, which requires dedicated engineering work.

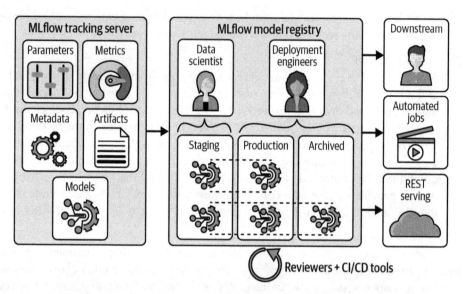

Figure 3-2. The two main MLflow components (courtesy of Databricks (https://oreil.ly/ iUkGX))

Software Components of the MLflow Platform

To better understand how it works, let's take a look at MLflow's software components:

Storage

MLflow provides support for connecting to multiple storage types (directories of files, databases, etc.) and leveraging them to track the machine learning work-flow. The storage contains all the information about the experiments, parameters, results of different runs, etc.

Backend server

This component is responsible for communicating information from the database/storage, UI, SDK, and CLI to the rest of the components, capturing logs from experiments, etc.

Frontend

This is the UI side, where we can interact with and track experiments and the results of different runs in a visual manner.

API and CLI

MLflow also has a Python API and command-line interface for interaction and experiment tracking.

We can interact with the MLflow platform via the API, the CLI, or the UI. Behind the scenes, it tracks all the information we provide it with. Using the API/CLI generates

---

dedicated directories that you can push to a Git repository to facilitate collaboration. Figure 3-3 shows an example of what the UI looks like when managing multiple runs of an experiment.

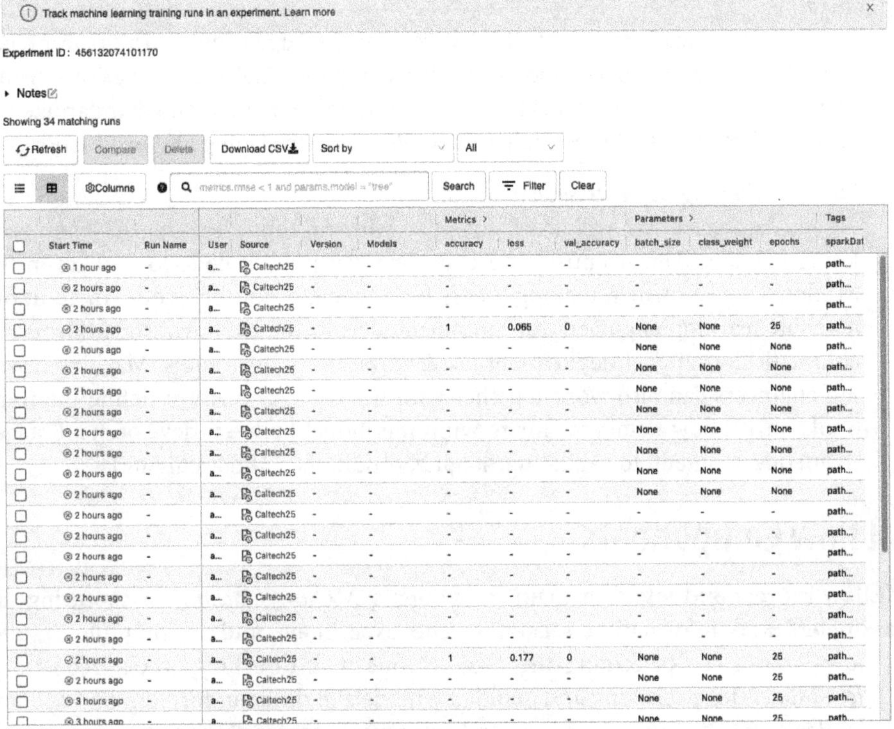

Figure 3-3. Tracking multiple runs as part of an experiment

Users of the MLflow Platform

As you can imagine, many teams and individuals are involved in the process of productionizing machine learning and developing and managing the lifecycle end to end. Because of this, MLflow has a broad range of potential users, including the following:

Individual users
> As an individual, you can use MLflow to track experiments locally on your machine, organize code in projects for future use, and output models that you can later test on fresh data. You can also use it for organizing your research work.

Data science teams
> Teams of data scientists working on the same problem and experimenting with different models can easily share and compare their results using MLflow. The

teams will often create a shared Git repository to hold the artifacts. Everyone on the team can save, track, download, and run their or another team member's model, or use the UI to track the various parameters and get a better understanding of the experiment stage.

Organizations
From an organizational point of view, you can package training and data preparation steps for team collaboration and compare results from various teams working on the same task. MLflow allows you to streamline and standardize the process of moving from research and development to staging and production.

Machine learning engineers/developers
Often, data scientists will work together with machine learning/AI engineers. Using MLflow, data scientists and engineers can publish code to GitHub in the MLflow Project format, making it easy for anyone to run their code. In addition, machine learning engineers can output models in the MLflow Model format to automatically support deployment using MLflow's built-in tools. Machine learning engineers can also work together with the DevOps team to define the webhooks in MLflow databases for moving the model between development stages (from development, to validating, staging, production, and archiving).

MLflow Components

MLflow is organized into four main components: *MLflow Tracking* for capturing the parameters and information related to the experiment and logging the results, *MLflow Projects* for packaging the project code in a directory or Git repository, *MLflow Models* for packaging and deploying models in different formats, and *MLflow Model Registry*, which provides a centralized repository for storing and tracking all the different versions of your models. Let's take a look at each of these in more detail.

MLflow Tracking

MLflow Tracking (*https://oreil.ly/uiJ87*) can be used in a standalone script (not bound to any specific framework) or notebook. It provides an API, UI, and CLI for logging experiment parameters, code itself and its versions, machine learning metrics, and output files produced when running your machine learning code so you can visualize them later. It also enables you to log and query experiments using Python and some other APIs.

MLflow Tracking is based on the concept of recording *runs*, or individual executions of some piece of data science code. The data that is recorded includes the code version, the start and end time, the source file or project, the parameters and metrics, and any artifacts that are generated (such as images, models, or data files). You can record runs from wherever you run your code using MLflow's Python, R, Java, and

REST APIs, and you can define where they are recorded: to local files, a database, or remotely to a tracking server. By default, the MLflow Python API logs runs locally to files in the *mlruns* directory. Runs can be organized into *experiments*, grouping together and providing easy access to all the runs for a specific task.

You can record runs in a standalone program, on a remote cloud machine, or in a notebook. If you record your runs in an MLflow Project (discussed in "MLflow Projects" on page 54), MLflow tracks the project URI and source version. Later, you can query all the recorded runs using the Tracking UI (*https://oreil.ly/N_qBg*) or the MLflow API.

Using MLflow Tracking to record runs

Let's assume we have a TensorFlow experiment that we want to run and track with MLflow. Depending on the flavor of the model we would like to track, we will import the relevant library as the first step. This will be either `mlflow.tensorflow` or `mlflow.keras`; use the one that supports the training algorithm you are using. Subsequently, we can leverage the platform's autologging capabilities or log the parameters and metrics programmatically—I'll show you how to do both.

To start the run, in Python we can use the `with` operator with `mlflow.start_run`. This API call starts a new run within an experiment, if one exists. If no experiment exists, it automatically creates a new one. You can create your own experiment with the `mlflow.create_experiment` API or via the UI. Within the run, you develop your training code and leverage `log_param` and `log_metric` for tracking important information. At the end, you log your model and all necessary artifacts (more on that later). Check out the following code snippet to better understand how the flow works:

```python
import mlflow
import mlflow.tensorflow
# Enable MLflow autologging to log the metrics, parameters, and artifacts
mlflow.tensorflow.autolog()

# Launch a run in a new experiment (or an existing one if one is passed in)
with mlflow.start_run():
    # Log parameters (key/value pairs)
    mlflow.log_param("num_dimensions", 8)

    # Log metrics that can be updated throughout the run
    mlflow.log_metric("alpha", 0.1)
    # ... some machine learning training code

    # Log artifacts (output files)
    mlflow.log_artifact("model.pkl")
    # Log the model
    mlflow.log_model("ml_model_path")
```

At the time of writing, `mlflow.tensorflow.autolog` is an experimental method in version 1.20.2. It uses the TensorFlow *callbacks* mechanism to perform different actions at particular stages in the training procedure. Callbacks can be passed to TensorFlow methods such as `fit`, `evaluate`, and `predict` in order to hook into the various stages of the model training and inference lifecycle. For example, you can leverage them to perform certain actions at the end of an epoch or to reduce compute costs by stopping training when it has reached the desired accuracy, by configuring parameters during the run.

An *epoch* is a single pass over the whole dataset. In each epoch, you can access the logs and programmatically make decisions using callbacks. Callbacks in TensorFlow are part of the Keras library `tf.keras.callbacks.Callback`, while in PyTorch they are part of `pytorch_lightning.callbacks`. In PyTorch, callbacks are often implemented with extensions, such as the open source PyTorch Lightning library, developed by Grid.AI.

At the beginning of the training, the `autolog` function logs all the configurations that are relevant for the training. Then, at the end of each epoch, it captures the log metrics. At the end of the training, it logs the model by calling `mlflow.log_model`. As a result, it covers logging the whole lifecycle, and you can add any other parameters and artifacts you wish to log with it using the available functions (`mlflow.log_param`, `mlflow.log_metric`, `mlflow.log_artifact`, etc.).

Autologging is also available for PyTorch, as demonstrated in the following code snippet:

```
import mlflow.pytorch
# Autolog all MLflow entities
mlflow.pytorch.autolog()
```

MLflow supports other frameworks and flavors of machine learning too, but not all of them are supported as part of the open source solution. For additional details, check out the fully managed and hosted version of MLflow provided by Databricks (*https://oreil.ly/sN3i0*).

 For now, it is recommended that you programmatically log the parameters, metrics, models, and artifacts as a general rule, as autologging is not currently fully supported in the open source version of MLflow. The same recommendation applies when working with Spark MLlib.

Logging your dataset path and version

For experiment tracking, reproducibility, and collaboration purposes, I advise logging the dataset path and version together with the model name and path during the training phase. In the future, this will enable you to reproduce the model given the exact dataset when necessary and to differentiate between models that were trained with the same algorithm but different versions of the input. Make sure to track all hyper-parameters, parameters, and seed data as well!

For that, I recommend using the `mlflow.log_param` function, as it enables you to log all the parameters in one call. This produces a batch log that is simpler to track later:

```
dataset_params = {"dataset_name": "twitter-accounts", "dataset_version": 2.1}
# Log a batch of parameters
with mlflow.start_run():
    mlflow.log_params(dataset_params)
```

Another recommended option is setting tags on the run by passing the `tags` argument to `start_run`:

```
with mlflow.start_run(tags=dataset_params):
```

MLflow provides a flexible API. It is up to you to decide how to structure your experiment logs, with these recommendations in mind. Figure 3-4 shows the MLflow dashboard, where you can track your experiments and view the parameters and tags, among other elements.

Experiment ID: 1384684472288350

▸ Notes ☑

Showing 5 matching runs

| | Refresh | Compare | Delete | Download CSV | Sort by | All | | | | Columns | | metrics.rmse < 1 and params.model = "tree" | | Search |

| State: | Active ∨ | Linked Models: | All Runs ∨ |

							Parameters		Tags	
☐	Start Time	Run Name	User	Source	Version	Models	dataset_name	dataset_version	dataset_name	dataset_version
☐	⊘ 2 minutes ago	-	ad...	Caltech25	-	-	caltech256	2	-	-
☐	⊘ 2 minutes ago	-	ad...	Caltech25	-	-	-	-	caltech256	2
☐	⊘ 5 days ago	-	ad...	Caltech25	-	-	-	-	-	-
☐	⊘ 13 days ago	-	ad...	Train - Ter	-	-	-	-	-	-
☐	⊘ 13 days ago	-	ad...	TrainingDi	-	-	-	-	-	-
						Load more				

Figure 3-4. The MLflow experiment dashboard

 MLflow provides the option to log all the contents of a local directory as artifacts of the run, creating a new active run if there isn't one: `mlflow.log_artifacts(local_dir, artifact_path=None)`. However, I advise against using this, since it copies everything in the given `local_dir` and writes it in the `artifact_path`. When I work with large-scale data for training, I prefer to avoid copying data unless it's really necessary.

By now, you understand the responsibility of the MLflow Tracking component: to log all the information needed to package up your project. Next, let's take a look at MLflow Projects.

MLflow Projects

An MLflow Project (*https://oreil.ly/jIfya*) is a standard format for packaging code in a reusable and reproducible way. The MLflow Projects component includes an API and command-line tools for executing projects and making it possible to chain projects together into workflows.

Each project is simply a directory or Git repository containing a set of code files and a descriptor file (a YAML file called *MLproject*) to specify its dependencies and how to run the code. The MLflow Project format captures all the relevant data that is needed to reproduce and deploy the model, including the environment data. According to the docs, at the time of writing, MLflow supports four different project environments: virtualenv environments (supporting Python packages available on the Python Package Index, aka PyPI), *conda environments* (supporting Python packages and native libraries), Docker container environments (allowing for non-Python dependencies such as Java libraries), and the system environment. The system environment is supplied at runtime, and all the project's dependencies must be installed before project execution. When using a conda environment, by default MLflow uses the system path to find and run the conda binary. You can decide to use a different conda installation by changing the MLFLOW_CONDA_HOME environment variable.

Your project may have multiple entry points for invoking runs with named parameters. Since MLflow Projects support conda, you can specify code dependencies through a conda environment by leveraging the MLflow CLI:

```
$ mlflow run example/conda-env/project -P alpha=0.5
```

Running the experiment using the -P command-line parameter gives us the flexibility to change parameters using the CLI. Here, we overwrite the parameter we passed to the log_metric function (mlflow.log_metric("alpha", 0.1)), changing the value to 0.5.

MLflow Models

The MLflow Models component (*https://oreil.ly/0SMx0*) is used for packaging machine learning models in multiple formats, called *flavors*. Deployment tools can use these flavors to understand the model, making it possible to write tools that work with models from any machine learning library. MLflow Models provides several standard flavors that MLflow's built-in deployment tools support, such as a python_function flavor that describes how to run the model as a Python function. A model of this flavor can be deployed to a Docker-based REST server, to a cloud server, or as a user-defined function. Since you output MLflow Models as artifacts using the tracking API during their run, MLFlow will automatically tag the correct project.

Running the experiment in "MLflow Tracking" on page 50 will record the run and output a model directory with the following outline:

```
--- 58dc6db17fb5471a9a46d87506da983f
------- artifacts
----------- model
----------- MLmodel
------------ conda.yaml
------------ input_example.json
------------ model.pkl
------- meta.yaml
------- metrics
----------- training_score
------- params
----------- A
------------ ...
------- tags
----------- mlflow.source.type
----------- mlflow.user
```

This directory contains all the information we need to reproduce the experiment. Let's look at the structure. The first line of output, 58dc6db17fb5471a9a46d 87506da983f, is the experiment's 128-bit universally unique identifier (UUID). At the root of the directory, there is a YAML file named *meta.yaml* that contains metadata about the experiment. With that, we already have extensive traceability information available to us and a solid foundation to continue our experiments. There are also four subdirectories: *artifacts*, which contains any artifacts that are logged; *metrics*, which contains the metrics that are logged; and *params* and *tags*, which contain the parameters and tags set for the run. The *MLmodel* file can define multiple flavors that the model supports as well as provide additional information about the model.

MLflow Model Registry

During experiments, we may generate a large number of models. The MLflow Model Registry (*https://oreil.ly/zKGAn*) provides a centralized storage for those models, as well as a set of APIs for interacting with them and a dedicated UI for visualization. It also allows us to manage the full lifecycle of an MLflow Model through the CLI. The Model Registry enables us to access a broad set of metadata about all our models, including which experiment and run created the model (its "lineage"), the model version and stage (e.g., staging, production, archived), and any annotations describing the model. We can also add comments about the models in the registry, rename them, transition them between stages, and serve them from the registry.

Registering models

During the training cycle, we produce multiple models so that we can ultimately pick the most suitable one. As you learned in Chapter 10, the models can be logged implicitly with `autolog` or explicitly with the `log_model` function. At this point, the model is not yet in the registry; to add it, we need to *register* it. There are a few different ways to do this. To register a model during a run, we can include the `registered_model_name` parameter, as shown here:

```
mlflow.keras.log_model(keras_model=model, registered_model_name='tfmodel',
                       artifact_path="path")
```

This registers the model as a new model with version 1, if no model with that name exists in the registry; if there's already a model with that name, it registers it as a new version. You can also use the `register_model` method after you've completed your experiment and decided which model you want to register, passing it the model's `run_id` and the name to register it as. For additional details on this and other registration options, see the documentation (*https://oreil.ly/1T-0O*).

Transitioning between model stages

At a high level, a machine learning model's lifecycle has five stages: development, validation, staging, production, and archived. MLflow allows us to connect to CI/CD tools to transition our models between these stages. For that, we need to write dedicated scripts that listen for model status change events and, upon an update, trigger the desired script. You can also leverage webhooks or other mechanisms of your preference.

When we first log a model using the `log_model` API of the corresponding model flavor (Keras or TensorFlow), it is assigned the status None, which means it's in the development stage. To promote the model from the development stage to staging in the database, use the `MlflowClient` API:

```
client = MlflowClient()
Model_version = client.transition_model_version_stage(
    name='tfmodel',
    version=3,
    stage="Staging"
)
```

`MlflowClient` is the Python client to interact with the tracking server. The `transition_model_version_stage` function allows us to update the model stage and invoke the desired CI/CD scripts. The `stage` parameter accepted the following values: `Staging|Archived|Production|None`. Setting this parameter to `Staging`, given a configured environment that tracks model status, will open a request to transition the model from None status to `Staging` status for integration testing in a staging environment. We will discuss this in more detail in Chapter 10.

Using MLflow at Scale

As mentioned earlier, MLflow Tracking stores information on experiments and runs as well as artifacts related to the runs (model-related files). It uses two components for storage, which can be either local or remote: a *backend store* for information about experiments (runs, parameters, metrics, tags, annotations, etc.) and an *artifact store* for storing the models themselves and any related files, objects, model summaries, etc. MLflow, like most frameworks, offers various configuration options, including what to use for storage. If you work locally on your machine, you can save artifacts and information about your experiments to your local disk. If you work from a note-book on a cloud or other remote server, you can save your projects to the storage you have available there. Figure 3-5 shows the different storage options.

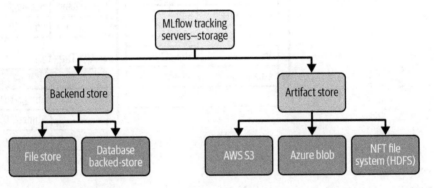

Figure 3-5. MLflow Tracking storage options

The artifact store can be any local or remote file store (though note that a local file store is not a scalable option). The backend store can be a local or remote file store or a database. When running MLflow on your local machine, the backend and artifact stores can share a single directory on the local filesystem, or you can choose to store experiment-related entities in a database such as PostgreSQL or SQLite. Figure 3-6 shows what the table hierarchy might look like in this case.

Experiments table

Columns	Type
experiment_id	Integer
name	String(256)
artifact_location	String(256)
lifecycle_stage	String(32)

Runs table

Columns	Type
run_uuid	String(256)
name	String(256)
source_type	String(20)
source_name	String(500)
entry_point_name	String(50)
user_id	String(256)
status	String(256)
start_time	BigInteger
end_time	BigInteger
source_version	String(50)
lifecycle_stage	String(20)
artifact_url	String(200)
experiment_id	Integer

Metrics table

Columns	Type
key	String(256)
value	Float
timestamp	BigInteger
run_uuid	String(32)

Params table

Columns	Type
key	String(256)
value	String(250)
timestamp	BigInteger
run_uuid	String(32)

Tags table

Columns	Type
key	String(256)
value	String(250)
timestamp	BigInteger
run_uuid	String(32)

Figure 3-6. MLflow tracking server SQL table hierarchy

Let's dive deeper into a potential scalable solution. MLflow supports distributed architectures, where the tracking server, backend store, and artifact store reside on remote hosts. For scaling and team collaboration, this configuration is preferable to running on *localhost*. Figure 3-7 shows what this might look like. As you can see, there can be multiple hosts. Here, the user runs MLflow on their local machine, and the tracking server itself and both stores reside remotely.

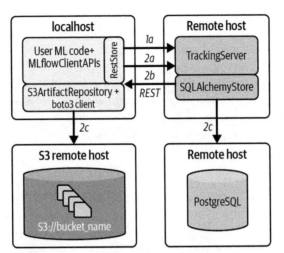

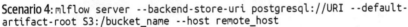

Scenario 4: `mlflow server --backend-store-uri postgresql://URI --default-artifact-root S3:/bucket_name --host remote_host`

Figure 3-7. Distributed configuration example

The backend store can be a file store or a database-backed store, but for a scalable approach we will use PostgreSQL (an open source database that has great support by the community). To connect with it using Python, MLflow uses SQLAlchemy (*https://www.sqlalchemy.org*). For our artifact store, where we will store our models, we should choose a location that is suitable for big data. We can configure this using the `artifact-root` parameter when we run the tracking server from the command line.

There is often a huge knowledge gap between developers and data scientists; while the former are experts in building software, the latter are experts in building machine learning models and solving business problems. That sometimes creates a dissonance between coding best practices and data science best practices, which leads to general software antipatterns, especially when dealing with large-scale data or complex systems. For example, if our dataset is relatively small (say, 100 MB), we can save the dataset together with the machine learning experiment code and output in a Git repository if we wish to do so. However, as we move through the stages of productionizing machine learning—development, validation, testing in staging, and so on—to comply with organizational rules around privacy, access control, etc., we often need to use cloud storage solutions instead (typically cloud-based object-storage services such as Azure Blob, AWS S3, and others). The takeaway: *don't store large data files as artifacts in MLflow.*

Summary

At this point, you have a decent understanding of what MLflow is and how to use it to manage your machine learning experiments. This is an important task, and the differentiator between experimenting with machine learning and actually using it as part of an organization's R&D lifecycle. We'll talk more about MLflow in Chapter 10, when we discuss deployment. In the next chapter, we'll dive into working with the data itself: ingesting it, preprocessing it, and exploring it.

## CHAPTER 4

Data Ingestion, Preprocessing, and Descriptive Statistics

You are most likely familiar with the phrase "garbage in, garbage out." It captures well the notion that flawed, incorrect, or nonsensical data input will always produce faulty output. In the context of machine learning, it also emphasizes the fact that the attention we devote to ingesting, preprocessing, and statistically understanding our data (exploring and preparing it) will have an effect on the success of the overall process. Faulty data ingestion has a direct impact on the quality of the data, and so does faulty preprocessing. To get a feel for the data in hand, and its correctness, we leverage descriptive statistics; this is a vital part of the process as it helps us verify that the data we are using is of good quality. Data scientists, machine learning engineers, and data engineers often spend significant time working on, researching, and improving these crucial steps, and I will walk you through them in this chapter.

Before we start, let's understand the flow. Let's assume that at the beginning, our data resides on disk, in a database, or in a cloud data lake. Here are the steps we will follow to get an understanding of our data:

1. *Ingestion.* We begin by moving the data in its current form into a DataFrame instance. This is also called *deserialization* of the data. More accurately, in Spark, in this step we define a plan for how to deserialize the data, transforming it into a DataFrame. This step often provides us with a basic schema inferred from the existing data.

2. *Preprocessing.* This involves marshaling the data to fit into our desired schema. If we load the data as strings and we need it as floats, we will cast the data type and tweak the values as needed to fit the desired schema. This can be a complex and error-prone process, especially when synchronizing data from multiple sources at a multi-terabyte scale, and requires planning ahead.

3. *Qualifying.* This step consists of using descriptive statistics to understand the data and how to work with it.

Steps 2 and 3 can overlap, as we may decide to do more preprocessing on the data depending on the statistics calculated in step 3.

Now that you have a general idea of what the steps are, let's dig a bit more deeply into each of them.

Data Ingestion with Spark

Apache Spark is generic enough to allow us to extend its API and develop dedicated connectors to any type of store for ingesting (and persisting/sinking/saving) data using the connector mechanism. Out of the box, it supports various file formats such as Parquet, CSV, binary files, JSON, ORC, image files, and more.

Spark also enables us to work with batch and streaming data. The Spark *batch API* is for processing offline data residing in a file store or database. With batch data, the dataset size is fixed and does not change, and we don't get any fresh data to process. For processing streaming data, Spark has an older API called DStream or simply Streaming, and a newer, improved API called *Structured Streaming*. Structured Streaming provides an API for distributed continuous processing of structured data streams. It allows you to process multiple data records at a time, dividing the input stream into microbatches. Keep in mind that if your data is not structured, or if the format varies, you will need to use the legacy DStream API instead, or build a solution to automate schema changes without failures.

In this chapter, we will focus on batch processing with offline, cold data. Building machine learning models using cold data is the most common approach across varied use cases such as video production, financial modeling, drug discovery, genomic research, recommendation engines, and more. We will look at working with streaming data in Chapter 10, where we discuss serving models with both kinds of data sources.

Specifying batch reading with a defined data format is done using the `format` function, for example:

```
df = spark.read.format("image")
```

The class that enables this is the `DataFrameReader class` (*https://oreil.ly/NTjyk*). You can configure it through its `options` API to define how to load the data and infer the schema if the file format doesn't provide it already, or extract the metadata if it does.

Different file formats may either have a schema or not, depending on whether the data is *structured*, *semi-structured*, or *unstructured*, and, of course, the format's implementation itself. For example, JSON format is considered semi-structured, and out of the box it doesn't maintain metadata about the rows, columns, and features. So with JSON, the schema is *inferred*.

On the other hand, structured data formats such as Avro and Parquet have a metadata section that describes the data schema. This enables the schema to be *extracted*.

Working with Images

An image file can store data in an uncompressed, compressed, or vector format. For example, JPEG is a compressed format, and TIFF is an uncompressed format.

We save digital data in these formats in order to easily convert them for a computer display or a printer. This is the result of *rasterization (https://oreil.ly/ezVss)*. Rasterization's main task is converting the image data into a grid of pixels, where each pixel has a number of bits that define its color and transparency. Rasterizing an image file for a specific device takes into account the number of bits per pixel (the color depth) that the device is designed to handle. When we work with images, we need to attend to the file format and understand if it's compressed or uncompressed (more on that in "Image compression and Parquet" on page 81).

In this chapter, we will use a Kaggle image dataset named Caltech 256 (*https://oreil.ly/8Pi_w*) that contains image files with the JPEG compression format. Our first step will be to load them into a Spark DataFrame instance. For this, we can choose between two format options: image or binary.

 When your program processes the DataFrame `load` operation, the Spark engine does not immediately load the images into memory. As described in Chapter 2, Spark uses lazy evaluation, which means that instead of actually loading them, it creates a plan of how to load them if and when that becomes necessary. The plan contains information about the actual data, such as table fields/columns, format, file addresses, etc.

Image format

Spark MLlib has a dedicated image data source that enables us to load images from a directory into a DataFrame, which uses OpenCV types to read and process the image data. In this section, you will learn more about it.

OpenCV (https://opencv.org) is a C/C++-based tool for computer vision workloads. MLlib functionality allows you to convert compressed images (*.jpeg, .png*, etc.) into the OpenCV data format. When loaded to a Spark DataFrame, each image is stored as a separate row.

The following are the supported uncompressed OpenCV types:

- CV_8U
- CV_8UC1
- CV_8UC3
- CV_8UC4

where 8 indicates the bit depth, U indicates unsigned, and Cx indicates the number of channels.

 As of Spark 3.1.1, the limit on image size is 1 GB. Since Spark is open source, you can follow the image size support updates in its source: the line assert(imageSize < 1e9, "image is too large") in the definition of the decode function of the Image Schema.scala object tells us that the limit is 1 GB.

To explore relatively small files, the image format Spark provides is a fantastic way to start working with images and actually see the rendered output. However, for the general workflow where there is no actual need to look at the images themselves during the process, I advise you to use the binary format, as it is more efficient and you will be able to process larger image files faster. Additionally, for larger images files (≥1 GB), binary format is the only way to process them. Whereas Spark's default behavior is to partition data, images are not partitioned. With spatial objects such as images, we instead refer to *tiling*, or decomposing the image into a set of segments (tiles) with the desired shape. Tiling images can be part of the preprocessing of the data itself. Going forward, to align the language, I will refer to partitions even when discussing images or spatial objects.

Binary format

Spark began supporting a binary file data source (*https://oreil.ly/VSQ7a*) with version 3.0. This enabled it to read binary files and convert them into a single record in a table. The record contains the raw content as BinaryType and a couple of metadata columns. Using binary format to read the data produces a DataFrame with the following columns:

---

1 The binary data source schema may change with new releases of Apache Spark or when using Spark in managed environments such as Databricks.

- path: StringType

- modificationTime: TimestampType

- length: LongType

- content: BinaryType

We'll use this format to load the Caltech 256 data, as shown in the following code snippet:

```
from pyspark.sql.types import BinaryType
spark.sql("set spark.sql.files.ignoreCorruptFiles=true")

df = spark.read.format("binaryFile")
                .option("pathGlobFilter", "*.jpg")
                .option("recursiveFileLookup", "true")
                .load(file_path)
```

As discussed in Chapter 2, the data within our dataset is in a nested folder hierarchy. recursiveFileLookup enables us to read the nested folders, while the pathGlob Filter option allows us to filter the files and read only the ones with a *.jpg* extension.

Again, note that this code does not actually load the data into the executors for computing. As discussed previously, because of Spark's lazy evaluation mechanism, the execution will not start until an action is triggered—the driver accumulates the various transformation requests and queries in a DAG, optimizes them, and only acts when there is a specific request for an action. This allows us to save on computation costs, optimize queries, and increase the overall manageability of our code.

Working with Tabular Data

Since Spark provides out-of-the-box connectors to various file format types, it makes working with tabular data pretty straightforward. For example, in the book's GitHub repository (*https://oreil.ly/smls-git*), under *datasets* you will find the CO_2 Emission by Vehicles dataset, where the data is in CSV format. With the connector function .format("csv"), or directly with .csv(file_path), we can easily load this into a DataFrame instance.

Do pay attention to the schema, though—even with the InferSchema option, Spark tends to define columns in CSV files as containing strings even when they contain integers, Boolean values, etc. Hence, at the beginning, our main job is to check and correct the columns' data types. For example, if a column in the input CSV file contains JSON strings, you'll need to write dedicated code to handle this JSON.

Notice that each Spark data source connector has unique properties that provide you with a set of options for dealing with corrupted data. For example, you can control the column-pruning behavior by setting spark.sql.csv .parser .column Pruning

`.enabled` to `False` if you don't wish to prune columns with a corrupted format or data, or use `True` for the opposite behavior. You can also leverage the `mode` parameter to make pruning more specific, with approaches such as `PERMISSIVE` to set the field to `null`, `DROPMALFORMED` to ignore the whole record, or `FAILFAST` to throw an exception upon processing a corrupted record. See the following code snippet for an example:

```
df = spark.read.option("mode","FAILFAST")
              .option("delimiter","\t")
              .csv(file_path)
```

After loading the data and deserializing it into a DataFrame, it is time to preprocess it. Before moving on, I advise saving your data in a format that has a typed schema with well-defined column names and types, such as Parquet or Avro.

Preprocessing Data

Preprocessing is the art of transforming the data into the desired state, be it a strongly typed schema or a specific data type required by the algorithm.

Preprocessing Versus Processing

Differentiating between preprocessing and processing can be difficult when you're just getting started with machine learning. *Preprocessing* refers to all the work we do before validating the dataset itself. This work is done before we attempt to get a feel for the data using descriptive statistics or perform feature engineering, both of which fall under the umbrella of *processing*. Those procedures are interlocked (see Figure 4-1), and we will likely repeat them again and again until we get the data into the desired state. Spark provides us with all the tools we need for these tasks, either through the MLlib library or SQL APIs.

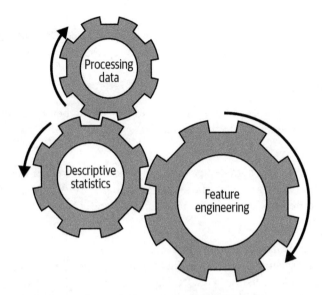

Figure 4-1. Interlocked procedures during machine learning

Why Preprocess the Data?

Preprocessing the data, or wrangling it into the desired schema, is a crucial step that must be completed before we can even start exploring the data, let alone engineering new features. The reason it's so important is because machine learning algorithms often have dedicated input requirements, such as specific data structures and/or data types. In some academic research papers, you might find this process referred to as *data marshaling*.

To give you an idea of what kind of preprocessing you might need to perform on your data before passing it to an MLlib algorithm, let's take a quick look at the high-level requirements of the different kinds of algorithms:

Classification and/or regression algorithms
    For classification and regression, you will want to transform your data into one column of type `vector` (dense or sparse) with `double` or `float` values. This column is often named `features`, but you have the flexibility to set the input column name later.

Recommendation algorithms
    For recommendation, you will want to have a `userCol` column with `integer` values representing the user IDs, an `itemCol` column with `integer` values representing the item IDs, and a `ratingCol` column with `double` or `float` values representing the items' ratings by the users.

Unsupervised learning

> When dealing with data that calls for an unsupervised learning approach, you will often need one column of type `vector` to represent your features.

Data Structures

Depending on its structure, data often requires processing before it can be fully utilized. Data can be classified into three categories:

Structured

> Structured data has a high degree of organization. It's stored in a predefined schematic format, such as a comma-separated values (*.csv*) file or a table in a database. It is sometimes also referred to as *tabular* data.

Semi-structured

> Semi-structured data has some degree of organization, but the structure is less rigid, and the schema is not fixed. There might be tags that separate elements and enforce hierarchies, like in a JSON file. Such data might require preprocessing before we can use it for machine learning algorithms.

Unstructured

> Unstructured data has no defined organization and no specific format—think of *.jpeg* images, *.mp4* video files, sound files, etc. This data often requires major preprocessing before we can use it to build models. Most of the data that we create today is unstructured data.

MLlib Data Types

MLlib has its own dedicated data types that it requires as input for machine learning algorithms. To work with Spark MLlib, you will need to transform your columns into one of these types—this is why preprocessing and transforming data are processes that you will perform in an interlocked manner. Under the hood, Spark uses the private objects `VectorUDT` and `MatrixUDF`, which abstract multiple types of local vectors (dense, sparse, labeled point) and matrices (both local and distributed). Those objects allow easy interaction with `spark.sql.Dataset` functionality. At a high level, the two types of objects are as follows:

Vector

> A vector object represents a numeric vector. You can think of it as an array, just like in Python, only here the index is of type `integer` and the value is of type `double`.

Matrix

> A matrix object represents a numeric matrix. It can be local to one machine or distributed across multiple machines. With the local version, indices are of type

integer and values are of type double. With the distributed version, indices are of type long and values are of type double. All matrix types are represented by vectors.

 To simplify our work with Python tools, MLlib recognizes NumPy arrays and Python lists as dense vectors and SciPy's csc_matrix (*https://oreil.ly/Tw5L3*) with a single column as a sparse vector. This enables us to transition more easily from one tool to the other. Bear it in mind when working with multiple tools.

It's good to understand how sparse and dense vectors are represented in MLlib, as you will encounter them in the documentation and your experiments. Spark decides which kind of vector to create for a given task behind the scenes.

 The third kind of vector is a labeled point; it represents features and labels of a data point and can be either dense or sparse. In MLlib, labeled points are used in supervised learning algorithms.

Let's start with a dense vector. Here's an example:

```
Row(features=DenseVector([1.2, 543.5, 0.0, 0.0, 0.0, 1.0, 0.0]))]
```

A DenseVector consists of a fixed-size array of values. It is considered less efficient than a SparseVector in terms of memory consumption because it explicitly creates memory space for the specified vector size, including any empty/default values. In our example, there are seven values in the DenseVector, but four of them are empty (0.0 is the default value, so these are considered empty values).

A SparseVector is an optimization of a DenseVector that has empty/default values. Let's take a look at how our example DenseVector would look translated into a SparseVector:

```
Row(features=SparseVector(7,{0:1.2, 1: 543.5, 5:1.0}))
```

The first number represents the size of the vector (7), and the map ({...}) represents the indices and their values. In this vector, there are only three values that need to be stored: the value at index 0 is 1.2, the value at index 2 is 543.5, and the value at index 5 is 1. The values at the other indices do not need to be stored, because they are all the default value.

Let's take a look at a bigger vector example:

```
[Row(features=SparseVector(50, {48: 9.9, 49: 6.7}))]
```

In this case, the vector size is 50, and we have only two values to store: `9.9` for index 48 and `6.7` for index 49.

A `SparseVector` can also look like this:

```
(50,[48,49],[9.9,6.7])
```

where the first number (here, 50) represents the size, the first array (`[48,49]`) represents the indices whose values are stored in the `SparseVector`, and the second array (`[9.9,6.7]`) represents the values at those indices. So in this example, the value at index 48 is `9.9`, and the value at index 49 is `6.7`. The rest of the vector indices all have a value of `0.0`.

Why do we need both kinds of vectors? In machine learning, some algorithms, such as the naive Bayes classifier, work better on dense vector features and consequently might perform poorly given sparse vector features.

What can you do if your machine learning algorithm doesn't work well with the kinds of features you have? First of all, the process described next will help you get a feel for your data and adapt it to fit your machine learning goal. If necessary, you can try collecting more data. You can also choose algorithms that perform better on sparse vectors. After all, this is part of the process of building machine learning models!

 Make sure to bookmark and use the MLlib documentation (*https://oreil.ly/DfP7R*). There is a community project dedicated to improving the Spark docs, which evolve and get better every day.

Preprocessing with MLlib Transformers

Transformers are part of the Apache Spark MLlib library named `pyspark.ml.feature`. In addition to transformers, it also provides *extractors* and *selectors*. Many of them are based on machine learning algorithms and statistical or mathematical computations. For preprocessing, we will leverage the transformers API, but you might find the other APIs helpful as well in different situations.

Transformers in Spark are algorithms or functions that take a DataFrame as an input and output a new DataFrame with the desired columns. In other words, you can think of them as translating a given input into a corresponding output. Transformers enable us to scale, convert, or modify existing columns. We can divide them loosely into the following categories: *text data transformers, categorical feature transformers, continuous numerical transformers,* and *others.*

The tables in the following sections will guide you on when to use each transformer. You should be aware that given the statistical nature of the transformers, some APIs may take longer to finish than others.

Working with text data

Text data typically consists of documents that represent words, sentences, or any form of free-flowing text. This is inherently unstructured data, which is often noisy. *Noisy data in machine learning is irrelevant or meaningless data that might significantly impact the model's performance.* Examples include stopwords such as *a*, *the*, *is*, and *are*. In MLlib, you'll find a dedicated function just for extracting stopwords, and so much more! MLlib provides a rich set of functionality for manipulating text data input.

With text, we want to ingest it and transform it into a format that can be easily fed into a machine learning algorithm. Most of the algorithms in MLlib expect structured data as input, in a tabular format with rows, columns, etc. On top of that, for efficiency in terms of memory consumption, we would typically hash the strings, since string values take up more space than integer, floating-point, or Boolean values. Before adding text data to your machine learning project, you first need to clean it up by using one of the text data transformers. To learn about the common APIs and their usage, take a look at Table 4-1.

Table 4-1. Text data transformers

API	Usage
Tokenizer	Maps a column of text into a list of words by splitting on whitespace. It is based on the regular expression (regex) \\s, which matches a single whitespace character. Under the hood, the Tokenizer API uses the java.lang.String.split function.
RegexToken izer	Splits the text based on the input regex (the default is \\s+, which matches one or more whitespace characters. It is typically used to split on whitespace and/or commas and other supported delimiters. RegexTokenizer is more computation-heavy than Tokenizer because it uses the scala.util.matching regex function. The supplied regex should conform to Java regular expression syntax.
HashingTF	Takes an array of strings and generates hashes from them. In many free-text scenarios, you will need to run the Tokenizer function first. This is one of the most widely used transformers.
NGram	Extracts a sequence of *n* tokens given an integer *n*. The input column can only be an array of strings. To convert a text string into an array of strings, use the Tokenizer function first.
StopWords Remover	Takes a sequence of text and drops the default stopwords. You can specify languages and case sensitivity and provide your own list of stopwords.

Before we proceed, let's generate a synthetic dataset to use in the examples that follow:

```
sentence_data_frame = spark.createDataFrame([
    (0, "Hi I think pyspark is cool ","happy"),
    (1, "All I want is a pyspark cluster","indifferent"),
    (2, "I finally understand how ML works","fulfilled"),
    (3, "Yet another sentence about pyspark and ML","indifferent"),
    (4, "Why didn't I know about mllib before","sad"),
    (5, "Yes, I can","happy")
], ["id", "sentence", "sentiment"])
```

Our dataset has three columns: id, of type int, and sentence and sentiment, of type string.

The transformation includes the following steps:

1. Free text → list of words
2. List of words → list of meaningful words
3. Select meaningful values

Ready? Set? Transform! Our first step is to transform the free text into a list of words. For that, we can use either the Tokenizer or the RegexTokenizer API, as shown here:

```
from pyspark.ml.feature import Tokenizer

tokenizer = Tokenizer(inputCol="sentence", outputCol="words")
tokenized = tokenizer.transform(sentence_data_frame)
```

This tells Tokenizer to take the sentence column as an input and generate a new DataFrame, adding an output column named words. Notice that we used the transform function—transformers always have this function. Figure 4-2 shows our new DataFrame with the added words column.

```
+---+--------------------------------------------+-----------+------------------------------------------------+
|id |sentence                                    |sentiment  |words                                           |
+---+--------------------------------------------+-----------+------------------------------------------------+
|0  |Hi I think pyspark is cool                  |happy      |[hi, i, think, pyspark, is, cool]               |
|1  |All I want is a pyspark cluster             |indifferent|[all, i, want, is, a, pyspark, cluster]         |
|2  |I finally understand how ML works           |fulfill    |[i, finally, understand, how, ml, works]        |
|3  |Yet another sentence about pyspark and ML   |indifferent|[yet, another, sentence, about, pyspark, and, ml]|
|4  |Why didn't I know about mllib before        |sad        |[why, didn't, i, know, about, mllib, before]    |
|5  |Yes, I can                                  |happy      |[yes,, i, can]                                  |
+---+--------------------------------------------+-----------+------------------------------------------------+
```

Figure 4-2. New DataFrame with words column

The next step is to remove stopwords, or words that are unlikely to provide much value in our machine learning process. For that, we will use StopWordsRemover:

```
from pyspark.ml.feature import StopWordsRemover

remover = StopWordsRemover(inputCol="words", outputCol="meaningful_words")
meaningful_data_frame = remover.transform(tokenized)
# I use the show function here for educational purposes only; with a large
# dataset, you should avoid it.
meaningful_data_frame.select("words","meaningful_words").show(5,truncate=False)
```

Example 4-1 shows the DataFrame with the new meaningful_words column.

Example 4-1. New DataFrame with `meaningful_words` column

```
+------------------------------------------------+--------------------------------------------+
|words                                           |meaningful_words                            |
+------------------------------------------------+--------------------------------------------+
|[hi, i, think, pyspark, is, cool]               |[hi, think, pyspark, cool]                  |
|[all, i, want, is, a, pyspark, cluster]         |[want, pyspark, cluster]                    |
|[i, finally, understand, how, ml, works]        |[finally, understand, ml, works]            |
|[yet, another, sentence, about, pyspark, and, ml]|[yet, another, sentence, pyspark, ml]|
|[why, didn't, i, know, about, ml, lib, before]  |[know, mllib]                               |
|[yes,, i, can]                                  |[yes,]                                      |
+------------------------------------------------+--------------------------------------------+
```

Stopwords Are Noisy Data

Removing stopwords can be viewed as part of the feature engineering process, as it involves removing noise from the array of words. I've decided to keep it as part of the discussion of preprocessing, since with natural language processing (NLP), you'll want to remove stopwords at the beginning.

Pay close attention to the list of stopwords you are using, and make sure the list stays consistent between developing the model, validating it, testing it, and putting it into production. You should try to avoid potential clashes caused by having different stopword lists. For example, imagine that you are using Spark 3.*x* functionality to remove stopwords. Later, your colleague pushes a fix list to the Spark 3.*y* version source and starts a cluster upgrading process that upgrades Spark version 3.*x* to 3.*y*. Since these two versions hold different stopword lists, this could create a problem with the expected model behavior and impact accuracy.

What's more, you will often use Spark to clean the data and train the model, and another framework to serve it, and that framework might have a different default list of stopwords. This is why it is frequently a better decision to manage the stopword list yourself. Of course, this is a more advanced approach that is suitable for production-izing machine learning while staying in control of the various parameters that can change from the environment where you develop the model to the environment where you serve the model (the production environment).

From nominal categorical features to indices

One of the strategies we can use to speed up the machine learning process is to turn discrete categorical values presented in `string` format into a numerical form using indices. The values can be discrete or continuous, depending on the machine learning models we plan to use. Table 4-2 lists the most common APIs and describes their usage.

Table 4-2. Categorical feature transformers

API	Usage
String Indexer	Encodes string columns into indices, where the first one (starting at index 0) is the most frequent value in the column, and so on. Used for faster training with supervised data where the columns are the categories/labels.
IndexTo String	The opposite of `StringIndexer`: maps a column of label indices back to a column containing the original labels as strings. Often used to retrieve the label categories after the training process.
OneHot Encoder	Maps a column of categorical features represented as label indices into a column of binary vectors, with at most one 1 value per row indicating the category. This allows machine learning algorithms that expect continuous features, such as logistic regression, to use categorical features by mapping them into continuous features.
Vector Indexer	Similar to `StringIndexer`; takes a vector column as input and converts it into category indices.

The DataFrame we generated includes a column representing the sentiment of the text. Our sentiment categories are happy, fulfilled, sad, and indifferent. Let's turn them into indices using `StringIndexer`:

```
from pyspark.ml.feature import StringIndexer
indexer = StringIndexer(inputCol="sentiment", outputCol="categoryIndex")
indexed = indexer.fit(meaningful_data_frame).transform(meaningful_data_frame)
indexed.show(5)
```

In this code snippet, we create a new `StringIndexer` instance that takes the senti ment column as an input and creates a new DataFrame with a `categoryIndex` column, of type double. We call the fit function first, providing it with the name of our DataFrame. This step is necessary for training the indexer before the transformation: it builds a map between indices and categories by scanning the sentiment column. This function is performed by another preprocessing tool called an *estimator*, which we'll look at in more detail in Chapter 6. After fitting the estimator, we call transform to calculate the new indices. Example 4-2 shows the DataFrame with the new categoryIndex column.

Example 4-2. DataFrame with `categoryIndex` column

```
+---+--------------------+-----------+--------------------+--------------------+-------------+
| id|            sentence|  sentiment|               words|     meaningful_words|categoryIndex|
+---+--------------------+-----------+--------------------+--------------------+-------------+
|  0|Hi I think pyspar...|      happy|[hi, i, think, py...|[i, think, pyspa... |          0.0|
|  1|All I want is a p...|indifferent|[all, i, want, is...|[want, pyspark, c...|          1.0|
|  2|I finally underst...|  fulfilled|[i, finally, unde...|[finally, underst...|          2.0|
|  3|Yet another sente...|indifferent|[yet, another, se...|[yet, another, se...|          1.0|
|  4|Why didn't I know...|        sad|[why, didn't, i, ...|     [know, mllib]|          3.0|
|  5|         Yes, I can|      happy|     [yes,, i, can]|            [yes,]|          0.0|
+---+--------------------+-----------+--------------------+--------------------+-------------+
```

Structuring continuous numerical data

In some cases, we may have continuous numeric data that we want to structure. We do this by providing a threshold, or multiple thresholds, for taking an action or deciding on a classification.

 Continuous numeric values are often represented in a vector, with common data types being `integer`, `float`, and `double`.

For example, when we have scores for specific sentiments, as shown in Example 4-3, we can take an action when a given score falls into a defined range. Think about a customer satisfaction system—we would like our machine learning model to recommend an action that is based on customer sentiment scores. Let's say our biggest customer has a `sad` score of `0.75` and our threshold for calling the customer to discuss how we can improve their experience is a `sad` score above `0.7`. In this instance, we would want to call the customer. The thresholds themselves can be defined manually or by using machine learning algorithms or plain statistics. Going forward, let's assume we have a DataFrame with a dedicated score for every sentiment. That score is a continuous number in the range `[0,1]` specifying the relevancy of the sentiment category. The business goal we want to achieve will determine the thresholds to use and the structure to give the data for future recommendations.

Example 4-3. DataFrame with sentiment score for each category

```
+-----------+-----+-----------+---------+----+
|sentence_id|happy|indifferent|fulfilled| sad|
+-----------+-----+-----------+---------+----+
|          0| 0.01|       0.43|      0.3| 0.5|
|          1|0.097|       0.21|      0.2| 0.9|
|          2|  0.4|      0.329|     0.97| 0.4|
|          3|  0.7|        0.4|      0.3|0.87|
|          4| 0.34|        0.4|      0.3|0.78|
|          5|  0.1|        0.3|     0.31|0.29|
+-----------+-----+-----------+---------+----+
```

Take into consideration the type of data you are working with and cast it when necessary. You can leverage the Spark SQL API for this, as shown here:

```
cast_data_frame = sentiment_data_frame.selectExpr("cast(happy as double)")
```

The following are some common strategies for handling continuous numerical data:

Fixed bucketing/binning
> This is done manually by either binarizing the data by providing a specific threshold or providing a range of buckets. This process is similar to what we discussed earlier with regard to structuring continuous data.

Adaptive bucketing/binning
　　The overall data may be skewed, with some values occurring frequently while others are rare. This might make it hard to manually specify a range for each bucket. Adaptive bucketing is a more advanced technique where the transformer calculates the distribution of the data and sets the bucket sizes so that each one contains approximately the same number of values.

Table 4-3 lists the most commonly used continuous numerical transformers available in MLlib. Remember to pick the one that fits your project based on your needs.

Table 4-3. Common continuous numerical transformers

API	Usage
Binarizer	Turns a numerical feature into a binary feature, given a threshold. For example, 5.1 with threshold 0.7 would turn into 1, and 0.6 would turn into 0.
Bucketizer	Takes a column of continuous numerical values and transforms it into a column of buckets, where each bucket represents a part of the range of values—for example, 0 to 1, 1 to 2, and so on.
MaxAbsScaler	Takes a vector of float values and divides each value by the maximum absolute value in the input columns.
MinMaxScaler	Scales the data to the desired min and max values, where the default range is [0,1].
Normalizer	Converts a vector of double values into normalized values that are nonnegative real numbers between 0 and 1. The default *p*-norm is 2, which implements the Euclidean norm for calculating a distance and reducing the float range to [0,1].
Quantile Discretizer	Takes a column of continuous numerical values and transforms it into a column with binned categorical values, with the input maximum number of bins optionally determining the approximate quantile values.
RobustScaler	Similar to StandardScaler; takes a vector of float values and produces a vector of scaled features given the input quantile range.
StandardScaler	Estimator that takes a vector of float values and aims to center the data given the input standard deviation and mean value.

Additional transformers

MLlib offers many additional transformers that use statistics or abstract other Spark functionality. Table 4-4 lists some of these and describes their usage. Bear in mind that more are added regularly, with code examples available in the *examples/src/main/python/ml/* directory of the Apache Spark GitHub repository (*https://oreil.ly/SQxG9*).

Table 4-4. Additional transformers

API	Usage
DCT	Implements a discrete cosine transform, taking a vector of data points in the time domain and translating them to the frequency domain. Used in signal processing and data compression (e.g., with images, audio, radio, and digital television).

API	Usage
Elementwise Product	Takes a column with vectors of data and a transforming vector of the same size and outputs a multiplication of them that is associative, distributive, and commutative (based on the Hadamard product). This is used to scale the existing vectors.
Imputer	Takes a column of numeric type and completes missing values in the dataset using the column mean or median value. Useful when using estimators that can't handle missing values.
Interaction	Takes one distinct vector or double-valued column and outputs a vector column containing the products of all the possible combinations of values.
PCA	Implements principal component analysis, turning a vector of potentially correlated values into non-correlated ones by outputting the most important components of the data (the principal components). This is useful in predictive models and dimensionality reduction, with a potential cost of interpretability.
Polynomial Expansion	Takes a vector of features and expands it into an n-degree polynomial space. A value of 1 means no expansion.
SQL Transformer	Takes an SQL statement (any SELECT clause that Spark supports) and transforms the input according to the statement.
Vector Assembler	Takes a list of vector columns and concatenates them into one column in the dataset. This is useful for various estimators that take only one column.

Preprocessing Image Data

Image data is common in machine learning applications, and it also requires preprocessing to move forward in the machine learning workflow. But images are different from the kinds of data we've seen before, and they require a different kind of procedure. There may be more or fewer steps involved, depending on the actual data, but the most common path consists of these three actions:

1. Extract labels

2. Transform labels to indices

3. Extract image size

Let's walk through these steps using our example dataset to see what they involve.

Extracting labels

Our images dataset has a nested structure where the directory name indicates the classification of the image. Hence, each image's path on the filesystem contains its label. We need to extract this in order to use it later on. Most raw image datasets follow this pattern, and this is an essential part of the preprocessing we will do with our images. After loading the images as BinaryType, we get a table with a column called path of type String. This contains our labels. Now, it's time to leverage string manipulation to extract that data. Let's take a look at one example path: .../256_Object Categories/198.spider/198_0089.jpg.

The label in this case is actually an index and a name: `198.spider`. This is the part we need to extract from the string. Fortunately, PySpark SQL functions provide us with the `regexp_extract` API that enables us to easily manipulate strings according to our needs.

Let's define a function that will take a `path_col` and use this API to extract the label, with the regex `"256_ObjectCategories/([^/]+)"`:

```
from pyspark.sql.functions import col, regexp_extract

def extract_label(path_col):
    """Extract label from file path using built-in SQL function"""
    return regexp_extract(path_col,"256_ObjectCategories/([^/]+)",1)
```

We can now create a new DataFrame with the labels by calling this function from a Spark SQL query:

```
images_with_label = df_result.select(
    col("path"),
    extract_label(col("path")).alias("label"),
    col("content"))
```

Our `images_with_label` DataFrame consists of three columns: two string columns called `path` and `label` and a binary column called `content`.

Now that we have our labels, it's time to transform them into indices.

Transforming labels to indices

As mentioned previously, our `label` column is a string column. This can pose a challenge for machine learning models, as strings tend to be heavy on memory usage. Ideally, every string in our table should be transformed into a more efficient representation before being ingested into a machine learning algorithm, unless it is a true necessity not to. Since our labels are of the format *{index.name}*, we have three options:

1. Extract the index from the string itself, leveraging string manipulation.

2. Provide a new index using Spark's `StringIndexer`, as discussed in "From nominal categorical features to indices" on page 73.

3. Use Python to define an index (in the Caltech 256 dataset, there are only 257 indices, in the range `[1,257]`).

In our case, the first option is the cleanest way to handle this. This approach will allow us to avoid maintaining a mapping between the indices in the original files and the indices in the dataset.

Extracting image size

The final step is to extract the image size. We do this as part of our preprocessing because we know for sure that our dataset contains images of different sizes, but it's often a useful operation to get a feel for the data and provide us with information to help us decide on an algorithm. Some machine learning algorithms will require us to have a unified size for images, and knowing in advance what image sizes we're working with can help us make better optimization decisions.

Since Spark doesn't yet provide this functionality out of the box, we'll use Pillow (*https://oreil.ly/kfoQR*) (aka PIL), a friendly Python library for working with images. To efficiently extract the width and height of all of our images, we will define a pandas user-defined function (UDF) that can run in a distributed fashion on our Spark executors. pandas UDFs, defined using `pandas_udf` as a decorator, are optimized with Apache Arrow and are faster for grouped operations (e.g., when applied after a `groupBy`).

Grouping allows pandas to perform vectorized operations. For these kinds of use cases, a pandas UDF on Spark will be more efficient. For simple operations like a*b, a Spark UDF will suffice and will be faster because it has less overhead.

Our UDF will take a series of rows and operate on them in parallel, making it much faster than the traditional one-row-at-a-time approach:

```
from pyspark.sql.functions import col, pandas_udf
from PIL import Image
import pandas as pd
@pandas_udf("width: int, height: int")
def extract_size_udf(content_series):
    sizes = content_series.apply(extract_size)
return pd.DataFrame(list(sizes))
```

Now that we have the function, we can pass it to Spark's `select` function to extract the image size information:

```
images_df = images_with_label.select(
    col("path"),
    col("label"),
    extract_size_udf(col("content")).alias("size"),
    col("content"))
```

The image size data will be extracted into a new DataFrame with a `size` column of type `struct` containing the `width` and `height`:

```
size:struct
    width:integer
    height:integer
```

Note that using the `extract_size_udf` function will transfer all of the images from the JVM (Spark uses Scala under the hood) to the Python runtime using Arrow, compute the sizes, and then transfer the sizes back to the JVM. For efficiency when working with large datasets, especially if you are not using grouping, it might be worth implementing the extraction of the sizes at the JVM/Scala level instead. Keep considerations like this in mind when implementing data preprocessing for the various stages of machine learning.

Save the Data and Avoid the Small Files Problem

When you've completed all of your preprocessing, it can be a good idea to save the data to cold or hot storage before continuing to the next step. This is sometimes referred to as a *checkpoint*, or a point in time where we save a version of the data we are happy with. One reason to save the data is to enable *fast recovery*: if our Spark cluster breaks completely, instead of needing to recalculate everything from scratch, we can recover from the last checkpoint. The second reason is to facilitate collaboration. If your preprocessed data is persisted to storage and available for your colleagues to use, they can leverage it to develop their own flows. This is especially useful when working with large datasets and on tasks requiring extensive computation resources and time. Spark provides us with functionality to both ingest and save data in numerous formats. Note that if you decide to save the data for collaboration purposes, it's important to document all the steps that you took: the preprocessing you carried out, the code you used to implement it, the current use cases, any tuning you performed, and any external resources you created, like stopword lists.

Avoiding small files

A *small file* is any file that is significantly smaller than the storage block size. Yes, there is a minimum block size, even with object stores such as Amazon S3, Azure Blob, etc.! Having files that are significantly smaller than the block size can result in wasted space on the disk, since the storage will use the whole block to save that file, no matter how small it is. This is an overhead that we should avoid. On top of that, storage is optimized to support fast reading and writing by block size. But don't worry—Spark API to the rescue! We can easily avoid wasting precious space and paying a high price for storing small files using Spark's `repartition` or `coalesce` functions.

In our case, because we are operating on offline data without a specific requirement to finish computation on the millisecond, we have more flexibility in which one to choose. `repartition` creates entirely new partitions, shuffling the data over the network with the goal of distributing it evenly over the specified number of partitions (which can be higher or lower than the existing number). It therefore has a high cost up front, but down the road, Spark functionality will execute faster because the data will be distributed optimally—in fact, executing a `repartition` operation can be useful in any stage of the machine learning workflow when we notice that computation is relatively slow and want to speed it up. The `coalesce` function, on the other hand, first detects the existing partitions and then shuffles only the necessary data. It can only be used to reduce the number of partitions, not to add partitions, and is known to run faster than `repartition` as it minimizes the amount of data shuffled over the network. In some cases, `coalesce` might not shuffle at all and will default to batch local partitions, which makes it super efficient for reduce functionality.

Since we want to be in control of the exact number of partitions and we don't require extremely fast execution, in our case it's okay to use the slower `repartition` function, as shown here:

```
output_df = output_df.repartition(NUM_EXECUTERS)
```

Bear in mind that if time, efficiency, and minimizing network load are of the essence, you should opt for the `coalesce` function instead.

Image compression and Parquet

Suppose we want to save our image dataset in Parquet format (if you're not familiar with it, Parquet is an open source, column-oriented data file format designed for efficient storage and retrieval). When saving to this format, by default Spark uses a compression codec named Snappy. However, since images are already compressed (e.g., with JPEG, PNG, etc.), it wouldn't make sense to compress them again. How can we avoid this?

We save the existing configured compression codec in a string instance, configure Spark to write to Parquet with the *uncompressed* codec, save the data in Parquet format, and assign the codec instance back to the Spark configuration for future work. The following code snippet demonstrates:

```
# Image data is already compressed, so we turn off Parquet compression
compression = spark.conf.get("spark.sql.parquet.compression.codec")
spark.conf.set("spark.sql.parquet.compression.codec", "uncompressed")

# Save the data stored in binary format as Parquet
output_df.write.mode("overwrite").parquet(save_path)
spark.conf.set("spark.sql.parquet.compression.codec", compression)
```

Descriptive Statistics: Getting a Feel for the Data

Machine learning is not magic—you will need to understand your data in order to work with it efficiently and effectively. Getting a solid understanding of the data before you start training your algorithms will save you much time and effort down the road. Fortunately, MLlib provides a dedicated library named `pyspark.ml.stat` that contains all the functionality you need for extracting basic statistics out of the data.

Don't worry if that sounds intimidating—you don't need to fully understand statistics to use MLlib, although some level of familiarity will definitely help you in your machine learning journey. Understanding the data using statistics enables us to better decide on which machine learning algorithm to use, identify biases, and estimate the quality of the data—as mentioned previously, if you put garbage in, you get garbage out. Ingesting low-quality data into a machine learning algorithm will result in a low-performing model. As a result, this part is a must!

Having said that, as long as we build conscious assumptions about what the data looks like, what we can accept, and what we cannot, we can conduct much better experiments and have a better idea of what to remove, what to input, and what we can be lenient about. Take into consideration that those assumptions and any data cleansing operations we perform can have big consequences in production, especially if they are aggressive (like dropping all nulls in a large number of rows or imputing too many default values, which screws up the entropy completely). Watch out for mismatches in assumptions made during the exploratory stages about the data input, quality measurements, and what constitutes "bad" or low-quality data.

 For deeper statistical analysis of a given dataset, many data scientists use the pandas (*https://oreil.ly/eZ8o9*) library. As mentioned in Chapter 2, pandas is a Python analysis library for working with relatively small data that can fit in one machine's memory (RAM). Its counterpart in the Apache Spark ecosystem is Koalas (*https://oreil.ly/HVzc9*), which has evolved into a pandas API on Spark. There is not 100% feature parity between the original pandas and pandas on Spark, but this API expands Spark's capabilities and takes them even further, so it's worth checking out.

In this section, we will shift gears from straightforward processes and will focus on getting a feel for the data with the Spark MLlib functionality for computing statistics.

Calculating Statistics

Welcome to the Machine Learning Zoo Project!

For learning about MLlib's statistics functions, we'll use the Zoo Animal Classification dataset from the Kaggle repository (*https://oreil.ly/RHuSJ*). This dataset, created in 1990, consists of 101 examples of zoo animals described by 16 Boolean-valued attributes capturing various traits. The animals can be classified into seven types: Mammal, Bird, Reptile, Fish, Amphibian, Bug, and Invertebrate.

The first thing you need to do to get a feel for the data to better plan your machine learning journey is calculate the feature statistics. Knowing how the data itself is distributed will provide you with valuable insights to determine which algorithms to select, how to evaluate the model, and overall how much effort you need to invest in the project.

Descriptive Statistics with Spark Summarizer

A *descriptive statistic* (*https://oreil.ly/Y174f*) is a summary statistic (*https://oreil.ly/6RFxO*) that quantitatively describes or summarizes features from a collection of information (*https://oreil.ly/iINTU*). MLlib provides us with a dedicated `Summarizer` object for computing statistical metrics from a specific column. This functionality is part of the MLlib `LinearRegression` algorithm for building the `LinearRegression Summary`. When building the `Summarizer`, we need to specify the desired metrics. Table 4-5 lists the functionality available in the Spark API.

Table 4-5. Summarizer metric options

Metric	Description
mean	Calculates the average value of a given numerical column
sum	Calculates the sum of the numerical column
variance	Calculates the variance of the column (how far the set of numbers in the column are spread out from its mean value, on average)
std	Calculates the standard deviation of the column (the square root of the variance value), to provide more weight to outliers in the column
count	Calculates the number of items/rows in the dataset
numNonZeros	Finds the number of nonzero values in the column
max	Finds the maximum value in the column
min	Finds the minimum value in the column
normL1	Calculates the L1 norm (similarity between the numeric values) of the column
normL2	Calculates the Euclidean norm of the column

> The L1 and L2 (aka Euclidean) norms are tools for calculating the distance between numeric points in an *N*-dimensional space. They are commonly used as metrics to measure the similarity between data points in fields such as geometry, data mining, and deep learning.

This code snippet illustrates how to create a `Summarizer` instance with metrics:

```
from pyspark.ml.stat import Summarizer
summarizer = Summarizer.metrics("mean","sum","variance","std")
```

Like the other MLlib functions, the Summarizer.metrics function expects a vector of numeric features as input. You can use MLlib's `VectorAssembler` function to assemble the vector.

Although there are many features in the Zoo Animal Classification dataset, we are going to examine just the following columns:

- feathers
- milk
- fins
- domestic

As discussed in "Data Ingestion with Spark" on page 62, we'll load the data into a DataFrame instance named zoo_data_for_statistics.

In the next code sample, you can see how to build the vector. Notice how we set the output column name to features, as expected by the summarizer:

```
from pyspark.ml.feature import VectorAssembler
# set the output col to features as expected as input for the summarizer
vecAssembler = VectorAssembler(outputCol="features")
# assemble only part of the columns for the example
vecAssembler.setInputCols(["feathers","milk","fins","domestic"])
vector_df = vecAssembler.transform(zoo_data_for_statistics)
```

Our vector is leveraging Apache Spark's Dataset functionality. A Dataset in Spark is a strongly typed collection of objects encapsulating the DataFrame. You can still call the DataFrame from a Dataset if needed, but the Dataset API enables you to access a specific column without the dedicated column functionality:

```
Vector_df.features
```

Now that we have a dedicated vector column and a summarizer, let's extract some statistics. We can call the summarizer.summary function to plot all the metrics or to compute a specific metric, as shown in the following example:

```
# compute statistics for multiple metrics
statistics_df = vector_df.select(summarizer.summary(vector_df.features))
# statistics_df will plot all the metrics
statistics_df.show(truncate=False)

# compute statistics for single metric (here, std) without the rest
vector_df.select(Summarizer.std(vector_df.features)).show(truncate=False)
```

Example 4-4 shows the output of calling std on the vector of features.

Example 4-4. std of the features column

```
+---------------------------------------------------------------------+
|std(features)                                                        |
+---------------------------------------------------------------------+
|[0.4004947435409863,0.4935223970962651,0.37601348195757744,0.33655211592363116]|
+---------------------------------------------------------------------+
```

The standard deviation (STD) is an indicator of the variation in a set of values. A low STD indicates that the values tend to be close to the mean (also called the expected value) of the set, while a high STD indicates that the values are spread out over a wider range.

 Summarizer.std is a global function that you can use without creating a Summarizer instance.

Since the features feathers, milk, fins, and domestic are inherently of type Boolean —milk can be 1 for true or 0 for false, and the same for fins and so on—calculating the STD doesn't provide us with much insight—the result will always be a decimal number between 0 and 1. That misses the value of STD in calculating how "spread out" the data is. Instead, let's try the sum function. This function will tell us *how many* animals in the dataset have feathers, milk, or fins or are domestic animals:

```
# compute statistics for single metric "sum" without the rest
vector_df.select(Summarizer.sum(vector_df.features)).show(truncate=False)
```

Take a look at the output of sum, shown in Example 4-5.

```
+--------------------+
|sum(features)       |
+--------------------+
|[20.0,41.0,17.0,13.0]|
+--------------------+
```

This tells us that there are 20 animals with feathers (the vector's first value), 41 animals that provide milk (the vector's second value), 17 animals with fins (the third value), and 13 domestic animals (the final value). The sum function provides us with more insights about the data itself than the std function, due to the Boolean nature of the data. However, the more complicated/diverse the dataset is, the more looking at all of the various metrics will help.

Data Skewness

Skewness in statistics is a measure of the asymmetry of a probability distribution. Think of a bell curve where the data points are not distributed symmetrically on the left and right sides of the curve's mean value. Assuming the dataset follows a normal distribution curve, skewness means it has a short tail on one end and a long tail on the other. The higher the skewness value is, the less evenly distributed the data is, and the more data points will fall on one side of the bell curve.

To measure skewness, or the asymmetry of the values around the mean, we need to extract the mean value and calculate the standard deviation. A statistical equation to accomplish this has already been implemented in Spark for us; check out the next code snippet to see how to take advantage of it:

```
from pyspark.sql.functions import skewness
df_with_skew = df.select(skewness("{column_name}"))
```

This code returns a new DataFrame with a dedicated column that measures the skewness of the column we requested. Spark also implements other statistical functions, such as *kurtosis*, which measures the tail of the data. Both are important when building a model based on the distribution of random variables and the assumption that the data follows a normal distribution; they can help you detect biases, data topology changes, and even data drift. We'll discuss data drift in more detail in Chapter 10, when we look at monitoring machine learning models in production).

Correlation

A *correlation* between two features means that if feature A increases or decreases, feature B does the same (a *positive* correlation) or does the exact opposite (a *negative* correlation). Determining correlation therefore involves measuring the linear relationship between the two variables/features. Since a machine learning algorithm's goal is to learn from data, perfectly correlated features are less likely to provide insights to improve model accuracy. This is why filtering them out can significantly improve our algorithm's performance while maintaining the quality of the results. The `test` method of the `ChiSquareTest` class (*https://oreil.ly/SmC6A*) in MLlib is a statistical test that helps us assess categorical data and labels by running a Pearson correlation on all pairs and outputting a matrix with correlation scores.

 Be mindful that correlation doesn't necessarily imply causation. When the values of two variables change in a correlated way, there is no guarantee that the change in one variable causes the change in the other. It takes more effort to prove a causative relationship.

In this section, you will learn about Pearson and Spearman correlations in Spark MLlib.

Pearson correlation

When looking into correlation, we look for positive or negative associations. Pearson correlation measures the strength of linear association between two variables. It produces a coefficient r that indicates how far away the data points are from a descriptive line. The range of r is $[-1,1]$, where:

- r=1 is a perfect positive correlation. Both variables act in the same way.

- r=-1 is perfect negative/inverse correlation, which means that when one variable increases, the other decreases.

- r=0 means no correlation.

Figure 4-3 shows some examples on a graph.

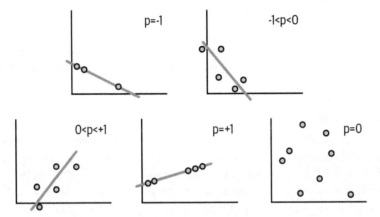

Figure 4-3. Pearson correlation examples on a graph

Pearson is the default correlation test with the MLlib `Correlation` object. Let's take a look at some example code and its results:

```
from pyspark.ml.stat import Correlation

# compute r1 0 Pearson correlation
r1 = Correlation.corr(vector_df, "features").head()
print("Pearson correlation matrix:\n" + str(r1[0])+ "\n")
```

The output is a row where the first value is a `DenseMatrix`, as shown in Example 4-6.

Example 4-6. Pearson correlation matrix

```
Pearson correlation matrix:
DenseMatrix([[ 1.          , -0.41076061, -0.22354106,  0.03158624],
             [-0.41076061,  1.          , -0.15632771,  0.16392762],
             [-0.22354106, -0.15632771,  1.          , -0.09388671],
             [ 0.03158624,  0.16392762, -0.09388671,  1.          ]])
```

Each line represents the correlation of a feature with all the other features, in a pairwise way: for example, `r1[0][0,1]` represents the correlation of `feathers` with `milk`, which is a negative value (-0.41076061) that indicates a negative correlation between animals that produce milk and animals with feathers.

Table 4-6 shows what the correlation table looks like, to make this clearer.

Table 4-6. Pearson correlation table

	feathers	milk	fins	domestic
feathers	1	-.41076061	-0.22354106	0.03158624
milk	-0.41076061	1	-0.15632771	0.16392762
fins	-0.22354106	-0.15632771	1	-0.09388671
domestic	0.03158624	0.16392762	-0.09388671	1

This table makes it easy to spot negative and positive correlations: for example, fins and milk have a negative correlation, while domestic and milk have a positive correlation.

Spearman correlation

Spearman correlation, also known as Spearman rank correlation, measures the strength and direction of the monotonic relationship between two variables. In contrast to Pearson, which measures the linear relationship, this is a curvilinear relationship, which means the association between the two variables changes as the values change (increase or decrease). Spearman correlation should be used when the data is discrete and the relationships between the data points are not necessarily linear, as shown in Figure 4-4, as well as when ranking is of interest. To decide which approach fits your data better, you need to understand the nature of the data itself: if it's on an ordinal scale, use Spearman, and if it's on an interval scale, use Pearson. To learn more about this, I recommend reading *Practical Statistics for Data Scientists* (*https://oreil.ly/prac-stats*) by Peter Bruce, Andrew Bruce, and Peter Gedeck (O'Reilly).

---

2 An ordinal scale has all its variables in a specific order, beyond just naming them.

3 An interval scale labels and orders its variables and specifies a defined, evenly spaced interval between them.

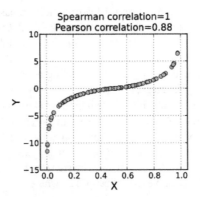

Figure 4-4. An example showing that Spearman correlation plots do not create a linear graph (image source: Wikipedia (https://oreil.ly/p0lFT), CC BY-SA 3.0)

Notice that to use Spearman, you have to specify it (the default is Pearson):

```
from pyspark.ml.stat import Correlation

# compute r2 0 Spearman correlation
r2 = Correlation.corr(vector_df, "features", "spearman").head()
print("Spearman correlation matrix:\n" + str(r2[0]))
```

As before, the output is a row where the first value is a `DenseMatrix`, and it follows the same rules and order described previously (see Example 4-7).

Example 4-7. Spearman correlation matrix

```
Spearman correlation matrix:
DenseMatrix([[ 1.        , -0.41076061, -0.22354106,  0.03158624],
             [-0.41076061,  1.        , -0.15632771,  0.16392762],
             [-0.22354106, -0.15632771,  1.        , -0.09388671],
             [ 0.03158624,  0.16392762, -0.09388671,  1.        ]])
```

Spark has an automation for feature selectors based on correlation and hypothesis tests, such as chi-squared, ANOVA F-test, and F-value (the `UnivariateFeatureSelector`; see Table 5-2 in Chapter 5). To speed up the process, it is best to use existing, implemented tests instead of calculating every hypothesis by yourself. If after the feature selection process you identify an insufficient set of features, you should use hypothesis tests such as `ChiSquareTest` to evaluate whether you need to enrich your data or find a larger set of data. I've provided you with a code example in the book's GitHub repository (*https://oreil.ly/smls-git*) demonstrating how to do this. Statistical hypothesis tests have a null hypothesis (H0) and alternative hypothesis (H1), where:

- H0: The sample data follows the hypothesized distribution.
- H1: The sample data does not follow the hypothesized distribution.

The outcome of the test is the *p*-value, which demonstrates the likelihood of H0 being true.

Tuning Linear Algebra Operations

Under the hood, Spark has a private object named `BLAS` that provides a set of Basic Linear Algebra Subprograms. These are routines that serve as building blocks for performing vector and matrix operations, with the aim of accelerating these operations. For advanced optimizations, `BLAS` uses a Java library named `netlib-java` that optimizes native linear algebra operations based on the operating system and hardware; check out the MLlib Linear Algebra Acceleration Guide (*https://oreil.ly/YJIw6*) to find the correct library for your OS. Spark MLlib will still work even if you don't configure it, but for optimization purposes, it is a good idea to leverage this capability.

Summary

In this chapter, we discussed three crucial steps in the machine learning workflow: ingesting data, preprocessing text and images, and gathering descriptive statistics. Data scientists and machine learning engineers typically spend a significant portion of their time on these tasks, and executing them mindfully sets us up for greater success and a better machine learning model that can meet the business goal in a much more profound way. As a rule of thumb, it's best to collaborate with your peers to validate and engineer these steps to ensure the resulting insights and data can be reused in multiple experiments. The tools introduced in this chapter will accompany us again and again throughout the machine learning process. In the next chapter, we will dive into feature engineering and build upon the outcomes from this chapter.

## CHAPTER 5

Feature Engineering

In machine learning, *feature engineering* is the process of using domain knowledge to select and transform the most relevant variables in the data to reach the goal of the machine learning process. *Domain knowledge* here refers to an understanding of the data and where it originated. In data science, it's less about the tools and more about the data and problem itself, encompassing the general background in a specific field or vertical. For example, in finance it might involve familiarity with financial terms and the various possible applications of the data, such as loan scoring. Depending on the experience of the team working on the project, it might be necessary to consult a financial expert to create a representative feature to solve the problem at hand. Similarly, in healthcare tech you might work with a medical doctor to design the features, and knowledge of anatomy, biological systems, and medical conditions may be required.

The goal of feature engineering is for the final features to serve as proxies to the information the data contains about the world or the specific context where the problem takes place. Domain experience is what enables you to make those links, often intuitively. Using domain knowledge can help you simplify the challenges inherent in machine learning, improving your chances of reaching your business goal. Indeed, to be successful, you must have a solid understanding of the problem and the data you are working with.

Here's another example. Let's assume you have a set of images of vehicles, and you are in charge of detecting the make, model, and year from a set of images. That can be a tough problem to solve! After all, a picture of a car can be taken from many angles, and you will need to differentiate and narrow down the options based on very specific features. Rather than asking your machine learning model to assess many individual features, instead, you can detect the vehicle's registration plate and translate the pixels into numbers and letters. Once you have this information, you can match it with other datasets to extract the information you need. Since extracting numbers/letters from images is a solved machine learning problem, you have leveraged your domain knowledge together with feature engineering to reach your business goal.

As this example suggests, your goal and your data will determine which features you will need for training your models. Interestingly enough, given that machine learning algorithms can be the same for different scenarios, like the classification of emails into spam or nonspam or the classification of Twitter accounts into bots or real users, *good quality features* might be the main driver for your model's performance. By "good" here, I mean features that are going to provide a lot of information about the data, explain the most variance, and have a strong relationship with the target variable.

Most machine learning algorithms are not intelligent enough to automatically extract meaningful features from raw data on their own. As a result, stacking multiple algorithms in a chain of executions, using *extractors* and *transformers* together with smart *selectors*, can help us identify noteworthy features. This process is also referred to as *featurization*, and it is a crucial part of processing the data in your machine learning pipeline.

In this chapter, we will explore some of the tools and techniques Spark provides for feature extraction. Before we proceed, here are a couple of terms you should know:

Estimator
    An algorithm that can be fit on a DataFrame to produce a transformer

Hashing function
    A function that is used to map data of arbitrary size to fixed-size values

Derived feature
    A feature obtained from feature engineering

Raw feature
    A feature obtained directly from the dataset with no extra data manipulation or engineering

At a high level, this chapter covers the following:

- Features and their impact on machine learning models
- MLlib featurization tools
- The image featurization process
- The text featurization process
- How to enrich your dataset

Let's get started by taking a closer look at features and the effect they have on our models.

Features and Their Impact on Models

Since our models are mathematical and statistical representations of the space from which the data was (estimated to be) drawn/generated, they might be impacted by outliers or suffer from internal biases or other problems that we would prefer to avoid. Suppose your data contains missing values, but your algorithm doesn't support these. You have to decide what to do: Do you fill in the missing values? Drop the columns with missing values altogether? Try using a different algorithm? The decisions you make can have a significant impact on your results with algorithms such as linear models, support vector machines (SVMs), neural networks, principal component analysis (PCA), and nearest neighbors, since each data point changes the outcome. Stated plainly: *if there are more missing values than real values, filling them with a default value can completely tilt the equation in favor of the default value.*

To better understand this, let's take a look at an SVM algorithm, as shown in Figure 5-1, where we need to develop a linear vector/function (H_1, H_2, H_3) to distinguish between two categories, an empty circle or a full circle, given X_1 and X_2 as inputs. If we had missing values for most of the X_2 data points in the empty circle category and we filled them with a default value, that would completely change our linear vector's direction and degree. So we have to think carefully about how we fill in missing data and how our features impact the models.

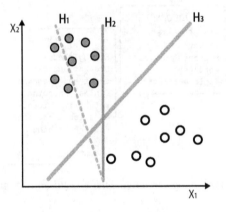

Figure 5-1. SVM with linear hard margin, describing (H1, H2, H3) as the hypotheses and dots as the actual data values

Another important aspect of featurization is the ability to identify and reduce noise, especially when using automated machine learning models that have built-in feature extraction mechanisms. Noisy data in algorithms creates a risk of producing an incorrect pattern that the algorithm starts to generalize from, which in turn creates an undesired model outcome that doesn't represent the business domain well. Understanding the data together with featurization is key here.

As shown in Figure 5-2, feature engineering is a rich world of tools and techniques.

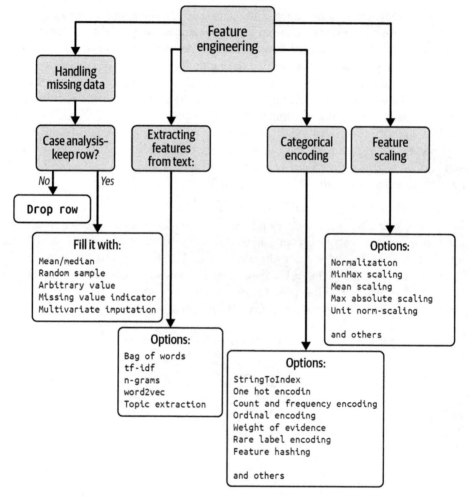

Figure 5-2. High-level view of feature engineering requirements and techniques

The best ones to use depend on the type of data you are working with and your requirements. There are no hard rules, but here are some of the things you'll need to keep in mind, depending on the problem you're dealing with:

Handling missing data

Do I use this data for a specific case analysis? What is the "price" of dropping the whole column/row versus filling it in with default data? What is the percentage of the missing data in my dataset? Is data missing in a whole row, or specific columns? Answer those questions and you've got yourself a plan!

Extracting features from text

Do I have only unstructured text data? How would I make sense of it? What is the nature of my data? How long is the text—a tweet with a limited number of characters, or a feature engineering chapter in a book? (More on this in "The Text Featurization Process" on page 109.)

Categorical encoding

This is the process of transforming categorical variables into a set of binary variables—yes or no, true or false, 0 or 1. The goal here is to boost the performance of the model. An example of categorical data is the city where a person lives: San Francisco, New York, Berlin, Tel Aviv, etc. Those are nominal categories, as there isn't a specific order to them. Categories can have an inherent order as well, as in the case of a student's grades: A+, A, A–, B+, etc. We will look at classification in Chapter 6; many algorithms take categorical features as input.

Feature scaling

We use this technique, also referred to as *data normalization,* to standardize the independent features in the dataset so they are all on a similar scale. We attend to it during the preprocessing phase, or as part of feature engineering when new, highly varying values show up. Feature scaling is commonly used when working with gradient descent algorithms, as it helps speed up convergence. Figure 5-3 demonstrates the ideal trajectory of how x moves closer to the smallest possible value in each gradient descent algorithm iteration until it finds the minimum value or reaches the maximum number of allowed iterations—this is what it means for normalization to facilitate convergence. Without normalization, the difference in the ranges of the features will result in each one having a different step size, which means they are updated at different rates and it takes longer to reach overall optimization. Normalization smooths things out and speeds up the process. You can think of it like a person stuck in the woods and trying to find their way back to their car; that person will wander around, collect information, and try to optimize their route. But what if most of the trees were transparent and the person could see through them? This is the effect that feature scaling has. Feature scaling is also useful for distance-based algorithms and regression. To accomplish it, we can leverage PCA, an unsupervised technique that enables us to filter a noisy dataset and reduce the dimensionality of the data.

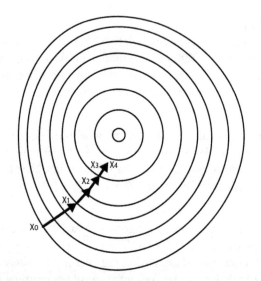

Figure 5-3. Gradient descent moving toward the minimum of a function on each iteration, from x_1 to x_2 and so on

MLlib Featurization Tools

MLlib provides many featurization functions in its `pyspark.ml.feature` package (the Scala-based APIs are in `spark.ml.feature`). The full list of up-to-date APIs can be found in the Apache Spark MLlib documentation (*https://oreil.ly/8rrMh*), and code examples can be found in the Apache Spark GitHub repository (*https://oreil.ly/SQxG9*), under the *examples/src/main/python/ml/* directory.

In this section, we will cover MLlib extractors and selectors.

Extractors

Extractors are MLlib APIs for drawing out features that are not necessarily meaningful on their own but that can help us with the exploration process. Remember Figure 4-1 from the previous chapter? Preprocessing, feature engineering, and statistical description are interlocking processes. Transformers (refer to "Preprocessing with MLlib Transformers" on page 70 if you need a refresher on these) can be used as extractors, and vice versa. Some extractors require us to use transformers first, like `TF-IDF`, which cannot operate directly on the raw data and requires preprocessing with the `Tokenizer` API for extracting words and `HashingTF` or `CountVectorizer` for converting the collections of words to vectors of token counts.

Table 5-1 presents the available extractor APIs and when to use each of them.

Table 5-1. Spark MLlib extractor APIs

API	Usage
TF-IDF	Calculates the term frequency–inverse document frequency, where term frequency is the number of times a term appears in a document in the corpus, and the document frequency is the number of documents the term appears in. Used in text mining for weighing the importance of a term to a document.
Word2Vec	Converts sequences of words into a fixed-size vector. Used for natural language processing.
Count Vectorizer	Converts fixed-size sequences of words into vectors of token counts, to be used in text classification. When sequence size varies, it will use the minimal size as the vocabulary size.
Feature Hasher	Takes a set of categorical or numerical features and hashes them into one feature vector. Often used to reduce features without significantly losing their value.

Selectors

After we use our transformers and extractors to develop a bunch of features, it's time to select the ones we would like to keep. For this we use selectors, which are APIs for selecting a subset from a large set of features. This can be done manually or adaptively using algorithms that estimate feature importance and aim to improve the performance of our machine learning models; it's important because too many features might lead to overfitting.

Spark provides the simple options that are listed in Table 5-2.

Table 5-2. Spark MLlib selector APIs

API	Usage
Vector Slicer	Takes a vector column of features and outputs a new column with a subset of the original features, determined by the indices we pass in.
RFormula	Selects columns with an R model formula (for users of the R programming language) using a set of basic supported operations and produces a vector column of features and a double or string column of labels.
ChiSq Selector	Takes a column with a vector of all the features and a label column and generates a DataFrame with a new column with a vector of selected features. Performs feature selection using a chi-squared statistical test based on one of five selection methods (top x most predictive features, top % most predictive features, features with a false positive rate below a threshold, etc.).
Univariate Feature Selector	Takes as input categorical/continuous labels with categorical/continuous vector features and generates a DataFrame with a new column with a vector of selected features. Spark chooses the score function to use for feature selection based on the specified label and feature types (chi-squared, ANOVA F-test, or F-value); the selection methods are the same as for ChiSqSelector.
Variance Threshold Selector	Takes a vector column of features and outputs a new column with all features below the provided variance threshold removed.

Example: Word2Vec

Many of the selectors and later machine learning models take vectors of features in the shape of one column in the DataFrame. This is why using a columnar storage format such as Parquet is not always more efficient, as all the features are represented as one column anyway. However, it can be more efficient when given a large DataFrame with many columns, where each one represents a different transformation or set of features. To accommodate this usage, the Spark MLlib API generates a new DataFrame with the same columns as the previous one and a new column to represent the selected features.

The output of many transformers can be persisted to disk and reused later. The following code snippet shows how we can stack multiple transformers, persist them to disk, and load them from disk:

```python
from pyspark.ml.feature import Word2Vec, Word2VecModel
from pyspark.ml.feature import Tokenizer

# Input data: Each row is a bag of words from a sentence or document.
sentence_data_frame = spark.createDataFrame([
    (0, "Hi I think pyspark is cool ","happy"),
    (1, "All I want is a pyspark cluster","indifferent"),
    (2, "I finally understand how ML works","fulfilled"),
    (3, "Yet another sentence about pyspark and ML","indifferent"),
    (4, "Why didn't I know about mllib before","sad"),
    (5, "Yes, I can","happy")
], ["id", "sentence", "sentiment"])

tokenizer = Tokenizer(inputCol="sentence", outputCol="words")
tokenized = tokenizer.transform(sentence_data_frame)

word2Vec = Word2Vec(inputCol="words", outputCol="result")
model = word2Vec.fit(tokenized)
model.write().overwrite().save("some_path")
model_from_disk = Word2VecModel.load("some_path")

df_with_word_vec = model_from_disk.transform(tokenized)
df_with_word_vec.show()
selector = VarianceThresholdSelector(varianceThreshold=0.0,
                                     outputCol="selectedFeatures")
result = selector.fit(df_with_word_vec).transform(df_with_word_vec)
```

In this code:

- sentence_data_frame is a mock DataFrame for demonstrating the functionality.

- Tokenizer creates a Tokenizer instance, providing input column and output column names.

- transform transforms the DataFrame and generates a new one named tokenized.

- Word2Vec creates a Word2Vec instance with the specified input column, output column, and vector size. Word2Vec is an estimator, so we need to run fit on the data before it is used for transformation. More on that in Chapter 6.

- .save persists the Word2Vec model to disk using the write function.

- Word2VecModel.load loads the Word2Vec model from disk.

- model_from_disk.transform uses the loaded model to transform the tokenized data.

- VarianceThresholdSelector creates a VarianceThresholdSelector instance for selecting features, with a threshold of 0, meaning it filters out the features with the same value in all samples. VarianceThresholdSelector expects a column named features as input. We call fit to fit the VarianceThresholdSelector on the data and use the model for selecting features.

Example 5-1 shows what the resulting DataFrame will look like.

Example 5-1. The DataFrame with all the new columns

```
Output: Features with variance lower than 0.000000 are removed.
+---+--------------------+-----------+--------------------+--------------------+--------------------+
| id|            sentence|  sentiment|               words|            features|    selectedFeatures|
+---+--------------------+-----------+--------------------+--------------------+--------------------+
|  0|Hi I think pyspar...|      happy|[hi, i, think, py...|[-6.2237260863184...|[-6.2237260863184...|
|  1|All I want is a p...|indifferent|[all, i, want, is...|[-7.1128298129354...|[-7.1128298129354...|
|  2|I finally underst...|    fulfill|[i, finally, unde...|[-8.2983014484246...|[-8.2983014484246...|
|  3|Yet another sente...|indifferent|[yet, another, se...|[0.0,0.0,0.0,0.0,...|[0.0,0.0,0.0,0.0,...|
|  4|Why didn't I know...|        sad|[why, didn't, i, ...|[-7.1128298129354...|[-7.1128298129354...|
|  5|          Yes, I can|      happy|     [yes,, i, can]|[-0.0016596602896...|[-0.0016596602896...|
+---+--------------------+-----------+--------------------+--------------------+--------------------+
```

For simplicity, we didn't normalize our feature vector to fit the range of [0,1], although doing so might be helpful with the selection process later. This is another route you should explore during the feature engineering process. As a side note, while in this example we saved the model to disk, you can save it to any store that you have a connector to and that supports Parquet format (since the model itself is saved in Parquet format unless you specify otherwise). We will discuss this further in Chapter 10.

The Image Featurization Process

There is a misconception in the industry regarding feature engineering when working with images. Many assume there is no need for it, but in practice, even when we are using a neural network algorithm that extracts and maps features—like a convolutional neural network (CNN), as shown in Figure 5-4—there is still a chance of introducing noise and computation overhead and missing features, since the algorithm itself doesn't possess any business knowledge or domain understanding of the given problem.

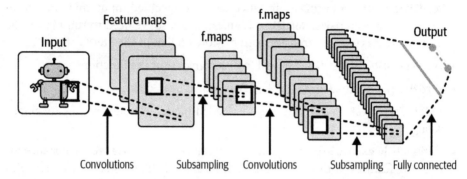

Figure 5-4. Typical CNN architecture describing convolutions, subsampling, etc. all the way to the output

There are many features we can extract from image data, depending on the domain we're working in. Our Caltech 256 image classification dataset is quite diverse, and we can try out multiple techniques until we find the best features. Also bear in mind that when it comes to images and layered neural network models, we can leverage an existing model and just add the last layer. I'll talk more about that later, but I mention it here because that model might require specific image features, such as a specific width, height, and number of channels:

Width and height

These represent the number of pixels in an image. For example, an image with the dimensions 180 × 200 is 180 pixels wide by 200 pixels high.

Channels

This is the number of conventional primary color layers that make up an image. For example, an RGB (red, green, blue) image is actually composed of three images (matrices of pixels): one for the red channel, one for the green, and one for the blue. Grayscale images often have only one channel. GeoTIFF and other formats used to encode satellite images can have up to 13 layers (or channels), 3 of which are RGB, the human-visible layers.

So for a full-color image in RGB format, we actually need three matrices (or channels) with values between 0 and 255, where a smaller number represents a dark color and a larger number indicates a light color (0 is black, 255 is white).

> There are other formats for storing image data; however, RGB is the most popular one, so that's what I'll focus on here.

How should we think about and define our features? Let's get a basic feel for what we can do with image manipulation.

Understanding Image Manipulation

How best to proceed depends on the image complexity—how many objects are in the image, the image background, the number of channels, whether color provides actionable value, etc. Based on these considerations, we have multiple options for manipulating the existing data and extracting features.

As shown in Figure 5-5, colored images have three layers of matrices that we can manipulate. We can add filtering, change the pixels, group them, or extract one channel only to get a grayscale image (as shown at the bottom of the figure).

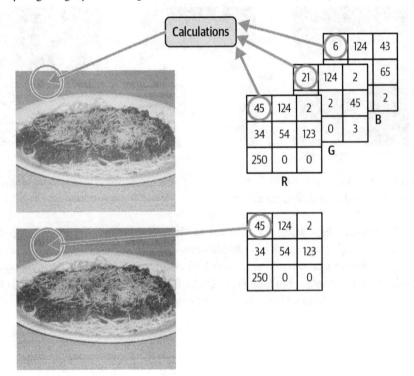

Figure 5-5. RGB image with three matrices (top) and grayscale image with one matrix (bottom)

Grayscale

When there is no meaning to the colors in RGB images, converting them to grayscale can assist in eliminating noise in our data. Grayscale images are single-channel images that carry information about the intensity of light in each pixel, using integer values between 0 and 255. These images are exclusively made up of shades of gray, encompassing the continuous range between white and black.

Defining image boundaries using image gradients

Let's take a look at another image from our repository, image 196_0070. This image is classified as spaghetti, but in the color version on the left, we can also see some other things in the picture, like tomatoes, some bread, a jar, a glass, a bowl, and what look like mussels. Without defining features, like image boundaries, such an image could introduce a lot of noise to our algorithms, and we might end up with a model that incorrectly classifies images of tomatoes, mussels, and other items as spaghetti!

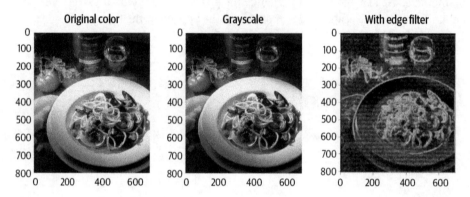

Figure 5-6. An image with multiple filters, classified simply as spaghetti in our dataset although it includes several other items

Extracting image edges using gradient calculations can be done by leveraging vector operators such as Laplace, which highlights areas of rapid intensity change. Using Pillow, we can define our own convolution kernel for edge detection with the `Kernel` method, or we can use the built-in `FIND_EDGES` filter that the library provides us with. The following code sample illustrates both approaches:

---

1 A *kernel* is a matrix that acts like an image filter. It slides across the image and multiplies the kernel values with the input data, extracting certain "features" from the input image.

```
from PIL import Image, ImageFilter

img = Image.open(r"sample.png")
# Input image to be of mode grayscale (L)
img = img.convert("L")
# Calculating edges by providing a kernel manually
final = img.filter(ImageFilter.Kernel((3, 3),
                   (-1, -1, -1, -1, 8, -1, -1, -1, -1), 1, 0))
# Calculating edges by leveraging Pillow filter defaults
edges = img.filter(ImageFilter.FIND_EDGES)
```

Pillow provides us with many other filters out of the box, such as BLUR, SMOOTH, and EDGE_ENHANCE, all of which are based on adding a filter to the image based on pixel gradient manipulation. Figure 5-6 captures how grayscale and edge filters are rendered.

Extracting Features with Spark APIs

We can use multiple techniques at once on the Caltech 256 dataset to extract features from the data. In Chapter 4, we touched a bit on UDFs and how to use them for extracting image size. Let's start by diving deeper into this topic, as it is our main tool for extracting features from images.

Until 2017, PySpark supported UDFs that operated on one row at a time. Those functions missed out on the Spark query engine's optimization capabilities, and because behind the scenes PySpark is translated into Scala code, many UDFs written in PySpark had high serialization and invocation overhead. To overcome these problems, data engineers and data scientists worked together to define UDFs in Java and Scala that could be invoked from Python. This made the code messy, however, and hard to navigate and maintain. Fortunately, Spark 2.3 introduced pandas UDFs, which allow vectorized operations and leverage Apache Arrow optimization for reducing serialization and deserialization operations. This addition enabled data scientists not only to scale their workloads but also to make use of pandas APIs within Spark.

Apache Arrow Optimization

When we transmit data over the network, or within a process running on the same machine, we need to provide a dedicated structure indicating how to convert the objects into sequences of bits (a process called *serialization*) and vice versa (known as *deserialization*). When Spark needed to translate Java objects to Python objects, there was a high overhead because of the serialization processes that were involved. To reduce this overhead, support for the Apache Arrow format was introduced into Spark. Arrow allows serializing and shipping of columnar data over the network in a standardized format, avoiding the need to copy and convert the data between different formats, as shown in Figure 5-7.

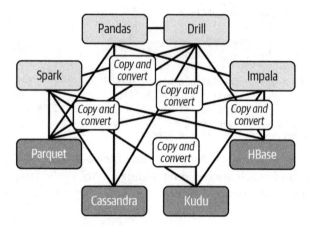

Figure 5-7. *Without Arrow, data needs to be copied and converted into the appropriate format for the destination framework (from the Arrow docs (https://oreil.ly/bQGeG))*

Using Apache Arrow allows us to avoid these expensive translations, as shown in Figure 5-8.

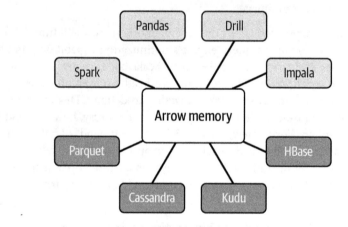

Figure 5-8. *Arrow's in-memory columnar data format avoids the need for serialization and deserialization (from the Arrow docs (https://oreil.ly/bQGeG))*

pyspark.sql.functions: pandas_udf and Python type hints

As mentioned in Chapter 4, pandas UDFs are defined using the `pandas_udf` decorator, which is part of the `pyspark.sql.functions` library. Prior to Apache Spark 3.0, which leverages Python type hints, you needed to specify the type of pandas UDF you were creating (depending on the type of transformation) with `PandasUDFType`, as shown in Table 5-3. Each type expects a certain kind of input and produces a certain kind of output. Use of Python type hints is preferred, as it gives a clear indication of what the function is supposed to do and makes it easier to perform static analysis; specifying the type with `PandasUDFType` will likely be deprecated in future releases. Certain types of transformations can now be performed with the dedicated functions `applyInPandas` and `mapInPandas`, discussed in the next section.

Table 5-3. Breakdown of Spark pandas UDF types

Spark PandasUDFType	Inputs and outputs	Python type hints
SCALAR (default)	A pandas Series	Doesn't need a specified scalar pandas data type; can take `long`, `double`, `float`, `int`, or `boolean`
SCALAR_ITER	An iterator of pandas Series	Requires pandas data type to be specified in the function signature to enable the compiler and runtime engine to create the correct iterator
GROUPED_MAP	A pandas DataFrame	Doesn't need a specific pandas data type; you can use the `mapInPandas` or `applyInPandas` function instead on top of a Spark DataFrame
GROUPED_AGG	A pandas DataFrame	Similar to GROUPED_MAP, doesn't need a specific pandas data type; you can use `applyInPandas` instead

In Chapter 4, we used a pandas UDF to calculate the size of each image in our dataset. Now let's calculate the average size for each image category so we can decide if we want to resize the images accordingly.

First, we'll flatten the `size` struct into two columns:

```
flattened = df.withColumn('width', col('size')['width'])
flattened = flattened.withColumn('height', col('size')['height'])
```

An excerpt from the resulting flattened DataFrame is shown in Example 5-2.

Example 5-2. Flattened width and height columns

```
+-----+------+
|width|height|
+-----+------+
|1500 |1500  |
|630  |537   |
|1792 |1200  |
+-----+------+
```

Next, we'll extract the mean width and height for each column, leveraging a pandas UDF with Python type hints:

```
@pandas_udf("int")
def pandas_mean(size: pd.Series) -> (int):
    return size.sum()

flattened.select(pandas_mean(flattened['width'])).show()
flattened.groupby("label").agg(pandas_mean(flattened['width'])).show()
```

```
flattened.select(pandas_mean(flattened['width'])
                 .over(Window.partitionBy('label'))).show()
```

The @pandas_udf("int") at the beginning and the -> (int) in the Python function give PySpark a hint about the data type we are using. This example shows how to calculate the mean width for a column, but we can use the same function for height as well.

Example 5-3 shows some example output.

Example 5-3. Example mean width and height values

```
+-------------+------------------+-------------------+
|        label|pandas_mean(width)|pandas_mean(height)|
+-------------+------------------+-------------------+
|196.spaghetti|             39019|              33160|
|    249.yo-yo|             40944|              37326|
|  234.tweezer|             34513|              27628|
|   212.teapot|             51516|              45729|
+-------------+------------------+-------------------+
```

Our final step is to decide whether or not we want to resize the images, based on the results. In our case, we can skip this step because we are going to leverage PyTorch and TensorFlow machine learning algorithms and resize them according to the algorithms' requirements.

pyspark.sql.GroupedData: applyInPandas and mapInPandas

applyInPandas and mapInPandas are functions that operate over a grouped Spark DataFrame and return a new DataFrame with the results. When we define a pandas_udf to work with them, it receives a pandas DataFrame as input and returns a pandas DataFrame as an output.

Although they have the same name, pandas DataFrames and Spark DataFrames are not the same thing, and it's important not to confuse the two. Table 5-4 highlights the main differences between the two.

Table 5-4. Key features of Spark and pandas DataFrames

	Spark DataFrame	pandas DataFrame
Supports parallel execution	Yes	No
Lazy operation	Yes	No
Immutable	Yes	No

As an example, let's take a look at how we can extract grayscale versions of our images using the applyInPandas function. Here are the steps we'll follow:

1. Define the function `add_grayscale_img`:

```python
def add_grayscale_img(input_df):
    input_df['grayscale_image'] = input_df.content.apply(lambda image:
            get_image_bytes(Image.open(io.BytesIO(image)).convert('L')))
    input_df['grayscale_format'] = "png"
    return input_df

def get_image_bytes(image):
    img_bytes = io.BytesIO()
    image.save(img_bytes,format="png")
    return img_bytes.getvalue()
```

   Within this function, we call the `convert` function from the PIL library to extract a grayscale version of the image. `get_image_bytes` is a supporting function that helps us get the right object class to use with `.convert('L')`.

2. Test the function. Image processing is often an expensive procedure, since it requires the Spark application to iterate over all the data and process the images. Therefore, it's best practice to test the function on a subset of the image data, so you can tweak and tune it and make sure it delivers on its expectations before running it on the whole dataset.

3. Specify the schema for the output DataFrame. We can do this easily by leveraging the existing DataFrame and adding dedicated blank (`None`) columns:

```python
rtn_schema = (df.select('content','label','path')
                .withColumn('grayscale_image',
                            lit(None).cast(BinaryType())) 
                .withColumn('grayscale_format',
                            lit(None).cast(StringType())) 
             )
```

   We can then extract the schema later by calling `DataFrame.schema`. This process makes schema definition in the function invocation easy and reduces the likelihood of schema mismatches.

4. Reduce the DataFrame columns to the minimum required, since (as described in the following sidebar) `groupBy` and `applyInPandas` are relatively expensive operations:

```python
limited_df = df.select('label','content','path')
```

5. Run the Python function on the Spark executors. Start by calling `groupby` to group the data (you can use any function to do this, but it's a precondition to run the next function). We can use any column to group the data and call the `applyInPandas` function with a pointer to the function to execute and the schema. In our example, `add_grayscale_img` is the function we want to execute, and `rtn_schema.schema` is our schema:

```
augmented_df = limited_df.groupBy('label')
                    .applyInPandas(add_grayscale_img,
                              schema=rtn_schema.schema)
```

6. Finally, rejoin the data from the original DataFrame with the augmented Data-
   Frame, leveraging leftouter in case the image transform needs to skip some
   rows:

```
output_df = df.join(augmented_df.select('path','grayscale_image'),
                              ['path'],"leftouter")
```

Beware of Out-of-Memory Exceptions

The groupBy function requires a full shuffle of the data, which requires all the data of
a specific group to be loaded into one executor's memory. In our example, we group
the data into categories, which means that all content from the same category will be
loaded into a single executor's memory as a pandas DataFrame. That can result in
out-of-memory (OOM) exceptions if the categories of data are too large. I've used
this example to simplify the solution, but I recommend using dedicated image IDs
and bucketing methods to make sure to avoid OOM errors.

What is an out-of-memory exception? Good question.

OOM errors are common in Java; they happen when an in-memory object requires
more RAM than is available in the managed heap. In PySpark, we run both JVM
Spark and Python Spark, and often we need to process exceptions that arise in JVM
Spark. This situation can occur because of an object leak, meaning the garbage collection didn't work, or because we've asked for too much memory, or because the Java
heap is not large enough for the application that is running.

OOM exceptions can also happen if the dataset itself is skewed, which, sadly, happens
frequently. For example, suppose our data is partitioned into fruit categories, and all
our data is classified into the category Apple. Even if we have four machines, Spark
might try to load all the data on one machine, due to the way RDDs operate on data
and the defined partitions (discussed in Chapter 2).

Those six steps provided us with two new features: one of type Array[Byte] named
grayscale_image and one of type String named grayscale_format.

Figure 5-9 shows the output_df table structure and some sample rows of data.

label	content	path	grayscale_image	grayscale_format
249.yo-yo	[255, 216, 255, 224, 0, 16, 74, 70, 73, 70, 0,...	file:/home/jovyan/256_sampledata/249.yo-yo/249...	b'\x89PNG\r\n\x1a\n\x00\x00\x00\rIHDR\x00\x00\...	png
196.spaghetti	[255, 216, 255, 224, 0, 16, 74, 70, 73, 70, 0,...	file:/home/jovyan/256_sampledata/196.spaghetti...	b'\x89PNG\r\n\x1a\n\x00\x00\x00\rIHDR\x00\x00\...	png
249.yo-yo	[255, 216, 255, 224, 0, 16, 74, 70, 73, 70, 0,...	file:/home/jovyan/256_sampledata/249.yo-yo/249...	b'\x89PNG\r\n\x1a\n\x00\x00\x00\rIHDR\x00\x00\...	png
249.yo-yo	[255, 216, 255, 224, 0, 16, 74, 70, 73, 70, 0,...	file:/home/jovyan/256_sampledata/249.yo-yo/249...	b'\x89PNG\r\n\x1a\n\x00\x00\x00\rIHDR\x00\x00\...	png
196.spaghetti	[255, 216, 255, 224, 0, 16, 74, 70, 73, 70, 0,...	file:/home/jovyan/256_sampledata/196.spaghetti...	b'\x89PNG\r\n\x1a\n\x00\x00\x00\rIHDR\x00\x00\...	png

Figure 5-9. Output example with the new columns

The Text Featurization Process

In "Example: Word2Vec" on page 98 you learned how to use the Tokenizer, Word2Vec, and other tools. In this section, we will use the Bot or Not dataset (*https:// oreil.ly/v_Rba*) to learn about the featurization process for short free-text strings such as Twitter user descriptions (bios).

Since our data is supervised (i.e., labeled), we can explore combinations of existing features with labels to develop new ones. Of course, this might result in the features being highly correlated, which means we need to think outside of the box. It's true that interpretable features (features that we have combined and where we fundamentally understand the relationships between them) and models are easier to debug than complex ones. However, interpretability does not always lead to the most accurate model.

Our dataset has a description column of plain text and a label column. Example 5-4 gives some examples of what these look like.

Example 5-4. Twitter Bot or Not description and label columns

```
+--------------------+-----+
|         description|label|
+--------------------+-----+
|Contributing Edit...|    1|
|       I live in Texas|    0|
|Fresh E3 rumours ...|    0|
|''The 'Hello Worl...|    0|
|Proud West Belcon...|    1|
|Hello, I am here ...|    0|
|Meow! I want to t...|    0|
|I have something ...|    0|
|I have more than ...|    0|
|If you have to st...|   13|
|I am a twitterbot...|    1|
|Designing and mak...|    0|
|Host of Vleeties ...|    0|
|Benefiting Refuge...|    0|
|Access Hollywood ...|    0|
|Producer/Songwrit...|    0|
|CEO @Shapeways. I...|    0|
|Two division UFC ...|    0|
```

```
|Moderator of @mee...|    0|
|Tweeting every le...|    0|
+--------------------+-----+
only showing top 20 rows
```

Let's take a look at some of the options we have for extracting features out of this data.

Bag-of-Words

Bag-of-words is one of the "bag-of-*x*" methods for turning text into flat vectors. In this approach, a text—in our case, a Twitter bio—is represented as a "bag" (multiset) of its component words, disregarding grammar and even word order. Often, the final representation will be the terms and their counts. Hence, as part of building a bag-of-words, we also extract *term frequency vectors* containing the words and their frequency (number of occurrences) in the given text. MLlib provides us with functionality to do just that, such as the `Tokenizer` (for splitting the text) together with the `HashingTF` transformer or `CountVectorizer` selector.

As an example, let's assume we have the following Twitter account description:

> Tweets on programming best practices, open-source, distributed systems, data & machine learning, dataops, Apache Spark, MLlib, PyTorch & TensorFlow.

In this case, there is no real need to generate the term frequency vectors, as each word has a frequency of 1. However, if we group the descriptions of all accounts that are labeled as bots, we'll almost certainly find many terms that appear more than once, which might allow some interesting insights. This brings us to a second option: TF-IDF.

TF-IDF

TF-IDF is a method from the field of information retrieval that is highly used in text mining. It allows us to quantify the importance of a term in a given document or corpus. As a reminder, *term frequency* (`TF(t,d)`) is the number of times that term `t` appears in document `d`, and *document frequency* (`DF(t,D)`) is the number of documents in the corpus `D` that contain term `t`.

IDF is the *inverse* document frequency, which provides us with a numerical measure of how much information a specific term provides based on how rare or frequent it is in the corpus; the more frequent the usage, the lower the score.

TF-IDF multiplies those outputs:

```
TFIDF(t,d,D)=TF(t,d)•IDF(t,D)
```

The TF and IDF functionality is separated in MLlib, which provides us with the flexibility of deciding how to work with them and whether to use them together or separately.

Let's calculate the TF for our dataset, using the `Tokenizer` API to extract words and the `HashingTF` function to map the terms to their frequencies:

```
from pyspark.ml.feature import HashingTF, IDF, Tokenizer

tokenizer = Tokenizer(inputCol="description", outputCol="words")
wordsData = tokenizer.transform(data)

hashingTF = HashingTF(inputCol="words", outputCol="frequencyFeatures",
                      numFeatures=20)
featurizedData = hashingTF.transform(wordsData)
```

`HashingTF` creates a new column named `frequencyFeatures` that contains a sparse vector of hashed words and the documents they appear in, as shown in Example 5-5.

Example 5-5. Hashed term frequency

```
+-----+--------------------+
|label|   frequencyFeatures|
+-----+--------------------+
|    1|(20,[0,2,3,4,5,7,...|
|    0|(20,[3,13,16,17],...|
|    0|(20,[1,2,4,5,6,7,...|
|    0|(20,[0,1,4,5,7,8,...|
|    1|(20,[0,1,3,4,5,6,...|
+-----+--------------------+
only showing top 5 rows
```

Our second step is to calculate the inverse document frequency. Since Spark's `IDF` is an estimator, we need to build it first using the `fit` method:

```
idf = IDF(inputCol="frequencyFeatures", outputCol="features")
idfModel = idf.fit(featurizedData)
```

This creates an `IDFModel` object instance named `idfModel`. Now, we can transform the data using the model:

```
rescaledData = idfModel.transform(featurizedData)
```

The `rescaledData` DataFrame instance has a column named `features` with the calculated importance of a term in a description given the whole dataset. Although this information is nice to have, TF-IDF is an unsupervised method that completely neglects the labels in the data. Next, we'll look at a supervised approach.

N-Gram

MLlib's `NGram` transformer allows us to take an array of strings (words) and convert it into an array of *n*-grams, where *n* is a parameter that we can define in the `NGram` function:

```
from pyspark.ml.feature import NGram

ngram = NGram(n=2, inputCol="words", outputCol="ngrams")
ngramDataFrame = ngram.transform(wordsData)
```

NGram can produce a nice feature if we know what to do with it later and the output provides value. For example, the output of:

```
[I, live, in, texas]
```

given n=2 provides us with the following array of strings:

```
[I live, live in, in texas]
```

As you can see from the output, NGram works as a sliding window, repeating words. It's useful when we are building tools for automatically completing sentences, checking spelling or grammar, extracting topics, etc.

Additional Techniques

There are many other techniques that you can leverage to extract features from text. For example, *topic extraction aims to identify* the topic of a given document by scanning for known impactful terms or a combination of terms. You can also leverage the frequent pattern mining functionality in MLlib, provided by its implementations of the FP-growth and PrefixSpan algorithms. All those methods, at their core, are based on the feature extraction methods discussed previously: bag-of-words, identifying frequency of terms or patterns in a corpus versus in a given document, N-gram, etc. To learn more, check out the following reputable resources from O'Reilly:

- *Applied Text Analysis with Python* (*https://oreil.ly/ata-py*) by Benjamin Bengfort, Rebecca Bilbro, and Tony Ojeda

- *Natural Language Processing with Spark NLP* (*https://oreil.ly/nlp-spark*) by Alex Thomas

- *Practical Natural Language Processing* (*https://oreil.ly/prac-nlp*) by Sowmya Vajjala et al.

Enriching the Dataset

Often, our datasets will require more data points and new features. Finding the right features is the beating heart of the machine learning workflow, and it is often more art than science. We have a few options for enriching our datasets. With the Bot or Not bot detection dataset, for example, we can leverage the Twitter API to extract new tweets and updates if we need more data. We can also make use of *transfer learning*, which is the process of leveraging knowledge gained while solving one problem to solve a different problem.

How can we leverage transfer learning for our Twitter bot detection problem? One option would be to pull in data from other social media with similar account names, such as LinkedIn. Learning if an account is real on LinkedIn can provide us with another data point to leverage.

Feature Stores—What Are They All About?

In 2017, Uber introduced the concept of *feature stores* with its machine learning platform, Michelangelo (*https://oreil.ly/xeSLS*). The main goal of a feature store is to store the features in optimized, relatively fast storage, with comprehensible metadata to allow fast access and low-latency querying by the machine learning algorithm. Feature stores can also help with caching, dealing with data types, and bridging multiple platforms (topics we will discuss in Chapter 7). Uber acknowledged that engineering good features is the hardest part of machine learning; hence, capturing those features and making them available in a dedicated location is essential as it helps speed up the data science workflow. This is why it's recommended to persist the data during the training and feature extraction steps, use version control, and make sure it is shareable.

As for Michelangelo, Uber designed it to support more than just featurization. The platform is intended to support the whole machine learning workflow, including the following steps:

1. Manage data

2. Train models

3. Evaluate models

4. Deploy models

5. Make predictions

6. Monitor predictions

Uber uses it for offline, large-scale distributed training of various kinds of models, from decision trees to linear and logistic models, time series models, and deep neural networks. Michelangelo is also responsible for serving the features in the production system. This is sometimes referred to as *inferencing*, when the machine learning application is deployed to production and serves the model. The goal here is low latency, being able to query the feature store in real time and get fast responses that support the machine learning application in production.

Summary

Spark and Spark MLlib implement many additional feature extraction functions that you might want to look into when building your models. There are numerous features that can improve model accuracy; for example, with images, you might want to try out a feature descriptor that only preserves the image outline and very unique characteristics of an image to differentiate one feature of the image from another.

You can leverage Spark's generic functions to do anything that you need with code, but be mindful of the resources and compute costs involved. Domain knowledge is the key for a successful featurization process, and it's important to handle feature engineering with great care. Next, we'll take a look at building a machine learning model using Spark MLlib.

## CHAPTER 6

Training Models with Spark MLlib

Now that you've learned about managing machine learning experiments, getting a feel for the data, and feature engineering, it's time to train some models.

What does that involve exactly? *Training* a model is the process of adjusting or changing model parameters so that its performance improves. The idea here is to feed your machine learning model training data that teaches it how to solve a specific task—for example, classifying an object on a photo as a cat by identifying its "cat" properties.

In this chapter, you will learn how machine learning algorithms work, when to use which tool, how to validate your model, and, most importantly, how to automate the process with the Spark MLlib Pipelines API.

At a high level, this chapter covers the following:

- Basic Spark machine learning algorithms
- Supervised machine learning with Spark machine learning
- Unsupervised machine learning with Spark machine learning
- Evaluating your model and testing it
- Hyperparameters and tuning your model
- Using Spark machine learning pipelines
- Persisting models and pipelines to disk

Algorithms

Let's start with algorithms, the essential part of your model training activities. The input of a machine learning algorithm is sample data, and its output is a model. The algorithm's goal is to generalize the problem and extract a set of logic for making predictions and decisions without being explicitly programmed to do so. Algorithms can be based on statistics, mathematical optimization, pattern detection, and so on. Spark MLlib provides us with distributed training implementations for the classic *supervised* machine learning algorithms, such as classification, regression, and recommendation. It also includes implementations for *unsupervised* machine learning algorithms, such as clustering and pattern mining, which are often used to detect anomalies.

It is worth noting that at the time of writing, there is not yet feature parity between the MLlib RDD-based (*https://oreil.ly/r0MAS*) and DataFrame-based (*https://oreil.ly/lQOLE*) APIs, so there may be cases where the functionality you need can only be found in the RDD-based API. Singular value decomposition (SVD) is one example.

How do you pick the right algorithm for the job? Your choice always depends on your objectives and your data.

While this chapter will cover many algorithms and their respective use cases, the topics of deep learning, integration with PyTorch, and TensorFlow distributed strategies will be discussed in Chapters 7 and 8.

I would like to draw your attention to the fact that the MLlib model instance has dedicated functionality for parameter documentation. The following code sample illustrates how you can immediately access the documentation for the individual parameters once you have created an instance of the model:

```
import pprint
pp = pprint.PrettyPrinter(indent=4)
params = model.explainParams()
pp.pprint(params)
```

Example 6-1 shows some sample output from the `model.explainParams` function. Since this is a `GaussianMixture` model (discussed in "Gaussian Mixture"), it contains descriptions of the params that are available for tuning with that type of model. This is a great tool to help you in your educational journey as you explore MLlib algorithms and learn about each one and their model outputs.

Example 6-1. Example of pretty-printing the `GaussianMixture` *model params*

```
('aggregationDepth: suggested depth for treeAggregate (>= 2). (default: 2)\n'
 'featuresCol: features column name. (default: features, current: '
 'selectedFeatures)\n'
 'k: Number of independent Gaussians in the mixture model. Must be > 1. '
 '(default: 2, current: 42)\n'
 'maxIter: max number of iterations (>= 0). (default: 100, current: 100)\n'
 'predictionCol: prediction column name. (default: prediction)\n'
 'probabilityCol: Column name for predicted class conditional probabilities. '
 'Note: Not all models output well-calibrated probability estimates! These '
 'probabilities should be treated as confidences, not precise probabilities. '
 '(default: probability)\n'
 'seed: random seed. (default: 4621526457424974748, current: 10)\n'
 'tol: the convergence tolerance for iterative algorithms (>= 0). (default: '
 '0.01, current: 0.01)\n'
 'weightCol: weight column name. If this is not set or empty, we treat all '
 'instance weights as 1.0. (undefined)')
```

Now that we've covered the basics, our learning journey for this chapter starts with supervised machine learning. Let's dive in.

Supervised Machine Learning

All supervised algorithms expect to have a `label` column as part of the data. This allows the algorithm to "validate" itself during the training phase and estimate how well it performs. In other words, the `label` column is what the algorithm uses to correct its decisions. In the testing phase, we use it to assess the quality of the algorithm by comparing the model's predictions to the real outcomes. The label can be a discrete/categorical variable—that is, a specific value among a set of all possible values, such as `apple` when you are categorizing between apples and oranges—or a continuous variable, such as a person's height or age. This difference defines which kind of task we want our model to solve: classification or regression.

In some cases, the label itself might be a set of labels; we'll talk about that possibility in the next section.

Classification

Classification is the task of calculating the probability of a data point belonging to discrete categories, or classes, by examining input features. The output of that process is a prediction of the probability of the data point belonging to each possible category. Many practitioners confuse regression and classification due to the existence of the *logistic regression* algorithm, often used for binary classification. While logistic regression outputs the probability of a discrete class, similar to classification algorithms, other regression algorithms are used for predicting continuous numeric values. Pay attention to this difference!

There are three types of classification:

Binary

> Each input is classified into one of two classes (yes or no, true or false, etc.).

Multiclass

> Each input is classified into one of a set of more than two classes.

Multilabel

> Each given input can have multiple labels in practice. For example, a sentence might have two sentiment classifications, such as *happy* and *fulfilled*. Spark does not support this out of the box; you will need to train each classifier separately and combine the outcomes.

In addition, the distribution of classes in the training data impacts the classification process. Data labels are said to be *imbalanced* when the input data is distributed unevenly across classes. You often see this in fraud detection and medical diagnosis use cases, and when facing such scenarios, you will need to consider and weight your features accordingly, if possible. Imbalances can also appear in the training, validation, and testing sets: all three need to be balanced in order to provide the desired results. We'll look more closely at this problem, and at dealing with multilabel classification scenarios, in the following subsections.

MLlib classification algorithms

Classification algorithms expect an indexed label (often in the range of [0,1]) and a vector of indexed features. APIs for transforming categorical features into indices, such as `StringIndexer` and `VectorIndexer`, were discussed in Chapter 4.

MLlib implements several popular classification algorithms, listed in Table 6-1. The class name pattern is typically *{name}*`Classifier` or just *{name}*, and after training, the classifiers produce a model with a corresponding name: *{name}*`Classification Model` or *{name}*`Model`. For example, MLlib's `GBTClassifier` fits a `GBT Classif icationModel`, and `NaiveBayes` fits a `NaiveBayesModel`.

Table 6-1. MLlib classification algorithms

API	Usage
Logistic Regression	Binary and multiclass classifier. Can be trained on streaming data with the RDD-based API. Expects an indexed label and a vector of indexed features.
DecisionTree Classifier	Binary and multiclass decision tree classifier. Expects an indexed label and a vector of indexed features.
RandomForest Classifier	Binary and multiclass classifier. A random forest is a group or ensemble of individual decision trees, each trained on discrete values. Expects an indexed label and a vector of indexed features.
GBTClassifier	Binary gradient boosted trees classifier (supported in Spark v3.1.1 and later). Like the `RandomFor estClassifier`, this is an ensemble of decision trees. However, its training process is different; as a result, it can be used for regression as well. Expects an indexed label and a vector of indexed features.

API	Usage
`Multilayer Perceptron Classifier`	Multiclass classifier based on a feed-forward artificial neural network. Expects layer sizes, a vector of indexed features, and indexed labels.
`LinearSVC`	Linear support vector machine classifier (binary). Expects an indexed label and a vector of indexed features.
`OneVsRest`	Used to reduce multiclass classification to binary classification, using a one-versus-all strategy. Expects a binary classifier, a vector of indexed features, and indexed labels.
`NaiveBayes`	Multiclass classifier, considered efficient as it runs only one pass over the training data. Expects a `Double` for the weight of a data point (to correct for a skewed label distribution), indexed labels, and a vector of indexed features. Returns the probability for each label.
`FMClassifier`	Binary factorization machines classifier. Expects indexed labels and a vector of indexed features.

Implementing multilabel classification support

MLlib doesn't support multilabel classification out of the box, but there are several approaches we can take to work around this:

1. Search for another tool that does and that can train on a large dataset.

2. Train binary classifiers for each of the labels and output multilabel classifications by running relevant/irrelevant predictions for each one.

3. Think of a way to leverage your existing tools by breaking the task into pieces, solving each subtask independently, and then combining the results using code.

The good news with regard to the first option is that PyTorch and TensorFlow both support multilabel classification algorithms, so we can take advantage of their capabilities for multilabel use cases.

As for the second option, if you are an AI engineer or an experienced Spark developer, Spark provides a rich API you can use to execute the following steps:

1. Add multiple columns to the existing DataFrame, each representing a given label. So, for example, if your original DataFrame had only the columns `id`, `sentence`, and `sentiment`, you would add each sentiment category as its own column. A row with the value `[happy]` in the `sentiment` column would get the value `1.0` in the new column named `is_happy` and `0.0` in the `is_indifferent`, `is_fulfilled`, and `is_sad` columns; a row with `[happy, indifferent]` in the `sentiment` column would get `1.0` in the `is_happy` and `is_indifferent` columns and `0.0` in the others. This way, a sentence can be classified as belonging to multiple categories. Figure 6-1 illustrates what this looks like.

```
+---+--------------------------------------+---------------------+---------+---------------+------------+------+
|id |sentence                              |sentiment            |is_happy|is_indifferent|is_fulfilled|is_sad|
+---+--------------------------------------+---------------------+---------+---------------+------------+------+
|0  |Hi I think pyspark is cool            |[happy]              |1.0      |0.0            |0.0         |0.0   |
|1  |All I want is a pyspark cluster       |[indifferent]        |0.0      |1.0            |0.0         |0.0   |
|2  |I finally understand how ML works     |[fulfill, happy]     |1.0      |0.0            |1.0         |0.0   |
|3  |Yet another sentence about pyspark and ML|[happy, indifferent]|1.0   |1.0            |0.0         |0.0   |
|4  |Why didn't I know about mllib before  |[sad, indifferent]   |0.0      |1.0            |0.0         |1.0   |
+---+--------------------------------------+---------------------+---------+---------------+------------+------+
only showing top 5 rows
```

Figure 6-1. DataFrame output example for multilabel classification

2. Continue the featurization process for each label. The book's GitHub repo (*https://oreil.ly/smls-git*) includes code that uses `HashingTF`, `IDF`, and other methods to prepare the DataFrame for training the classifier, as shown in Example 6-2.

Example 6-2. DataFrame ready for training the first classifier for the happy label

```
+------------------------------------------+-----------+
|features                                  |happy_label|
+------------------------------------------+-----------+
|(65536,[16887,26010],[0.0,0.0])           |0.0        |
|(65536,[575871,[0.0])                     |1.0        |
|(65536,[34782,397581,[0.0,0.0])           |0.0        |
|(65536,[11730,34744,49304],[0.0,0.0,0.0])|0.0        |
|(65536,[],[])                             |1.0        |
+------------------------------------------+-----------+
only showing top 5 rows
```

3. Build a binary classifier for each of the labels. This code snippet shows you how to build a `LogisticRegression` classifier after the transformations of adding columns and indexing:

```
from pyspark.ml.classification import LogisticRegression

happy_lr = LogisticRegression(maxIter=10, labelCol="happy_label")
happy_lr_model = happy_lr.fit(train_df)
```

You'll need to apply the same process to all the rest of the labels.

Remember, there are more steps to the machine learning pipeline, like evaluating the outcome with the testing dataset and using the classifiers you just built together.

For testing the model, you call the `transform` function on your test DataFrame:

```
result = happy_lr_model.transform(test_dataframe)
```

Example 6-3 shows the output of testing the model.

Example 6-3. Spearman correlation matrix

```
Spearman correlation matrix:
DenseMatrix([[ 1.        , -0.41076061, -0.22354106,  0.03158624],
             [-0.41076061,  1.        , -0.15632771,  0.16392762],
             [-0.22354106, -0.15632771,  1.        , -0.09388671],
             [ 0.03158624,  0.16392762, -0.09388671,  1.        ]])
```

This is a `DenseMatrix`, as discussed in Chapter 4, that enables us to understand the result of the `LogisticRegression` prediction. You can find it in the `rawPrediction` column (a vector of doubles giving the measure of confidence in each possible label) of the prediction DataFrame, followed by the probability vector (the conditional probability for each class) in the `probability` column and the prediction itself in the `prediction` column. Note that not all models output accurate probabilities; therefore, the probability vector should be used with caution.

What about imbalanced class labels?

As mentioned earlier, imbalanced data can be problematic in classification tasks. If you have one class label with a very high number of observations and another with a very low number of observations, this can produce a biased model. The bias will be toward the class label with the higher number of observations, as it is statistically more dominant in the training dataset.

It is possible to introduce bias in various phases of the model's development. Insufficient data, inconsistent data collection, and poor data practices can all lead to bias in a model's decisions. We are not going to delve into how to solve existing model bias problems here but rather will focus on strategies for working with the dataset to mitigate potential sources of bias. These strategies include the following:

1. Filtering the more representative classes and sampling them to downsize the number of entries in the overall dataset.

2. Using ensemble algorithms based on decision trees, such as `GBTClassifier`, `GBTRegressor`, and `RandomForestClassifier`. During the training process, these algorithms have a dedicated `featureSubsetStrategy` parameter that you can set, with supported values of `auto`, `all`, `sqrt`, `log2`, and `onethird`. With the default of `auto`, the algorithm chooses the best strategy to go with based on the given features. In every tree node, the algorithm processes a random subset of features and uses the result to build the next node. It iterates on the same procedure until it finishes using all the datasets. This is useful because of its random approach to the parameters, but depending on the distribution of the observations, there can still be bias in the resulting model. Imagine that you have an apples and oranges dataset with 99 apples and 1 orange. Suppose that in a random process the

algorithm picks a batch of 10 units. It will include at most 1 orange and either 9 or 10 apples. The distribution remains heavily skewed toward apples, so the model will likely end up predicting `apple` 100% of the time—which is correct for the training dataset but might be completely off the mark in the real world. You can read more about this issue in the documentation (*https://oreil.ly/6sFNX*).

Here is how to set the strategy:

```
from pyspark.ml.classification import RandomForestClassifier
# Train a RandomForestClassifier model with a dedicated feature
# subset strategy
rf = RandomForestClassifier(labelCol="label", featuresCol="features",
                            featureSubsetStrategy="log2")
model = rf.fit(train_df)
```

Regression

It's time to learn about regression! This task is also known as *regression analysis*—the process of estimating the relationships between one or more dependent variables and one or more independent variables. The values of the independent variables should allow us to predict the values of the dependent variables. If that is not the case, you can use the APIs discussed in Chapter 5 to select only the features that add value.

From a bird's-eye view, there are three types of regression:

Simple
  There is only one independent and one dependent variable: one value for training and one to predict.

Multiple
  Here we have one dependent variable to predict using multiple independent variables for training and input.

Multivariate
  Similar to multilabel classification, there are multiple variables to predict with multiple independent variables for training and input. Accordingly, the input and output are vectors of numeric values.

Many of the algorithms used for classification are also used for simple and multiple regression tasks. This is because they support both discrete and continuous numerical predictions.

There is no dedicated API available for multivariate regression at the time of writing, so you'll need to architect your system to support this use case. This process is similar to what we did for multilabel classification: prepare the data, train each variant independently, test and tune multiple models, and finally assemble the predictions.

To learn about regression, we are going to try to predict a vehicle's CO_2 emissions using the CO_2 Emission by Vehicles dataset on Kaggle (*https://oreil.ly/GND1E*). To do this, we are going to look at features such as company, car model, engine size, fuel type, consumption, and more!

As you will see, working with data to solve a problem like this requires featurization, cleaning, and formatting it to fit into the algorithm.

There are 13 columns in the dataset. To speed up the process of indexing and hashing, we will use `FeatureHasher` on only the continuous features. This selector asks us to specify the nature of the numeric features, discrete or continuous:

```
from pyspark.ml.feature import FeatureHasher

cols_only_continuous = ["Fuel Consumption City (L/100 km)",
                        "Fuel Consumption Hwy (L/100 km)",
                        "Fuel Consumption Comb (L/100 km)"]
hasher = FeatureHasher(outputCol="hashed_features",
                       inputCols=cols_only_continuous)
co2_data = hasher.transform(co2_data)
```

Notice how nicely `inputCols` takes a list—this makes reusing our code and developing cleaner code easier!

`hashed_features` is of type `SparseVector`. Take a look at Example 6-4. Due to the complexity of the hashing function, we ended up with a vector of size 262,144.

Example 6-4. The hashed_features sparse vector

```
+------------------------------------------------+
|hashed_features                                 |
+------------------------------------------------+
|(262144,[38607,109231,228390],[0.0,9.9,6.7]) |
|(262144,[38607,109231,228390],[0.0,11.2,7.7])|
|(262144,[38607,109231,228390],[0.0,6.0,5.8]) |
|(262144,[38607,109231,228390],[0.0,12.7,9.1])|
|(262144,[38607,109231,228390],[0.0,12.1,8.7])|
+------------------------------------------------+
only showing top 5 rows
```

There's lots of room for improvement here, since most of the vectors are sparse and might not be meaningful for us. So it's time to select the features automatically:

```
from pyspark.ml.feature import UnivariateFeatureSelector

selector = UnivariateFeatureSelector(outputCol="selectedFeatures",
                                     featuresCol="hashed_features",
                                     labelCol="co2")

selector.setFeatureType("continuous")
selector.setLabelType("continuous")
```

```
model = selector.fit(co2_data_train)
output = model.transform(co2_data_test)
```

The selector reduces the number of features from 262,144 to 50.

 Note that we actually increased the dimensions with `Feature Hasher`. This is because we didn't normalize the data first to make it simpler for us to backtrack the experiment. For real use cases, it is best to normalize the data before hashing.

The next step is to build the machine learning model. MLlib provides multiple algorithms that we can choose from, such as `AFTSurvivalRegression`, `DecisionTreeRegressor`, and `GBTRegressor` (for a full list, see the documentation (*https://oreil.ly/IYkDB*)). AFT stands for *accelerated failure time*; this algorithm can be used to discover how long a machine in a factory will last. The `DecisionTreeRegressor` operates at its best on categorical features, which have a finite number of categories. As a result, it won't be able to predict unseen values, like other regressors. The `GBTRegressor` is a gradient boosted trees regressor that uses an ensemble of decision trees trained in a serial fashion. It splits the training data into a training dataset and a validation dataset and uses the validation set to reduce the error on each iteration of the algorithm over the training data.

If you're wondering how it differs from the `RandomForestClassifier` we saw earlier, the main difference is that a GBT algorithm builds one tree at a time that helps correct the errors made by the previous one, while a random forest algorithm builds the trees randomly in parallel: each subset of worker nodes forms its own tree, and these are then collected on the main node, which assembles the workers' output into the final model. Both `GBTRegressor` and `RandomForestClassifier` support continuous and categorical features.

In the next example, we'll try out MLlib's `GBTRegressor` to see if it performs any better. While training might take longer due to its sequential nature, the optimization function should help it to produce more accurate results:

```
from pyspark.ml.regression import GBTRegressor
# define the classifier
gbtr = GBTRegressor(maxDepth=3, featuresCol="selectedFeatures", labelCol="co2")
# build the model
model = gbtr.fit(input_data)
# use the model
test01 = model.transform(test_data)
```

Now that we have a model, we can ingest the data we will use to train it. We'll also need to validate that there is no overfitting. If `test01`'s predictions are 100% accurate, it is highly probable that it is overfitting—this can happen with lower accuracy as well, but any time you see accuracy at or close to 100%, you should be suspicious. We'll talk more about evaluating models in "Machine Learning Pipelines" on page 138. For now, let's take a look at a sample from the prediction column, shown in Example 6-5.

Example 6-5. Predicted versus actual CO_2 emissions of vehicles

```
+---------+----------+--------------+----+-------------------+
|Fuel Type|    Model|Vehicle Class| co2|         prediction|
+---------+----------+--------------+----+-------------------+
|     AS5|      ILX|      COMPACT|33.0| 32.87984310695771|
|      M6|      ILX|      COMPACT|29.0|28.261976730819185|
|     AV7|ILX HYBRID|      COMPACT|48.0| 49.88632059287859|
|     AS6|  MDX 4WD| SUV - SMALL|25.0|24.864078951152344|
|     AS6|  RDX 4WD| SUV - SMALL|27.0| 26.95552579785164|
+---------+----------+--------------+----+-------------------+
only showing top 5 rows
```

As you can see, the prediction column is outputting data points that are very similar to the actual data in the co2 column. For example, in the first line, the prediction was 32.879... and the actual co2 value is 33.0. The error here is manageable, and this holds true for the rest of the rows. This fact acts as a leading indicator that the algorithm training is heading in the right direction, as the predicted results are not identical to the actual values (which means there's a low probability of overfitting), yet they are pretty close. As mentioned previously, we still need to run statistical evaluation tests to measure the overall effectiveness of the model.

MLlib supports other machine learning algorithms that can solve this problem too, such as FMRegression (FM stands for *factorized machines*). This algorithm is based on a gradient descent algorithm with a dedicated loss function, also called an *optimization function*. Gradient descent is an iterative optimization algorithm. It iterates over the data, searching for rules or definitions that result in the minimum loss of accuracy. In theory, its performance improves with every iteration until it reaches the optimum value for the loss function.

The FMRegression algorithm's maximum number of iterations is set to 100 by default, but we can tweak this using the setMaxIter function. The optimization function used here is SquaredError. SquaredError implements the MSE function, which calculates the overall mean squared error in every iteration. This is what the algorithm seeks to reduce: the sum of squares of "distances" between the actual value and the predicted value in a given iteration. MSE is considered an unbiased estimator of error variance under standard assumptions of linear models.

If FM sounds familiar, this is because there is also an FMClassifier. The main difference between them is the loss function. The classifier uses LogisticLoss, sometimes referred to as *entropy loss* or *log loss*. The LogisticLoss function is used in Logistic

`Regression` as well. We will not dive into the theoretical math behind it as there are many introductory machine learning books that cover this (such as Hala Nelson's *Essential Math for AI* (*https://oreil.ly/ess-math-ai*), also from O'Reilly). However, it is important that you grasp the similarities and differences between classification and regression algorithms.

Recommendation systems

Recommendation systems are often taught using a movie dataset, such as MovieLens (*https://movielens.org*), where the objective is recommending movies to users based on what other users liked and/or user preferences like genres. You can find recommendation systems implemented in many online platforms—for instance, ecommerce systems such as Amazon or streaming platforms like Netflix. They are based on *association rule learning*, where the algorithm aims to learn the associations between movies and users.

At a high level, we can split them into three categories, depending on the data available (metadata about the users and content, and data about the interactions between the users and the content):

Content-based
> Algorithms use the available metadata about the content and the users, including what content the user has watched before and rated, favorite genres, movie genres, etc., and produce a recommendation based on this information. This can be implemented with rule-based functionality and doesn't necessarily require machine learning.

Collaborative filtering
> In this instance, no metadata is available about the movies and users; we only have the *interaction matrix* defining the interactions between the users and the content (i.e., which movies each user has watched or rated). The algorithm searches for similarities between the user interactions to provide a recommendation.

Neural networks
> Given metadata on the users and content together with the interaction matrix, you can leverage neural networks to make recommendations.

ALS for collaborative filtering

MLlib provides a well-documented solution for collaborative filtering called `ALS` (alternating least squares). Its goal is to fill in missing values in a user–item interaction matrix. It also provides a solution to cold-start scenarios where the user is new to the system and there is no previous data to draw upon to make accurate recommendations. You can read more about it in the MLlib docs (*https://oreil.ly/66Vyt*).

Unsupervised Machine Learning

Unsupervised algorithms are used when the data doesn't have labels but we still want to automatically find interesting patterns, predict behaviors, or calculate resemblance without knowing the desired outcome. Those algorithms can be used interchangeably with supervised algorithms as part of the feature extraction procedure. Common unsupervised machine learning tasks include frequent pattern mining and clustering. Let's take a look at how MLlib supports these tasks.

Frequent Pattern Mining

Frequent pattern mining falls into the category of *association rule learning*, based on identifying rules to uncover relationships between variables in the data. Association rule mining algorithms typically first look for frequent items in the dataset, then for frequent pairs or itemsets (e.g., items that are often viewed or purchased together). The rules follow the basic structure of *antecedent* (if) and *consequent* (then).

MLlib provides two frequent pattern mining functions that can be used as preprocessing procedures for recommendation engines, like extracting meaningful patterns out of a corpus of text to detect user sentiment toward a movie: FPGrowth and Prefix Span. I'll focus on the clustering algorithms here, because those can be used on their own, whereas you'll often need to stack more than one of these algorithms together to reach the end result. You are invited to read more about the frequent pattern mining algorithms in the MLlib docs (*https://oreil.ly/VQQCQ*).

Clustering

Clustering is a grouping technique for discovering hidden relationships between data points. Clustering is regularly used for customer segmentation, image processing and detection, spam filtering, anomaly detection, and more.

In the clustering process, each item is assigned to a group, defined by its center. The likelihood of an item belonging to a group is calculated by its distance from the center. The algorithms usually try to optimize the model by changing the center points of the groups.

The names of clustering algorithms often include the letter k, as in k-nearest neighbors (k-NN) and k-means. Its meaning depends on the algorithm itself. It often represents the number of predefined clusters/topics. MLlib algorithms have a default integer k value, and you can set it using the method setK or pass it as a parameter. Some algorithms require the data to have a weightCol—specifically, MLlib's KMeans,

`GaussianMixture`, `PowerIterationClustering`, and `BisectingMeans` expect a non-negative `weightCol` in the training dataset that represents the data points' weights relative to the center of the cluster. If a specific data point has a high weight and is relatively far from the cluster center, the "cost" it imposes on the optimization function (in other words, the loss for that point) will be high. The algorithm will try to minimize the loss across all data points by moving the cluster center closer to such data points, if possible, to reduce the overall loss.

Almost all clustering algorithms require seed values (the exception is `Power Iteration Clustering`). The seed value is used to initialize a set of cluster center points at random (think x and y coordinates), and with every iteration of the algorithm, the centers are updated based on the optimization function.

Now that you know what clustering is, we can return to our CO_2 emissions prediction objective and see if we can identify commonalities between columns such as fuel type, consumption, cylinders, etc. MLlib provides five clustering algorithms. Let's take a look at these to see which ones might be appropriate for this task:

LDA

> LDA (Latent Dirichlet Allocation) is a generic statistical algorithm used in evolutionary biology, biomedicine, and natural language processing. It expects a vector representing the counts of individual words in a document; since in our scenario we're focusing on variables like fuel type, LDA does not match our data.

GaussianMixture

> The `GaussianMixture` algorithm is often used to identify the presence of a group within a bigger group. In our context, it could be useful for identifying the subgroups of different classes inside each car manufacturer's group, such as the compact car class in the Audi group and the Bentley group. However, `Gaussian Mixture` is known to perform poorly on high-dimensional data, making it hard for the algorithm to converge to a satisfying conclusion. Data is said to be high-dimensional when the number of features/columns is close to or larger than the number of observations/rows. For example, if I have five columns and four rows, my data is considered high-dimensional. In the world of large datasets, this is less likely to be the case.

KMeans

> KMeans is the most popular algorithm for clustering, due to its simplicity and efficiency. It takes a group of classes, creates random centers, and starts iterating over the data points and the centers, aiming to group similar data points together and find the optimal centers. The algorithm always converges, but the quality of the results depends on the number of clusters (k) and the number of iterations.

BisectingKMeans

> BisectingKMeans is based on the KMeans algorithm with the hierarchy of groups. It supports calculating distance in two ways: euclidean or cosine. The model can be visualized as a tree, with leaf clusters; when training begins, there is only a root node, and the nodes are split in two on each iteration to optimize the model. This is a great option if you want to represent groups and subgroups.

PowerIterationClustering

> PowerIterationClustering (PIC) implements the Lin and Cohen algorithm (*https://oreil.ly/-Gu9c*). It's a scalable and efficient option for clustering vertices of a graph given pairwise similarities as edge properties. Note that this algorithm cannot be used in Spark pipelines as it does not yet implement the Estimator/Transformer pattern (more on that in "Machine Learning Pipelines" on page 138).

Cool, cool, cool! Now that we understand our options, let's try one out. We'll go with GaussianMixture, since our dataset has only 11 columns and much more data than that. We are going to use the CO_2 Emission by Vehicles dataset after preprocessing and feature engineering with all the columns, including the label column (for the end-to-end tutorial, check out the file *ch06_gm_pipeline.ipynb* in the book's GitHub repository (*https://oreil.ly/Dl9nO*)).

The value of k in this case will be the number of car manufacturers in our dataset. To extract it, we use distinct().count():

```
dataset.select("Make").distinct().count()
```

The result is 42. What an interesting number. :) We'll pass this in to the constructor, along with setting a few other parameters:

```
from pyspark.ml.clustering import GaussianMixture
gm = GaussianMixture(k=42, tol=0.01, seed=10,
                     featuresCol="selectedFeatures", maxIter=100)
model = gm.fit(dataset)
```

Now that we have the model, we can get the summary object that represents the model:

```
summary = model.summary
```

All clustering and classification algorithms have a summary object. In clustering, it contains the predicted cluster centers, the transformed predictions, the cluster size (i.e., the number of objects in each cluster), and dedicated parameters based on the specific algorithm.

For example, we can understand how many groups the algorithm has converged to at the end by running `distinct().count()` on the summary:

```
summary.cluster.select("prediction").distinct().count()
```

In our case, we get 17. Now, we can try reducing the value of k to see if we get better convergence or try increasing the number of iterations to see if this has an effect on that number. Of course, the more iterations the algorithm does, the more processing time it takes, so when running on a large set of data, you should be cautious with this amount. Determining how many iterations you need is a matter of trial and error. Be sure to add this to your experiment testing, together with trying different measures of performance.

Another way to measure the model's performance is by looking at the `logLikeli` `hood`, which represents the statistical significance of the difference between the groups the model found:

```
summary.logLikelihood
```

With 200 iterations, we received about 508,076 likelihood scores. These scores are not normalized, and it's hard to compare them directly; however, a higher score indicates a greater likelihood of an instance being related to its cluster. All we know is that a higher score means a greater likelihood of instances being related to their cluster. Therefore, this is a good way of comparing the performance of one model against another on the same data but not necessarily of evaluating the performance of a model on its own. This is one reason why it's important to define the objectives of your experiments up front. If you would like to learn more about statistics and likelihood measurement, I recommend reading *Practical Statistics for Data Scientists* (*https://oreil.ly/prac-stats*), by Peter Bruce, Andrew Bruce, and Peter Gedeck (O'Reilly).

Suppose we continue our explorations using maxIter = 200 and receive the same number of distinct predictions: 17. Based on this, we decide to change *k* to 17.

Our next step might be to examine the cluster sizes, to make sure there are no groups with zero data points in them:

```
summary.clusterSizes
```

This produces the following output, where the indices represent the group index:

```
[2200, 7, 1733, 11, 17, 259, 562, 12, 63, 56, 1765, 441, 89, 88, 61, 13, 8]
```

Since `clusterSizes` is of type `Array`, you can use tools such as `numpy` and `matplotlib` to create a histogram of the values. Figure 6-2 shows the resulting distribution of group/cluster sizes.

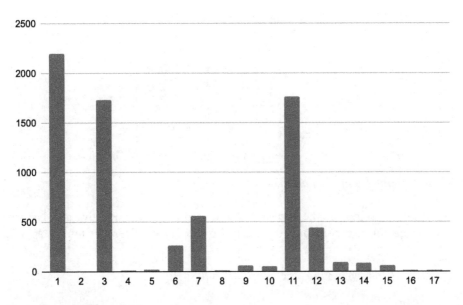

Figure 6-2. Histogram of clusters or group sizes

Evaluating

The evaluation phase is an essential part of the machine learning process—this is how we estimate the model's performance. MLlib has six evaluators, all of which implement the Spark abstract class `Evaluator`. They can be roughly split into two groups: supervised and unsupervised.

> `Evaluator` is a class that allows us to see how a given model performs according to specific machine learning evaluation criteria.

Supervised Evaluators

In supervised learning, we have the labels for the test data, so we can produce multiple metrics for estimating performance. To allow us to do this, the estimator first calculates the *confusion matrix*, which compares the predicted labels and the actual labels. For a binary classification task, conceptually the result would look like Figure 6-3, with each box having a range of [`0,dataset_size`].

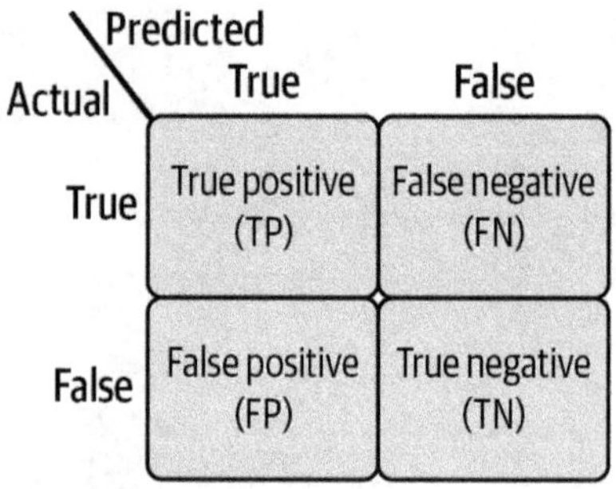

Figure 6-3. Binary confusion matrix

True and False stand for the accuracy of the prediction, and Positive and Negative stand for the binary predictions (these can also be 1 and 0). There are four categories:

True positive (TP)
    Positive labels where the prediction is also positive

True negative (TN)
    Negative labels where the prediction is also negative

False positive (FP)
    Negative labels where the prediction is positive

False negative (FN)
    Positive labels where the prediction is negative

Based on those values, Spark's estimators can provide many metrics; you can find full details in the documentation (*https://oreil.ly/knYwj*).

When we want to use the same process for *multiclass* and *multilabel* classification, the confusion matrix will grow accordingly to capture all of the labeling possibilities. In the case of imbalanced data, you would probably need to write your own evaluator. You can do that using Spark's extensive API.

In addition to the base `Evaluator`, Spark provides the following APIs to calculate performance metrics:

`BinaryClassificationEvaluator`
    A binary evaluator that expects the input columns `rawPrediction`, `label`, and `weight` (optional). It can be used to output the area under the receiver operating characteristic (ROC) and precision–recall (PR) curves.

`MulticlassClassificationEvaluator`
    An evaluator for multiclass classification that expects the input columns `predic tion`, `label`, `weight` (optional), and `probabilityCol` (only for `logLoss`). It has

dedicated metrics such as `precisionByLabel`, `recallByLabel`, etc., and a special matrix `hammingLoss` that calculates the fraction of labels that are incorrectly predicted. When comparing binary and multiclass classification models, remember that precision, recall, and F1 score are designed for the binary classification models; therefore, it is better to compare the `hammingLoss` to `accuracy`.

`MultilabelClassificationEvaluator`
An evaluator for multilabel classification (added in Spark 3.0). This evaluator is still in the experimental phase at the time of writing. It expects two input columns, `prediction` and `label`, and provides dedicated metrics such as `microPrecision`, `microRecall`, etc. that are averages across all the prediction classes.

> A feature in the experimental phase is usually still under development and not yet ready to be implemented fully. In most cases, these features are limited to just a few modules and are incorporated mainly to allow the developers to gain knowledge and insights for the future development of the software. Open source technologies frequently introduce experimental features that can be leveraged in production code, but these features might change in future versions of the software, and the contributors are not committing to continue supporting them or to turn them into well-polished features.

`RegressionEvaluator`
This evaluator expects the input columns `prediction`, `label`, and `weight` (optional) and produces metrics such as `mse` (the mean squared error of the distances between the predictions and the actual labels) and `rmse` (the root of the previous value).

`RankingEvaluator`
This evaluator (added in Spark 3.0 and also still in the experimental phase at the time of writing) expects the input columns `prediction` and `label`. It is often used for evaluating the ranking of search results. It has a variable k that you can set to get the matrix averages across the *k* first results. Think of a movie recommendation system that can output either 5 or 10 recommendations: the averages will change depending on the number of recommendations returned, and evaluating the results can help you make an informed decision about which movie to select. This evaluator's output is based on MLlib's RDD-based `RankingMetrics` API; you can read more about it in the docs (*https://oreil.ly/vobZH*).

Unsupervised Evaluators

MLlib also provides an evaluator for unsupervised learning, and we can access even more options by bridging to TensorFlow, PyTorch, or other libraries that can process Spark DataFrames. MLlib's evaluator for clustering results is the `ClusteringEva luator`. It expects two input columns, `prediction` and `features`, and an optional `weight` column. It computes the *Silhouette measure*, where you can choose between two distance measures: `squaredEuclidean` and `cosine`. Silhouette is a method to evaluate the consistency and validity of the clusters; it does this by calculating the distance between each data point and the other data points in its cluster and comparing this to its distance from the points in other clusters. The output is the mean Silhouette values of all points based on point weight.

Reflecting back on our classification example with `GaussianMixture` and `KMeans`, we can evaluate the models to make better decisions. You can find this and the other code from this chapter in the book's GitHub repository (*https://oreil.ly/smls-git6*):

```
from pyspark.ml.evaluation import ClusteringEvaluator
evaluator = ClusteringEvaluator(featuresCol='selectedFeatures')
evaluator.setPredictionCol("prediction")

print("kmeans: "+str(evaluator.evaluate(kmeans_predictions)))
print("GM: "+ str(evaluator.evaluate(gm_predictions)))
```

The default distance computation method is the squared Euclidean distance. It gives the following output:

```
kmeans: 0.7264903574632652
GM: -0.1517797715036008
```

How can we tell which one is better? The evaluator has a dedicated function named `isLargerBetter` that can help us determine this:

```
evaluator.isLargerBetter()
```

In our case, it returns `True`, suggesting that `KMeans` performs better on our data. We're not done yet, though—let's take a look at the `cosine` distance:

```
evaluator.setDistanceMeasure("cosine")
print("kmeans: "+str(evaluator.evaluate(kmeans_predictions)))
print("GM: "+ str(evaluator.evaluate(gm_predictions)))
```

Its output is:

```
kmeans: 0.05987140304400901
GM: -0.19012403274289733
```

`KMeans` still performs better, but in this case, the difference is much less pronounced. This is likely because of how the models themselves are implemented; for example, `KMeans` uses Euclidean distance as the default distance measure for clustering and so generally performs better when evaluating based on squared Euclidean distance. In other words, it's important to interpret indicators like this carefully. To add more clarity, we can combine the evaluating process with adjustments to the test and training datasets, the algorithms, and the evaluators. Time for tuning!

Hyperparameters and Tuning Experiments

What if I told you that there are tools that allow us to run multiple experiments, produce numerous models, and extract the best one in an automated manner? This is precisely what we are going to cover in this section!

All machine learning processes require tuning and experimentation before they can accurately predict real-world events. This is done by splitting the dataset into multiple training and test sets and/or tweaking the algorithms' parameters.

Building a Parameter Grid

In the following code, for example, we build a parameter (param) grid by using `Param GridBuilder().addGrid` to define multiple max iteration values for building k-means models using both available distance metrics:

```
from pyspark.ml.tuning import ParamGridBuilder

grid = ParamGridBuilder().addGrid(kmeans.maxIter, [20,50,100])
        .addGrid(kmeans.distanceMeasure, ['euclidean','cosine']).build()
```

A parameter grid is a grid or table of parameters with a discrete number of values for each one that can be used to iterate over different parameter value combinations as part of the training process, looking for the optimum values. `ParamGridBuilder` is just a tool that allows us to build it faster. You can use it with any MLlib function that takes in an array of params. Before continuing, let's tweak the params of our evaluator as well by adding a dedicated grid for it:

```
grid = ParamGridBuilder().addGrid(kmeans.maxIter, [20,50,100])
        .addGrid(kmeans.distanceMeasure, ['euclidean','cosine'])
        .addGrid(evaluator.distanceMeasure, ['euclidean','cosine']).build()
```

Splitting the Data into Training and Test Sets

Next, we'll use `TrainValidationSplit` to randomly split our data into a training set and a test set, which will be used to evaluate each parameter combination:

```
from pyspark.ml.tuning import TrainValidationSplit
tvs = TrainValidationSplit(estimator=kmeans, estimatorParamMaps=grid,
                            evaluator=evaluator, collectSubModels=True, seed=42)
tvs_model = tvs.fit(data)
```

By default, `TrainValidationSplit` uses 75% of the data for training and 25% testing. You can change this by setting the param `trainRatio` on initialization. `Train`

ValidationSplit is an estimator, so it implements fit and outputs a transformer. tvs_model represents the best model that was identified after validating various parameter combinations. We can also tell TrainValidationSplit to collect all the submodels that performed less well, rather than keeping only the best one; we do this by setting the collectSubModels param to True, as shown in this example.

 Use collectSubModels with caution. Consider this option when you want to stack multiple machine learning models as part of your workload or when you get similar results for the validation metrics and want to keep all the models to continue experimenting to identify the best one. For details on accessing the submodels and on why you should be careful when doing this, see "How Can I Access Various Models?" on page 137.

How can you tell that it's picked the best model? Let's check out the validation metrics:

```
tvs_model.validationMetrics
```

This gives us a view of how the various experiments performed given our evaluator, as shown in Example 6-6.

Example 6-6. Validation metrics output

```
[0.04353869289393124,
 0.04353869289393124,
 0.6226612814858505,
 0.6226612814858505,
 0.04353869289393124,
 0.04353869289393124,
 0.6226612814858505,
 0.6226612814858505,
 0.04353869289393124,
 0.04353869289393124,
 0.6226612814858505,
 0.6226612814858505]
```

Remember that every param in the process can be added to ParamGridBuilder. You can also set the specific columns for labels and features using this function. If you have a parameter dictionary or a list of (*parameter, value*) pairs, instead of adding them one by one with addGrid, you can leverage the baseOn function, which behind the scenes runs a foreach loop for you.

How Can I Access Various Models?

Good question. Remember we set `collectSubModels=True`? This saved all the sub-models, and you can access them from the `subModels` instance using this snippet of code:

```
arr_models = tvs_model.subModels
```

Bear in mind, however, that this operation will collect all the information from the executors to the driver, and if you are working with a large set of data, this might cause out-of-memory exceptions. So, while it's great for educational purposes, you should definitely avoid using this feature for real-world use cases!

`arr_models` is a Python array instance that holds our models and some metadata, as shown in Figure 6-4. The array index corresponds to the index of the validation metrics output shown earlier.

```
[KMeansModel: uid=KMeans_0695dc19e9ae, k=2, distanceMeasure=euclidean, numFeatures=50,
 KMeansModel: uid=KMeans_0695dc19e9ae, k=2, distanceMeasure=euclidean, numFeatures=50,
 KMeansModel: uid=KMeans_0695dc19e9ae, k=2, distanceMeasure=cosine, numFeatures=50,
 KMeansModel: uid=KMeans_0695dc19e9ae, k=2, distanceMeasure=cosine, numFeatures=50,
 KMeansModel: uid=KMeans_0695dc19e9ae, k=2, distanceMeasure=euclidean, numFeatures=50,
 KMeansModel: uid=KMeans_0695dc19e9ae, k=2, distanceMeasure=euclidean, numFeatures=50,
 KMeansModel: uid=KMeans_0695dc19e9ae, k=2, distanceMeasure=cosine, numFeatures=50,
 KMeansModel: uid=KMeans_0695dc19e9ae, k=2, distanceMeasure=cosine, numFeatures=50,
 KMeansModel: uid=KMeans_0695dc19e9ae, k=2, distanceMeasure=euclidean, numFeatures=50,
 KMeansModel: uid=KMeans_0695dc19e9ae, k=2, distanceMeasure=euclidean, numFeatures=50,
 KMeansModel: uid=KMeans_0695dc19e9ae, k=2, distanceMeasure=cosine, numFeatures=50,
 KMeansModel: uid=KMeans_0695dc19e9ae, k=2, distanceMeasure=cosine, numFeatures=50]
```

Figure 6-4. An example of the `subModels` array

The `tvs_model` instance itself has access to all the submodels. When we use the instance itself for testing or predicting, it picks the best-performing model out of all the submodels produced. When multiple models perform equally well, as in our case, it takes the first one in the list.

Cross-Validation: A Better Way to Test Your Models

One thing we can't do with `TrainValidationSplit` is try out multiple combinations of data splits. For that, MLlib provides us with `CrossValidator`, an estimator that implements *k*-fold cross-validation. This is a technique that splits the dataset into a set of nonoverlapping randomly partitioned "folds" used separately as training and test sets.

This operation is considered computation-heavy since when using it, we train *k* times the number of parameter maps models. In other words, if `numFolds` is 3, and we have one parameter grid with 2 values, we will train 6 machine learning models. With numFolds=3 and the previous param grid for the evaluator and the algorithm, we will train numFolds times the grid size, which is 12, machine learning models—i.e., a total of 36.

This is how we define it:

```
from pyspark.ml.tuning import CrossValidator
cv = CrossValidator(estimator=kmeans, estimatorParamMaps=grid,
                    evaluator=evaluator, collectSubModels=True,
                    parallelism=2, numFolds=3)
cv_model = cv.fit(data)
```

Similar to `TrainValidationSplit`'s `validationMetrics`, `CrossValidatorModel` has an `avgMetrics` parameter that can be used to retrieve the training metrics. For every parameter grid combination, it holds the average evaluation of the `numFold` `.parallelism` is used for evaluating models in parallel; when set to 1, sequential evaluation is performed. `parallelism` has the same meaning in `TrainValidationSplit`.

Executing `cv_model.avgMetrics` would result in the output shown in Example 6-7.

Example 6-7. Model training average evaluation metrics output

```
[0.057746040674997036,
 0.057746040674997036,
 0.5811536043895275,
 0.5811536043895275,
 0.057746040674997036,
 0.057746040674997036,
 0.5811536043895275,
 0.5811536043895275,
 0.057746040674997036,
 0.057746040674997036,
 0.5811536043895275,
 0.5811536043895275]
```

Each cell in the `avgMetrics` array is calculated using the following equation:

$$averageEval = \frac{\text{sum}(EvalForFold)}{NumOfFold}$$

Machine Learning Pipelines

This section introduces the concept of the machine learning pipeline, which is constructed from the various building blocks you've learned about so far: featurization, model training, model evaluation, and model tuning. Figure 6-5 visualizes the end-to-end process: ingesting data, preprocessing and cleaning it, transforming the data, building and tuning the model, and evaluating it.

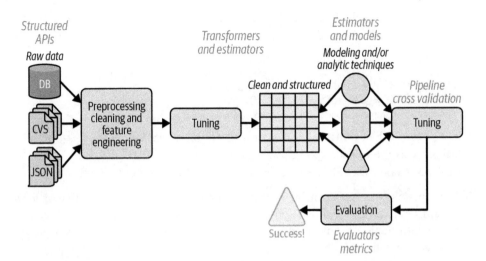

Figure 6-5. The machine learning workflow in Spark

The Pipelines API provides two main components, built on top of DataFrames and Datasets:

Transformer

A function that converts data in some way. As you learned in Chapter 4, a transformer takes in a DataFrame and outputs a new DataFrame with the columns modified as desired. Transformers can take in Spark parameters as well, as you'll see in the following example; this allows us to influence the function itself, including specifying the names of input and output columns. Providing temporary parameters gives us the flexibility to evaluate and test multiple variations using the same object.

All transformers implement the function `Transformer.transform`.

Estimator

An object that abstracts the concept of any algorithm that fits or trains on data. An estimator outputs a model or a transformer. For example, a learning algorithm such as `GaussianMixture` is an estimator, and calling its `fit` method trains a `GaussianMixtureModel`, which is a model and thus a transformer. Like a transformer, an estimator can take parameters as input.

All estimators implement the function `Estimator.fit`.

Going back to our CO_2 emissions prediction example, our `UnivariateFeatureSelec` `tor` is an estimator. As we specified in the `outputCol` and `featuresCol` parameters, it takes in a column called hashed_features and produces a new DataFrame with a new column called selectedFeatures appended:

```
selector = UnivariateFeatureSelector(outputCol="selectedFeatures",
                                     featuresCol="hashed_features",
                                     labelCol="CO2")
model_select = selector.fit(data)
transformed_data = model_select.transform(data)
```

Calling fit on the estimator creates an instance of UnivariateFeatureSelectorMo del that we assign to model_select. model_select is now a transformer that we can use to create a new DataFrame with the appended column, selectedFeatures.

Both estimators and transformers on their own are stateless. This means that once we use them to create a model or another transformer instance, they do not change or keep any information about the input data. They solely retain the parameters and the model representation.

For machine learning, that means that the model's state does not change over time. Hence, for online/adaptive machine learning, where new real-time data becomes available in sequential order and is used to update the model, you'll need to use PyTorch, TensorFlow, or another framework that supports this.

Constructing a Pipeline

In machine learning, it is common to run multiple steps in a sequential order to produce and evaluate a model. MLlib provides a dedicated Pipeline object for constructing a sequence of stages to run as a unit. An MLlib pipeline is an estimator with a dedicated stages param; each stage is a transformer or estimator.

Earlier in this chapter we defined a hasher, a selector, and a Gaussian mixture algorithm. Now, we are going to put them all together in a pipeline by assigning an array to the stages param:

```
from pyspark.ml import Pipeline
pipeline = Pipeline(stages=[hasher, selector, gm])
# Fit the pipeline to training data
model = pipeline.fit(data)
```

Remember to set the input and output columns according to the stage's sequence! For example, the hasher's output columns can be inputs for either the selector or the gm stage. Try to produce only the columns you will use.

Your pipelines may fail with all kinds of exceptions if you don't initialize them correctly. If you are adding stages on the fly, make sure to initialize the stages property with an empty list, as follows:

```
Pipeline(stages=[])
```

How Does Splitting Work with the Pipeline API?

Since the pipeline instance is an estimator, we can pass the pipeline to any function that takes an estimator as an argument. That includes all the functions for splitting a dataset that we learned about earlier, like CrossValidator.

Here's an example of how this works:

```
from pyspark.ml import Pipeline
pipeline = Pipeline(stages=[hasher,selector, gm])

cv = CrossValidator(estimator=pipeline, estimatorParamMaps=grid,
                    evaluator=evaluator, collectSubModels=True,
                    numFolds=3)
```

As you can see, it's pretty straightforward!

Persistence

An important part of the machine learning pipeline is persisting the output by saving it to disk. This will enable you to deploy the model to a staging or production environment, share it with colleagues for collaborative work, or just save it for future reference. MLlib provides this functionality using .write().save(*model_path*) for all of its models, including the PipelineModel:

```
path = "/cv_model"
cv_model.write().save(path)
```

To load an MLlib model from disk, you must know the model class used for saving it. In our case, CrossValidator produces a CrossValidatorModel, and this is what we use to load the model via the load function:

```
from pyspark.ml.tuning import CrossValidatorModel
read_model_from_disk = CrossValidatorModel.load(path)
```

Now we have loaded our model into memory, and it is ready for use.

You can also export your model to a portable format like ONNX and then use the ONNX runtime to run the model, though not all MLlib models support this. We will discuss this and other formats in Chapter 8.

Summary

This chapter provided an introduction to MLlib's supervised and unsupervised machine learning algorithms, training and evaluating them, and constructing a pipeline for collaborative, structured work. It contained a lot of information and insights into working with MLlib that you might want to revisit as you learn more about machine learning and Spark.

The next chapters are going to show you how to leverage all the work you've done thus far and extend Spark's machine learning capabilities by bridging into other frameworks, such as PyTorch and TensorFlow.

## CHAPTER 7

Bridging Spark and Deep Learning Frameworks

So far, the main focus of this book has been on leveraging Spark's capabilities for scaling machine learning workloads. But Spark is often a natural choice for scalable analytics workloads, and in many organizations, data scientists can take advantage of the existing teams supporting it. In this scenario, data scientists, data engineers, machine learning engineers, and analytics engineers are all consumers and/or creators of the data and share responsibility for the machine learning infrastructure. Using a scalable, multipurpose, generic tool such as Apache Spark facilitates this collaborative work.

But while Spark is a powerful general-purpose engine with rich capabilities, it lacks some critical features needed to fully support scalable deep learning workflows. This is the natural curse of development frameworks: in the distributed world, every framework needs to make decisions at the infrastructure level that later limit the possibilities of the API and constrain its performance. Spark's limitations are mostly bound to its underlying premise that all algorithm implementations must be able to scale without limit, which requires the model to be able to perform its learning process at scale, with each step/iteration distributed across multiple machines. This is in keeping with the Spark framework's philosophy that *the size of the cluster changes the duration of the job, not its capacity to run an algorithm*. This implies that partial training must be implemented in a monoid fashion, which means that the operations on the dataset are a closed set that implement the rules of associative binary operation—which is not always easy to ensure, especially with deep learning algorithms.

What Is a Monoid?

From a mathematical point of view, a *monoid* is an algebraic structure that includes a set, an associative binary operation, and an identity element. From a programming standpoint, monoids enable developers to break up a task into smaller subtasks almost arbitrarily, so breaking the task down doesn't require heavy computation. These subtasks can then be spread out among different workers and run individually, with their outputs later collected together into a final result—basically, a MapReduce operation. Let's take a closer look at the two properties of a monoid that enable this:

Associative binary operations
> Binary operations are operations that combine two elements of the same set to produce another element that is also in the set. These include addition, subtraction, multiplication, and division. With an associative operation, the order in which the elements are grouped can change without impacting the equation result. For example, multiplication and addition are associative because, for every set of numbers S, $(a * b) * c = a * (b * c)$ and $(a + b) + c = a + (b + c)$. However, subtraction and division are not. For example, $(2 - 3) - 4$ does not provide the same results as $2 - (3 - 4)$: $(-1) - 4 = -5$, while $2 - (-1) = 2 + 1 = 3$.

Identity element
> Operations have an identity or "empty" value (a value that, when combined with another one by a specified binary operation, has no effect). For example, with addition of nonnegative numbers, the empty value is 0. You can consider it to be the starting point of the set: 0, 1, 2, and so on. With multiplication, it's 1: $1 * 1 = 1$, $1 * 2 = 2$, $1 * 3 = 3$, and so on. From a programming perspective, you can call it the *null value* that doesn't add anything to the system. If a worker is running an addition task, it will start from its identity, which is 0.

> Because of these two properties, we can create a hierarchy of operations where their order of grouping doesn't change the end result. This is also the challenge of deep learning, where the operations are not always associative per se.

With deep learning algorithms, it can be hard to break each learning step into subtasks that can be aggregated afterward following the traditional MapReduce paradigm Spark is built upon. These algorithms are not easily distributable because their activation function needs to see the whole dataset, or accept a degree of imprecision. This can sometimes make it hard for data scientists working on deep learning applications (such as natural language processing and image processing) to fully take advantage of Spark. These systems can also be trained on large datasets with various technologies, which means that it is likely that to effectively develop deep learning models, you will have to rely on a broader range of algorithms.

This chapter will discuss how to bridge from Spark to deep learning frameworks, rather than completely using other tools. Why? In organizations, when there is a well-supported distributed system for processing and digesting data, it is a best practice to work with what exists and take full advantage of it, rather than introducing new complex frameworks. Introducing a new distributed framework can take months or even years, depending on the team size, the workloads, the importance of the task to the business goals, and short-term versus long-term investment efforts. If Spark is already used in your organization, you can leverage familiarity with that tool to get a solution up and running much faster.

Google's article "Hidden Technical Debt in Machine Learning Systems" (*https://oreil.ly/E2NBJ*) taught us that training machine learning models is only one piece of the puzzle—and a relatively small one at that. Figure 7-1, based on this article, shows the relationship between the machine learning/training code itself and the various other parts of the system that it relies on for support. The functionality of all of those elements influences the viability of the machine learning code; bugs in any of those components will, at some point in time, affect the machine learning code as well. For example, if my data collection process is flawed and provides a dataset with a completely different schema than the machine learning code expects, I will run into problems when trying to train the model.

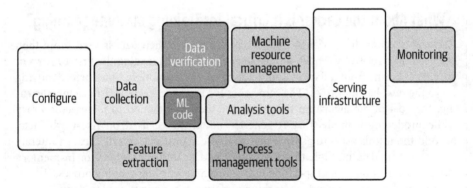

Figure 7-1. The required surrounding infrastructure for machine learning code

Ensuring all of the individual parts of a machine learning system are in good shape and will work well together requires more engineers, more frameworks, and more overall organizational investment than simply developing the model itself. The challenge of gaining the engineering support required to implement distributed clusters can more easily be overcome if you leverage tools that are already in use in your organization rather than increasing complexity by trying to introduce new ones. In our case, we can use Apache Spark for data collection, verification, feature extraction, analysis, and more, then bridge into other frameworks just for the capabilities that

Spark does not provide, enabling us take advantage of algorithms that exist in those frameworks while more easily securing buy-in from the rest of the organization.

Now that you have a better understanding of the why, let's explore some of the technologies that enable us to execute a distributed training workflow. I'll focus here on two tools that have good industry traction and are trusted by reputable organizations: PyTorch and TensorFlow. Off the shelf, both provide capabilities to ingest and preprocess large datasets, but this is often trickier to achieve than with Spark, and the team you are working with may not have experience with these dedicated machine learning-focused frameworks.

Even if your team agreed to put in the time and effort required to get up to speed with one of these tools, asking peer teams to shift their data ingestion, data processing, feature extraction, and other processes to a new framework would require a massive change in the infrastructure for the rest of the workloads, which would impact your ability to execute on the task at hand. A more efficient solution is to figure out how to combine the tools we're already using for the majority of our work with tools that provide the additional capabilities we need to address our deep learning requirements, taking advantage of just that subset of their functionality. This lowers the learning curve and keeps things simpler.

What About the Cache? Is It Critical for Training Machine Learning?

Caching is generally known to improve performance when data is used more than once and in a relatively sequential manner—for example, loading the first 10 rows of specific columns from a dataset and iterating on them multiple times before moving on to the next batch of rows. The same goes for machine learning. In machine learning, the goal of the algorithm is to optimize the loss function to increase accuracy while producing a model that is generic enough to be used on real-world data, beyond the test dataset. To achieve that goal, the algorithm typically needs to iterate over the same data multiple times. Storing the data in dedicated fast or in-memory storage has the potential of speeding up the machine learning training process. When looking at cloud storage options, caching is often a criterion we need to define as customers. Not all storage allows for caching out of the box; for example, with Amazon S3, we might need to leverage a dedicated caching service. While it is important to understand the concepts, we are not going to cover cloud caching in this book since it frequently requires a more specific solution.

To help you achieve this goal, this chapter covers the following topics:

- Data and the two clusters approach
- What a data access layer is and why and when to use it

- An introduction to and examples of using Petastorm
- Spark's Project Hydrogen and barrier execution mode
- A brief introduction to the Horovod Estimator API

The Two Clusters Approach

When your application calls for deep learning algorithms that are not implemented in MLlib, the *two clusters approach* can come in handy. As the name suggests, with this approach you maintain a dedicated cluster for running all your Spark workloads, such as data cleansing, preprocessing, processing, and feature engineering. As shown in Figure 7-2, the data is later saved into a distributed filesystem (such as Hadoop) or object store (such as S3 or Azure Blob) and is available for the second cluster—the dedicated deep learning cluster—to load it and use it for building and testing models.

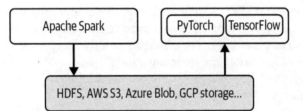

Figure 7-2. The two clusters approach: a dedicated cluster for Spark and a dedicated cluster for PyTorch and/or TensorFlow, with a distributed storage layer to save the data to

TensorFlow (TF) has a dedicated Data API that allows you to create a `Dataset` object and tell it where to get the data from when ingesting data into a TF cluster. It can read text files (such as CSV files), binary files with fixed-size records, and a dedicated TFRecord format for records of varying size. These are all row-oriented formats; TFRecords are the default data format for TensorFlow and are optimized using Google's Protocol Buffers. It is possible to read and write TFRecord data from Spark, but with Spark, the best practice is to work with a columnar format. When working with TFRecords, it's often best to stick with TensorFlow.

This brings us back to the question of when it is appropriate or necessary to work with multiple machine learning tools. Would just TensorFlow be enough for your needs? Would PyTorch be better? What happens if, as a data scientist, you need to implement algorithms from another library?

---

1 Protocol Buffers, also known as Protobufs, is an open source, language- and platform-neutral extensible mechanism for serializing structured data, similar to JSON.

To work with multiple platforms, we need to rethink our data formats and adjust them to fit each platform independently. Moreover, we'll need to adjust the data types. As you learned in Chapter 4, Spark has dedicated MLlib data types. When bridging to either PyTorch or TensorFlow—for example, saving an MLlib sparse vector into Parquet and later trying to load it directly into the PyTorch equivalent data type—we might experience type and format mismatches. While we can overcome issues like this with Apache Arrow's `pyarrow.parquet` and build our own translation layer, doing so will require us to understand how Arrow works, define the batches, and handle it ourselves. This process is error-prone and can rapidly become grueling. Instead, we should consider introducing an independent translation/data access layer that supports Parquet and will simplify data management by unifying file formats across different types of machine learning frameworks. We'll look at that next.

Implementing a Dedicated Data Access Layer

A data access layer (DAL) is a dedicated layer in an application, separate from the business logic and presentation layer, that provides simplified access to data stored in some kind of persistent storage. The concept was introduced by Microsoft, but it can be used outside of Microsoft environments as well. The actual storage can vary, and a DAL can support multiple storage connectors in addition to providing features such as data translation, caching, etc.

A DAL is not responsible for the *reliability* of the storage itself but only the *accessibility*—i.e., making the data available for different apps to consume. It provides a level of abstraction that makes it easier for us to consume data that was written with other tools. When working with multiple machine learning training platforms, it can help us close the gaps in data types, formats, access control, etc. We don't see the complexity of the underlying data store, because the DAL hides it.

Features of a DAL

Our DAL should be scalable and support distributed systems—which is to say, it should be able to save data to distributed storage and also leverage existing distributed server architecture to write and read data in a distributed manner. It should support the various data types needed to bridge the gap between Spark and other distributed machine learning frameworks, and ideally it should have a rich software ecosystem capable of supporting emerging machine learning frameworks. Additionally, there should be some notion of caching the data, since machine learning algorithms

---

2 Spark leverages Arrow heavily, but it is abstracted, and we rarely work directly with it.

3 *Data management* refers to the process of inputting, storing, organizing, and maintaining the data that an organization creates and collects.

iterate over data multiple times to improve the model's accuracy and reduce loss (we'll talk more about caching in the next section, when we discuss Petastorm).

Another great benefit of having a dedicated DAL is *discoverability*. The DAL should have a dedicated data catalog with information about the data it stores. This enables multiple teams to find and interact with the data easily and independently. One well-known and often, used data catalog is Hive Metastore. Sometimes referred to as a *metadata catalog*, meaning it holds data about the data, Hive Metastore is essentially a central repository of all the Hive tables; it includes information about their schemas, location, partitions, and so on, to enable users to access the data efficiently.

Regardless of what kind of data storage solution we use, our data access layer should act the same way: it should serve as a centralized repository of metadata that enables us to access and gain visibility into our data. With machine learning this is critical, since we often work collaboratively and need to find creative ways to enrich our training data and develop new features that may reside in other datasets. Similarly, after preprocessing and feature engineering, we need our data to be indexed and saved in a way that will speed up the learning process. For example, if we filter on specific fields in our machine learning experiments, our DAL should be able to support *columnar formats*. This enables us to create a single table for everyone to use, and to execute various experiments while filtering only with the desired columns for each experiment. Autonomous driving datasets are a good example, where data is coupled with information from sensors (such as radar and LiDAR sensors) that actively project signals and measure their responses. We might not want to load sensor information for every training iteration, and columnar support allows us to be more efficient.

If we use machine learning algorithms that sample the data during training cycles, our DAL should allow for *row filtering* as well. Some machine learning algorithms sample the data multiple times during training cycles and don't read it all at once. An example is long short-term memory (LSTM), a deep learning algorithm used for time series forecasting. With LSTM, a model is required to learn from a series of past observations to predict the next value in the sequence. Here, it might be necessary to filter the rows in each iteration based on time steps in the time series. You can think about it like a sliding window over a timeline, where each step computes a window of observed values bounded by a time range, learns from it, and tries to predict the next value. It will then update the loss function based on the success of the prediction.. This requires us to design our data in such a way that the model can pull information about a time window relatively fast. One option is to make this part of the actual file hierarchy. We can achieve that by integrating the time step as part of the file path, as in *../table_name/ts=1342428418/partition-...*, where *ts=* stands for the time step this folder holds information for.

Another feature that our DAL should enable is *data versioning*. As discussed in Chapter 3, one of the requirements of producing machine learning-driven applications is that it must be possible to reproduce the model-building experiment. For that, our DAL needs to be able to support access to various versions of the data over time.

To sum up, here's a recap of the key features that a DAL should support:

Distributed systems
It should be able to leverage existing systems to enable scaling.

Rich software ecosystem
This allows it to grow to encompass new machine learning frameworks and ensures that it will continue to be supported, bugs will be fixed, and new features will be developed.

Columnar file formats
Columnar file formats store data by column, not by row, which allows greater efficiency when filtering on specific fields during the training and testing process.

Row filtering
Some machine learning algorithms require sampling specific rows, so we need a mechanism to filter on rows, not only on columns.

Data versioning
It should be possible to travel back in time, to support reproducibility of experiments.

Selecting a DAL

So now that we know we need a DAL, how do we pick one? There are a range of solutions available, both proprietary and open source. You will need to do some research to understand your specific requirements, prioritize them, and then compare the various options to figure out which ones might work best for you. Before choosing a DAL, if you are planning on implementing it for work, make sure that you test it out on your real workloads. One of the big mistakes people often make is running only the benchmarks the vendor provides and not validating the tool on their own workloads, which might be quite different. Also remember to calculate potential risk and costs.

In this book, I focus solely on open source solutions. There are many such solutions that come to mind that support bridging, from Spark to TensorFlow or PyTorch, to enrich the capabilities of our machine learning algorithms. We'll take a look at the one I've chosen to cover here, Petastorm, in the next section.

What Is Petastorm?

Petastorm is an open source data access library developed by Uber ATG that allows us to train and evaluate deep learning models directly using multiterabyte datasets in Apache Parquet format. It does this by enabling us to read and write Parquet files with TensorFlow, PyTorch, and other Python-based machine learning training frameworks. Several features of Petastorm support the training of deep learning algorithms, including efficient implementations of row filtering, data sharding, and shuffling and the ability to access a subset of fields and handle time series data. Figure 7-3 shows how it fits into the overall architecture of a machine learning system.

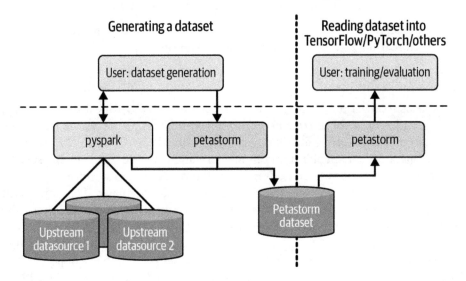

Figure 7-3. Architecture diagram with Petastorm dataset as the bridge

This figure actually tells the story of two processes: dataset generation and training/evaluation. Basically, we have a producer and a consumer of data (a common pattern in many machine learning workloads). Data from various sources is combined and processed with PySpark, then made available in Parquet columnar format to distributed training frameworks such as PyTorch and TensorFlow, which can use it as many times as needed for model training and evaluation.

Figures 7-4 and 7-5, in the following sections, demonstrate two different options for how to use Petastorm. The first one is to leverage Petastorm simply as a converter or translator and keep the data in strict Parquet format. The second approach is to integrate the Petastorm format with the Apache Parquet store; this leverages the translator and saves the data into a dedicated Petastorm dataset.

As of v.0.12.0, Petastorm only supports converting/translating and saving uniformly sized images. It cannot handle any variance in image size. Therefore, it's important to take image size into consideration as part of the preprocessing when working with this type of data.

Depending on how we use the dataset, both options can be useful. Choosing between them depends on how complex our system is: if the only frameworks we're using are TensorFlow, PyTorch, and Spark, having Petastorm as a store might make sense, but if our data system is more complex, it might be best to keep the data in a non-Petastorm store and just leverage Petastorm as a converter/translator.

Let's examine the first approach of training a model from an existing non-Petastorm Parquet store using Petastorm's `SparkDatasetConverter`.

SparkDatasetConverter

`SparkDatasetConverter` is an API that can do the "boring" work for us of saving, loading, and parsing the intermediate files, so we can focus on the unique part of the deep learning project. How does it work? Imagine the data was previously processed using a Spark DataFrame. It's stored in memory and is not yet saved in any specific offline store or files. We can take advantage of that and save it to a dedicated store, or intermediate files, which Petastorm manages. Interestingly enough, Petastorm itself has a caching mechanism, where it persists the data into a staging store. When the DataFrame is converted using Petastorm's `SparkDatasetConverter`, for each access to it, Petastorm will check if the data is already in the cache and persisted in the distributed filesystem. If so, it will read it from the cache, and if not, it will persist it in Parquet file format. The converter will then load the persisted file into a TensorFlow dataset or PyTorch data loader, as shown in Figure 7-4.

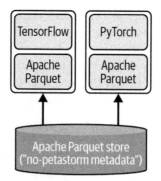

Figure 7-4. Using Petastorm as a converter

To achieve this in practice, we first need to define the cache path (a cache_path instance of type String) to specify the directory path for the intermediate files:

```
from petastorm.spark import SparkDatasetConverter
# Set a cache directory on DBFS FUSE for intermediate data
spark.conf.set(SparkDatasetConverter.PARENT_CACHE_DIR_URL_CONF,cache_path)
```

Later, SparkDatasetConverter (on its own) is able to recognize whether a DataFrame was cached or not by analyzing Spark's DataFrame query plan. At the end, the data will be persisted in the path with this directory format:

{datetime}-{appid}-{spark_application_id}-{uuid4}

To read the file paths in the cache directory, you will need to understand what each of these elements indicates:

- *{datetime}* is a string of the shape '%Y%m%d%H%M%S' that represents the time of DataFrame materialization (when the DataFrame was processed).

- *{appid}* is the application ID.

- *{spark_application_id}* is the Spark application ID. We can pull this directly from the running Spark session with .sparkContext.applicationId.

- *{uuid4}* is a random number that serves as a unique identifier.

Using Petastorm as a converter has many benefits. It caches intermediate files and cleans out the cache when the program exits. Additionally, it automatically converts Spark's unique MLlib vector into 1D arrays. This approach provides the decoupling that removes the necessity to use Spark and specifically MLlib for training machine learning models.

 In the event that the caching functionality fails, you will have to manage the ephemeral persisted files that may remain after a failed operation. Ensure that all created files and directories have been validated, deleted, or safely stored somewhere else before writing again.

After setting up the cache, it's time to create a simple converter. The converter's input is as follows:

parquet_row_group_size_bytes
  This is a critical component that defines the performance of the converter itself (i.e., how fast it operates) and also can help prevent out-of-memory errors. It is of type Int and defines the size in bytes of a row group in Parquet after materialization. The official Parquet documentation recommends a row group size of 512 to 1,024 MB on HDFS. The optimal block size will depend on what type of data you have and whether you're using cloud or on-prem storage. On cloud storage like

Amazon S3 or Azure Blob, the object sizes themselves are often optimized for a smaller block: with Azure it's between 64 KB and 100 MB, and with S3 it's between about 5 MB and 100 MB (these numbers are subject to change, and it is always a good practice to check with the cloud providers which sizes they are optimizing for). With images, for instance, you'll want to figure out how much space they take up on disk. Remember that this parameter is in bytes, so optimizing for HDFS with 512 MB is equal to 512 * 1,024 * 1,024 = 536,870,912 bytes. If we ran our example in the cloud, we might want to use 1,000,000 bytes, or 1 MB, as this size works nicely with our Caltech image dataset.

compression_codec

As discussed in Chapter 4, Parquet supports multiple compression codecs, and since Petastorm works with Parquet, it allows us to define the codec as well. The default is None. Don't mistake the image data compression codec (JPEG, PNG) with the compression_codec used as part of the Spark converter's functionality; the latter refers to Parquet compression.

dtype

This defines the precision of the floating-point elements in our data. In machine learning, when we convert data from one state to another, there is always a risk of losing information. This is especially the case if we convert strings to numbers and later round them up or change their representation again. The converter allows us to be very specific with this definition as well; the default type is float32.

 All of these configurations should be in global variables, so it's easier for you to remember them and easier for teams to collaborate. You can define a separate configuration file for defining data types across operations and transformations. They can also be defined as part of the Spark configuration or *.env* files when necessary.

Once you understand the configuration options, the code itself is straightforward:

```
# TIP: Use a low value for parquet_row_group_size_bytes. The default of 32 MiB
# can be too high for our image use case if we run it in the cloud.
# Convert the training DataFrame:
converter_train = make_spark_converter(df_train,
                                        parquet_row_group_size_bytes=32000000)
# Convert the test DataFrame:
converter_test_val = make_spark_converter(df_val,
                                        parquet_row_group_size_bytes=32000000)
```

At this stage, the DataFrame is materialized.

Petastorm enables us to define additional preprocessing functions using Transform Spec. All the transformations we define here are going to be applied to each row processed by the Spark workers. We need to pay attention to the columns we want to keep, their data types, the order of the columns, and the final schema. The following code example illustrates defining the `TransformSpec`:

```
# The output shape of the TransformSpec is not automatically known by Petastorm,
# so you need to specify the shape for new columns in edit_fields and specify
# the order of the output columns in selected_fields.
transform_spec_fn = TransformSpec(
    func=transform_row,
    edit_fields=[('features', np.uint8, IMG_SHAPE, False)],
    selected_fields=['features', 'label_index']
)
```

In this code snippet, we define a function that is going to operate in the Spark workers, named `transform_row`. This callable function performs the transformation of the *pre-transform-schema* dataset into the *post-transform-schema* dataset.

Here, we use this function to prepare the data to be injected into a dedicated TensorFlow MobileNetV2 neural network (more on MobileNetV2 in Chapter 8):

```
def preprocess(grayscale_image):
    """
    Preprocess an image file's bytes for MobileNetV2 (ImageNet).
    """
    image = Image.open(io.BytesIO(grayscale_image)).resize([224, 224])
    image_array = keras.preprocessing.image.img_to_array(image)
    return preprocess_input(image_array)

def transform_row(pd_batch):
    """
    The input and output of this function are pandas DataFrames.
    """
    pd_batch['features'] = pd_batch['content'].map(lambda x: preprocess(x))
    pd_batch = pd_batch.drop(labels=['content'], axis=1)
    return pd_batch
```

Using Python's mapping functionality, `transform_row` goes over the data in the content column and translates it into processed image data with the size and preprocessing requested by MobileNetV2. Although this is the case for our example, `transform_row` doesn't have to take a pandas DataFrame as input; it can be any other type. If you recall, in Chapter 5 we used Spark's pandas APIs to batch rows from a Spark DataFrame into a pandas DataFrame to iterate on them and extract features. That was where I first introduced the pandas DataFrame instance. This is an example of what we can do with those APIs, using them to transform the rows. It's also a good example of how the machine learning algorithm we use can have an effect: this algorithm doesn't allow any missing values, and resizing the images is necessary since their sizes in the original dataset vary and the algorithm requires a uniform size and shape (as do most). We can handle both of those requirements at once by running `transform_row`.

If `transform_row` is not defined correctly, during the actual transformation we might encounter the following error:

```
File "/opt/conda/lib/python3.9/site-packages/petastorm/arrow_reader_worker.py",
        line 176, in _check_shape_and_ravel
    raise ValueError('field {name} must be the shape {shape}'

ValueError: field features must be the shape (224, 224, 3)
```

This error won't show up until we run the converter and create the desired datasets. That means we need to decide which training framework we want to use and convert the data to the desired instance type.

Note the Pythonic way in which we handle the pandas DataFrame. We process the rows into *tuples*, not *namedtuples*, since this is what TensorFlow expects in our scenario.

Last, the `selected_fields` parameter (`selected_fields=['features', 'label_index']`) dictates the order and names of the columns.

Next, let's see how to connect these together with TensorFlow. Here is a code snippet that demonstrates how we make the actual TensorFlow dataset by calling the `make_tf_dataset` function and providing it with the `transform_spec_fn` and `batch_size` described earlier:

```
with converter_train.make_tf_dataset(transform_spec=transform_spec_fn,
                                     batch_size=BATCH_SIZE) as train_dataset,
        converter_test_val.make_tf_dataset(transform_spec=transform_spec_fn,
                                           batch_size=BATCH_SIZE) as val_dataset:
```

This code snippet creates `train_dataset` and `val_dataset` in TF dataset format, which can be used downstream with Keras and TensorFlow. We will dive into the possibilities of training using this data loading approach in Chapter 8.

Petastorm as a Parquet Store

The second option, rather than using Petastorm only as a converter, is to build a Petastorm store with Parquet as the data format. This is the classic variation of the DAL. It requires us to introduce Petastorm code in all our services, and it couples using Petastorm with all the data consumers, as shown in Figure 7-5.

---

4 *Tuples* are one of four Python data types used to store collections of data. The data is stored in a fixed, immutable order, and duplicate values are allowed.

5 A *namedtuple* in Python is a tuple with named fields, where the data is stored as keys and values. To learn more about this collection type, check out the Python docs (*https://oreil.ly/nFcKA*).

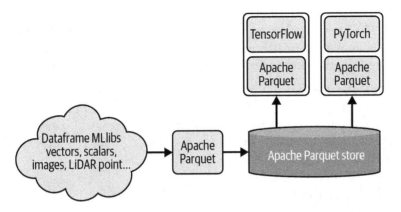

Figure 7-5. Using Petastorm as a dedicated store with metadata on top of the Parquet store

Petastorm on its own is not a complete store. It enables support for storing tensors (arrays) that were stored in Parquet format by saving additional metadata about the fields translated into NumPy data types. To create a Petastorm store, you can define a new schema by creating a Petastorm `Unischema` instance with dedicated fields and leveraging the `dict_to_spark_row` function:

```
from petastorm.unischema import Unischema, UnischemaField
imageSchema = Unischema('caltech256schema', [
    UnischemaField('content', np.uint8, (224, 224, 3), False),
    UnischemaField('label_index', np.int32, (), ScalarCodec(LongType()), False)])
```

`UnischemaField` is a type used to describe a single immutable field in the schema. You must provide it with the name, `numpy_dtype`, and shape. As you can see from this example, you can also specify a codec. Petastorm supports various codec types for images, scalar data, etc., such as `ScalarCodec` (encodes a scalar into a Spark Data‐Frame field), `NdarrayCodec` (encodes/decodes a NumPy `ndarray` into/from a Spark DataFrame field), `CompressedImageCodec` (compresses/decompresses images), and more. Generally speaking, all codecs define the encoding/decoding processes to use during serialization. Sometimes Petastorm can determine the codec needed on its own, as is the case for the `content` field in this example, but sometimes it will need your help, like for the `label_index` field.

Let's take a deeper look at our fields. The `content` field is of Spark SQL type `Binary Type`, and the `label_index` field is of type `LongType`. While mapping the latter to a `numpy_dtype` is straightforward, for the first one, it isn't. `BinaryType` in Spark is implemented as a Scala byte array. When choosing a `numpy_dtype`, we need to go back and assess the origin of the data. The `content` field is based on images. Their numeric representation range is [0,255]. For that range, `np.uint8` is a good fit. `uint` stands for *unsigned integer*, and this type can only hold positive numbers.

After defining the schema, you can leverage the `dict_to_spark_row` function with the Spark RDD to verify that the data conforms with the `Unischema` definition's types and encodes the data using the codec specified. In our example, we provided a `Scalar Codec`. Later, we can write the data into the store with the `spark.write` function.

This section was dense: you learned about caching, what Petastorm is, and how to leverage it to use processed Spark data with TensorFlow and PyTorch and improve accessibility. The next section will discuss Project Hydrogen, which aims to facilitate connecting Spark with other frameworks by enabling scheduling more suitable for machine learning. Let's jump right in!

Project Hydrogen

Project Hydrogen is a community-driven project to improve Apache Spark's support for deep learning/neural network distributed training. Earlier, we discussed the two clusters approach, where we have separate dedicated clusters for processing data with Spark and for deep learning. The reason for this setup is that the Spark MapReduce scheduler's approach isn't always suited to deep learning training with a cyclic training process. The algorithm's tasks must be coordinated and optimized for communication and support backpropagation and forward propagation. For that, Project Hydrogen offers another scheduling primitive called the Gang scheduler as part of its barrier execution mode as well as accelerator-aware scheduling (which is critical for deep learning training performance).

Barrier Execution Mode

In a neural network, *backpropagation* means "backward propagation of errors." In every iteration over a subset of the data, the neural network calculates the gradient of a loss function with respect to the weights in the network. Later, it propagates the error back into the previous network layer and adjusts the parameters of that layer, aiming to improve the accuracy of the predictions. The backpropagation occurs from the output layer all the way back to the input layer. The opposite behavior happens with forward propagation (sometimes referred to as *feed-forward*), where the calculated gradient of a loss function propagates to the layer that comes after it.

These are complex topics that I can only brush the surface of in this book; check out Josh Patterson and Adam Gibson's *Deep Learning* (*https://oreil.ly/dp-learn*) (O'Reilly) to learn more about the mathematics and behavior of deep learning.

To better understand the scheduler challenge, take a look at Figure 7-6. At the top, there is a depiction of the parallel execution model that Spark follows. While there might be dependencies among tasks, because of the nature of Spark and its use of monoids, breaking the tasks down into associative operations of the same type, the tasks are linear and Spark executes them in parallel. In distributed training, on the other hand, the tasks' dependency tree is more complex, and we can't necessarily execute them in parallel. For example, task 3 in the distributed training process may depend on tasks 2, 1, and n, while task n depends on task 5, which depends on task 3. That means we have a circle of operations here, and there is no one directed graph anymore. We need to support all of these dependencies and decide how and when to compute each.

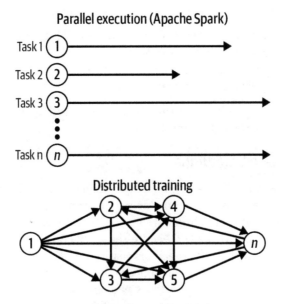

Figure 7-6. Linear/parallel execution versus distributed training

To solve the scheduler challenge, Project Hydrogen introduced *barrier execution mode*. This allows us to define a specific code block where barrier execution is being used. The barrier model enables us to create gates, or barriers, between sets of operations and makes the operations across barriers sequential. This means that each set of operations can be performed in parallel and that the whole process can operate as one directed graph, without circles. By establishing a fixed sequence of operations across barriers, this model also allows us to carry information over to dependent tasks.

In order to work with barrier execution mode, we need to use a barrier RDD with a barrier context and Spark's RDD functions, such as mapPartitions. Using a barrier RDD signals that all tasks performed on this RDD are going to run with a barrier context. The barrier context within the task enables us to decide which operations should be coordinated. First, we define the stage logic itself with BarrierTaskContext:

```
from pyspark import BarrierTaskContext

def stage_logic(row):
    context = BarrierTaskContext.get()
    # some logic that needs to be coordinated
    context.barrier()
    return row
```

Then we define the barrier RDD and call `stage_logic` with `mapPartitions`:

```
barrierRdd = df.rdd.barrier()
rdd = barrierRdd.mapPartitions(lambda x: stage_logic(x))
```

That's it. All the functionality we defined in the stage logic up until the `context`
`.barrier` call will take place in the barrier execution mode. This mode leverages the
MPI programming model discussed in Chapter 1 to allow for better communication
and a coordinated cyclic training process over the Spark cluster.

Now that we are able to define stages and barriers, let's level up and take a look at the
next challenge Project Hydrogen aims to solve.

Accelerator-Aware Scheduling

The goal of accelerator-aware scheduling is to validate that the distributed system
scheduler, responsible for managing the operations and available resources, is aware
of the availability of GPUs for hardware acceleration. Essentially, it's a feature that
allows us to expose the cluster's GPU addresses so that Spark can take advantage of
them. We already know that data executors that run on CPUs are sufficient for preprocessing, whereas for training we often need GPUs. To find the GPUs programmatically, we must configure Spark properties with the number of GPUs and provide
discovery scripts. Table 7-1 demonstrates some of the configuration options available
to us with Spark to enable accelerator-aware scheduling.

Table 7-1. Configuration for GPU scheduling awareness

Configuration key	Configuration value example
`spark.executor.resource.gpu.amount`	5
`spark.executor.resource.gpu. discoveryScript`	/home/ubuntu/ getGpusResources.sh
`spark.driver.resource.gpu.amount`	1
`spark.driver.resource.gpu. discoveryScript`	/home/ubuntu/ getGpusResources Driver.sh
`spark.task.resource.gpu.amount`	1

The discovery script can also be used to configure NVIDIA's RAPIDS Accelerator for
Apache Spark as a plug-in/add-on (to learn more, check out the tutorial (*https://
oreil.ly/FFO_R*) in the docs). RAPIDS provides better performance for operations
such as joins, aggregations, etc. Essentially, making Spark aware of RAPIDS will allow

it to replace certain SQL operations with GPU-accelerated versions. While it's an important piece of the puzzle, its role is actually about optimizing the hardware itself, not the operations. Note also that Kubernetes clusters might behave differently from clusters where the resources are controlled by YARN or standalone clusters.

With accelerator-aware scheduling, we source the GPU addresses from within a task that runs in an executor using TaskContext (*https://oreil.ly/FBPpI*):

```
context = TaskContext.get()
resources = context.resources()
gpus = resources['gpu'].addresses
# feed the GPU addresses into a dedicated program
```

From the driver, we can leverage the SparkContext with similar logic to before:

```
sc = spark.sparkContext
gpus = sc.resources['gpu'].addresses
# feed the GPU addresses into a dedicated program
```

We've seen how we can source the GPUs addresses themselves; now we can feed them into a TensorFlow or other AI program.

We've only covered the basics here; for further tips on optimizing resources, check out the "Resource Management" (*https://oreil.ly/t_dRI*) section of the Spark documentation.

A Brief Introduction to the Horovod Estimator API

As with most aspects of machine learning, the tools and resources we have at our disposal today may change tomorrow. So this section will walk through some criteria that will help you assess which dedicated management platform may work best for you today to stitch your software and hardware together for scale—and prepare you for tomorrow. For this, we need our software to act as a layer between the software designed for training and the software designed for tuning the hardware. This means that as well as supporting that software, it also needs to be able to support the hardware we're using currently and any hardware we might want to integrate in the future.

To tie together the tools we're using in this book in an automated way, we can leverage *Horovod*. Horovod, similar to Petastorm, is an open source framework for distributed deep learning training. It was also developed by Uber and later donated to Linux's LF AI & Data Foundation (*https://lfdl.io*). Horovod's core goal is to allow for single-GPU training to be distributed across multiple GPUs. Because of Uber's heavy use of Spark, the engineers also introduced the *Estimator API*. The Horovod Estimator hides the complexity of gluing Spark DataFrames to a deep learning training script. This is yet another tool that helps us to read in our data in a format interpretable by the training framework, and we can then distribute the training itself using Horovod. As users, we need to provide a TensorFlow, Keras, or PyTorch model, and the Estimator does the work of fitting it to the DataFrame. After training the model, the Estimator returns an instance of a Spark Transformer representing the trained model. Later, this can be used like any Spark machine learning transformer to make predictions on an input DataFrame, as discussed in Chapter 6.

Horovod helps us configure GPUs and define a distributed training strategy. It also takes care of Spark's broadcast mechanism using the BroadcastGlobalVariables Hook, which supports initializing a dedicated value on all processes before computation starts. This enables consistency when we want to start with random weights for training that are the same across processes. Working with Horovod (even as an exercise) requires dedicated hardware that goes beyond the scope of this book; if this is something you would like to explore further, check out the Horovod documentation (*https://oreil.ly/p9PS3*).

Summary

The goal of this chapter was to show you a creative way to bridge the gap between technologies such as Spark and TensorFlow/PyTorch and start thinking outside the box about what is possible. We discussed leveraging data in a Spark DataFrame saved in Parquet format and how to create a bridge to manage and load it into TensorFlow and PyTorch. We covered the two clusters approach, using a dedicated data access layer, Petastorm, and other tools you may want to have in your arsenal to bridge Spark and deep learning clusters. We also discussed combining hardware and software to a degree where the software is aware of the hardware, as well as an example of how to configure it.

It's important to remember that this world is still evolving and is going through a massive transformation. There is no one approach that fits all scenarios, and every organization will have slightly different requirements. The basic concepts and needs will stay the same, but the technology itself may change; so it's essential to assess your own specific criteria for a dedicated data management platform. Even though this book won't get into every aspect of data management and the hardware environment, it's essential to remember that code + data + environment go hand in hand.

This chapter should also have prepared you for Chapter 8, where you will learn about distributed training with TensorFlow—we'll start with the basics, the various patterns and architecture that are unique to TensorFlow, and will finish up with a step-by-step tutorial that uses Petastorm to process Parquet data and run a distributed training job.

## CHAPTER 8

TensorFlow Distributed Machine Learning Approach

TensorFlow (TF) is an open source software library developed by the Google Brain team to further advance deep learning in the industry. Their goal was, and still is, to close the gap between research and practice.

When TF was released in 2015, it blew the data science crowd away. Today, it's one of the most used libraries for deep learning. To provide a holistic solution allowing for a full production pipeline, the TF team released TensorFlow Extended (TFX) to the public in 2019. On top of that, Google created its own processing units, called *tensor processing units* (TPUs), to accelerate machine learning workloads that are developed with TF. If the acronym looks familiar, that's because it's intentionally similar to GPU, which stands for *graphics processing unit*. While TPUs provide some advanced capabilities, using them largely ties the technological stack to Google technologies. GPUs are more agnostic and flexible, so using them as accelerators will make your application hardware plan more cross-platform.

TF provides various distributed training strategies for GPUs, CPUs, and TPUs. Using TF, you can enrich your machine learning capabilities beyond what Apache Spark provides out of the box. To connect the machine learning workflow of preprocessing the data with Spark and training a TF model, you can use MLflow (discussed in Chapter 3).

In the previous chapter, we discussed how to bridge Spark and TensorFlow by using Petastorm to enable TF to ingest Parquet data. This chapter continues along that path and shows you how to use TF to train a large set of data. Basically, the same data we processed with Spark and saved to Parquet is now available to use with TF to train a model!

This chapter covers the following:

- A quick overview of TF basics
- How to load Parquet data into a TensorFlow dataset
- TF distributed strategies for training models
- TF training APIs and when to use them
- Putting it all together, from Petastorm to building a model with TF

Let's start by taking a look at the main components of TensorFlow.

A Quick Overview of TensorFlow

TensorFlow's basics consist of tensors, variables, operations, functions, graphs, and modules. Let's do a quick overview of them:

tf.Tensor
> Similar to a Spark DataFrame, this is an immutable object: its state cannot be changed after it has been created. A tf.Tensor represents a multidimensional array. It has two properties, shape and dtype. shape is the size of the tensor along its axes (for example, (2, 3)), and dtype is the data type of the elements in the tensor (for example, float32). All the elements in a tensor must be of the same type.

tf.Variable
> In contrast to tf.Tensors, tf.Variables are mutable objects, which means their state can be modified at any time. Variables are shared and represent the current state of the data—you can think of them as mutable multidimensional arrays, similar to tensors whose values can be changed by running operations on them. TF uses variables in machine learning training to store the model's parameters (for example, weights or other mutable state).

tf.Operation
> A tf.Operation is a node in a graph that performs some computation on tensors (for example, adding scalar values). It takes zero or more Tensor objects as input and produces zero or more Tensor objects as output.

tf.function
> Those paying attention will notice that function is lowercase, whereas the names of the other items in this list (Tensor, etc.) are capitalized. This is because tf.function is an *annotation*, not a TF object: it compiles a function into a callable TF graph. This annotation provides us with a Pythonic approach to building

a custom-made `tf.Operation` on tensors. The following code example shows a simple add function:

```
@tf.function
def add(x):
    return x + 1
```

tf.Graph

In TensorFlow, there are two execution models: *eager execution*, where TF functions execute operations immediately, and *graph execution*, where operations are added to a `tf.Graph` to be executed later. The graph holds the plan for execution; it contains both the data (tensors) and operations. Similar to Spark DAGs, TF graphs can be optimized. The default graph optimization system in the TF runtime is *Grappler*. It provides various optimizers that you can enable on demand, including a pruning optimizer—if your computation graph has nodes that don't affect the output, the pruning optimizer will reduce the graph's size by pruning the not-used nodes before execution, so TF won't run those computations at all. This is similar to the optimization performed by the Spark Catalyst engine, discussed in Chapter 2, which prunes nodes and optimizes the operations.

tf.Module

`tf.Module` is the base class for both TF machine learning layers and models. A module is a container for variables (including variables that can be modified either during or after training, as well as variables that can be modified but are not for training purposes—any user input, essentially), other modules, and functions that apply to input from the user.

The variables may include training parameters that change throughout the process and hyperparameters that don't change. In the case of linear regression models, for instance, the parameters can be the weighted coefficients that are being calculated. An example of a hyperparameter is the number of clusters in *k*-means clustering.

A few other important concepts to be aware of are the `model.compile` method in the `tf.keras` library and TensorBoard, the TF visualization kit for machine learning experimentation. `model.compile` configures a model for training, specifying the loss function, graph optimizers, and metrics. Regarding TensorBoard, to present the data, the TF cluster collects and logs information that is later visualized here. TensorBoard also leverages the TF callback mechanism, which (as discussed in Chapter 3) enables us to inject a function into the training process to, for example, capture the performance of the training. This is called *profiling*. The profiling process quantifies the performance of the machine learning application to ensure it is running an optimized version. Profiling capabilities are critical since the algorithms are typically computationally expensive. To enable it, make sure to install the TensorFlow Profiler as part of your cluster. You can do this with the following `pip` command:

```
pip install -U tensorboard_plugin_profile
```

And later, define the callback and incorporate it into the `model.fit` call, as shown in the following code snippet:

```
tboard_callback = tf.keras.callbacks.TensorBoard(log_dir = logs,
                    histogram_freq = 1,
                    profile_batch = '500,520')

model.fit(df_train,
        epochs=8,
        validation_data=df_test,
        callbacks = [tboard_callback])
```

This book won't go into more detail on the mechanisms behind TF callbacks and how to work with TensorBoard; for further information, consult an introductory text like Aurélien Géron's *Hands-On Machine Learning with Scikit-Learn, Keras, and Tensor-Flow*, 3rd edition (*https://oreil.ly/ml-slktf*) (O'Reilly).

Before we dig further into the mechanics of TensorFlow, let's take a closer look at the primary purpose it was designed to support—deep learning with neural networks—and the different roles and responsibilities in a TF cluster.

What Is a Neural Network?

Good question! Let's run through it quickly, as an understanding of this concept will come in handy for the next chapters as well!

A neural network, sometimes called an *artificial neural network* (ANN) or simulated neural network, is a system that attempts to mimic how the human brain operates. The algorithm creates multiple layers of nodes or "neurons" that communicate and train weights given input data. There is an input layer and an output layer, and between these are one or more *hidden layers* that are responsible for transforming the data, performing feature extraction, etc. The size of each layer and the number of hidden layers depends on how we configure the algorithm. Figure 8-1 is an abstraction of a neural network, with an input layer x, two hidden layers, and an output layer y.

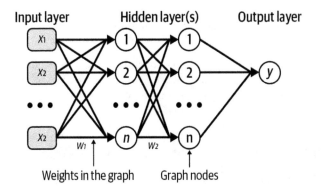

Figure 8-1. Example of a neural network graph

Let's assume we have only one neuron in our input layer, and we feed it with our input data. The function inside the neuron calculates the output based on some preconfigured weights (the trainable parameters), a bias function, and some additional information. This neuron produces an output that can then be fed into the next neuron. As mentioned in the previous chapter, this is called *forward propagation*; a neural network where information flows in only this direction is known as a *feed-forward network*. Training is reflected by adjusting the weights in each neuron according to a *loss function*, which measures the difference between the predicted and expected outcome. Because the expected outcome is known, this is a supervised learning approach.

After the loss (or gradient) is calculated, this information can be fed back into the previous neuron so its weights can be adjusted to improve the performance. This is known as *backward propagation*, or *backpropagation*. When working with neural networks in TensorFlow, we will typically use its dedicated Keras API. Keras (discussed in more detail later in this chapter) is a neural network library built into Python that provides a high-level API for training models. The TensorFlow Keras API, `tf.keras`, has a number of machine learning algorithms already implemented and ready for use. Two key classes in this API are the `Layer` class and the `Model` class:

`tf.keras.layers.Layer`
This is the base class from which all layers inherit. Each layer takes one or more tensors as input, runs the designated operation, and outputs one or more tensors. It has a `call` method that applies the layer to the inputs and state (its weight variables).

`tf.keras.Model`
This is the base class used to define a model architecture. Its main goal is to run a group of operations on tensors. A `Model` groups layers into an object, together with features for training and inference. To use the model in Figure 8-1 for

prediction, for example, all we need to do is run a forward pass with the given data input (*x1, x2, ...*) to extract the prediction (*y*).

 For a comprehensive walkthrough of using TensorFlow, I recommend reading "Getting Started with TensorFlow" (*https://oreil.ly/LT23z*) from Aurélien Géron's book *Hands-On Machine Learning with Scikit-Learn, Keras, and TensorFlow*.

TensorFlow Cluster Process Roles and Responsibilities

TensorFlow clusters follow a client/server model. As in Spark, you leverage numerous machines to accomplish the heavy lifting of the compute requirements. When a TF task is run, a session is created on one of those machines and the graph is optimized and computed, with parts of it potentially distributed to different machines in the cluster.

Generally speaking, in a TensorFlow cluster there are multiple processes running, either on the same machine (as threads) or on multiple machines. Each of them has a distinct role and responsibilities, as they are each in charge of completing a certain activity that is part of the larger processing plan. As with a Spark cluster, each process is running a task or a TF server and has its own IP address and port number. The roles include the following:

Worker
    A worker performs computations on behalf of the application.

Parameter server (PS)
    The parameter server keeps track of variables' values and state. More on this in "An Inside Look at TensorFlow's Distributed Machine Learning Strategies" on page 171.

Chief
    The chief is similar to a worker, but it is assigned additional responsibilities related to the cluster health, such as writing to TensorBoard logs or saving checkpoints.

Evaluator
    This is the process that is responsible for the evaluation of the model.

Figure 8-2 shows communications between the various processes. The chief is responsible for starting the program; it also takes care of providing the configuration and the context for the rest of the workers.

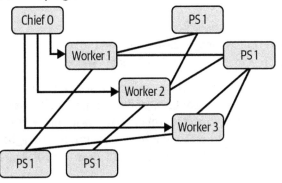

Figure 8-2. *Distributed compute with TF and the various processes' responsibilities*

Processes' roles and responsibilities are configured in the `TF_CONFIG` config property of the cluster. I will share an example of configuring it later in this chapter.

Now that you have a better understanding of TensorFlow's basic components, it's time to learn how to load Parquet data into a TF dataset.

Loading Parquet Data into a TensorFlow Dataset

Like every machine learning process, this one starts with loading data. In TensorFlow, this is done with the load function of the `tf.data.Dataset` object.

A TF dataset acts as an abstraction of the actual data (similar to a Spark DataFrame), whether it's on disk or in memory. This enables you to iterate over the distributed data. You can ingest data from multiple sources that can then be used with any TF model.

The load function is all you need if you're using TensorFlow on its own. It fetches the data from the source iteratively; later, you can preprocess it into a standard format while the TF engine itself collects statistics on the data. After preprocessing, TF will enable you to save the data to disk. Once the data is saved to disk, it is ready for the next step: being used by TF to build the model.

There's a caveat, though: while this is true for CSV and other file formats, such as images, this is not the case for Parquet. TF doesn't support loading Parquet out of the box.

How do you get around this? And why is it a problem? As described in Chapter 4, often you will want to take advantage of existing preprocessed data that you, your team, or other teams in your organization have prepared. And more often than not, the data will have been preprocessed with Spark and saved into Parquet format, which TF datasets' `load` function cannot load accurately.

In the previous chapter, we used Petastorm as a bridge between the frameworks. Petastorm has a `make_petastorm_dataset` function that creates a `tf.data.Dataset` instance, using an instance of `petastorm.reader.Reader`.

As developers, after creating a Petastorm reader, it's our responsibility to programmatically pass it to the `make_petastorm_dataset` function. As discussed in Chapter 7, we can choose to save the data in Parquet format without relying on the Petastorm store directly. In this case, to create the reader, we use the `make_batch_reader` function (instead of `make_reader`). It creates a non-Petastorm Parquet reader, which is precisely what we need.

The `make_batch_reader` function performs the following steps:

1. Normalize the dataset URL according to where it runs and what we give it.
2. Locate the filesystem paths for the data pieces.
3. Analyze the Parquet metadata to determine the schema. This function supports all standard Parquet types.
4. If there is a cache format, validate it.
5. Determine the type of reader pool. This can be one of the following:
   - `'thread'` (a pool of threads)
   - `'process'` (often a dedicated `ArrowTableSeralizer`)
   - `'dummy'` (executes all `read` calls locally in the main thread)
6. Return the reader instance configured with the filesystem and ready for use.

This logic returns a reader instance that reads data from a Petastorm dataset and encapsulates `ArrowReaderWorker`. `ArrowReaderWorker` is a Petastorm object that, in turn, encapsulates `pyarrow` and enables us to work with the Parquet data using the standard Arrow interconnecting format (discussed in Chapter 5).

Now that you understand the logic, let's write some code! The next code snippet shows how to import the function and use it in Python syntax. The second line creates a reader that is ready to be used within the Python function scope:

```
from petastorm import make_batch_reader
with make_batch_reader(petastorm_dataset_url) as reader:
    ...
```

We now have a Parquet reader, but it has limitations—not all `Dataset` features will work. To remove those limitations, we can build the `petastorm.reader.Reader` itself by providing the following arguments to the constructor:

1. `Dataset` has a dedicated `repeat` function that allows us to select how many iterations to run over the dataset. Instead of `repeat`, use `num_epochs` when building the reader itself, as Petastorm doesn't support `repeat` in the way TensorFlow does.

2. Instead of using the `filter` function, use the `predicate` function to leverage the power of Parquet as a columnar data format and load only the columns that the `predicate` function has operated on before loading and decoding other columns.

Now that we have a reader, let's create the dataset instance! For that, we will use the `make_petastorm_dataset` function. It will create a `tensorflow.data.Dataset` instance that we can use to train a TensorFlow model. Remember to import the function from `petastorm.tf_utils`, as shown in the following code snippet. We can then call this function later, providing it with the reader we just created. Here's an example of what the code might look like, with `num_epochs` configured as part of the reader:

```
from petastorm.tf_utils import make_petastorm_dataset
...
with make_batch_reader(petastorm_dataset_url, num_epochs=100) as reader:
    dataset = make_petastorm_dataset(reader)
```

You now know how to load data in Parquet format into a TF dataset instance. `make_petastorm_dataset` uses TF's `tf.data.Dataset.from_generator` function, which fetches the next piece of data from the dataset URL and filesystem. With this dataset instance, we can begin training a distributed machine learning model.

The next section will discuss multiple distributed TF training strategies. It will also help you understand how TensorFlow's distributed approach differs from Spark's.

An Inside Look at TensorFlow's Distributed Machine Learning Strategies

TF supports a variety of encapsulated strategies for distributed training: synchronous versus asynchronous, all-reduce versus parameter servers, in-graph versus between graphs, and CPUs/GPUs versus TPUs. All the strategies are available via the *tf.distribute.Strategy* library.

TF supports data parallelism out of the box, so our dataset is split across machines, and during training each machine in our cluster processes a different piece of the data. The training operations' logic is replicated across multiple devices, and the algorithm's variables are shared across them. Each copy of the operations' logic updates these variables via a mechanism that's specific to the used strategy. Therefore, during the training process, the machine learning algorithm is changing the model's variables (the trained ones), until it consolidates. To support efficient consolidation of the algorithm, we need to pick an appropriate strategy based on the data size, our cluster resources, etc.

What's nice about the TF distributed strategy design is that it enables us to write modular code, separating the functionality of training the model and defining the training strategy. This allows us to incorporate multiple training functions in the same strategy and to use different strategies while training. The following code snippet shows how easy it is to switch between strategies. Each strategy instance can be created from `tf.distribute`:

```
import tensorflow as tf
strategy = tf.distribute.MirroredStrategy()

with strategy.scope():
    some_model = ...
    some_model.compile([...])
    ...
```

The decoupling of the training strategy from the model training code allows for more experimentation. Take note of the `scope` function that defines where the strategy takes place. In our example, within the scope, the training is leveraging the `tf.distribute.MirroredStrategy` strategy.

TF supports five distributed training strategies and three different APIs for training a machine learning model—you can use `tf.Keras` or the TF Estimator API or build a custom training loop. Table 8-1 (from the TensorFlow docs) provides a breakdown of the support the different training APIs, discussed in more detail in "Training APIs" on page 182, offer for the individual strategies at the time of writing. You can refer back to this table as you progress through this chapter and to help you decide which combinations might be best for your own projects. Bear in mind that some strategies currently have limited or even experimental support, which means that this feature has not yet been fully validated and is still under development; for up-to-date information on the level of support, see the docs (*https://oreil.ly/NsUs0*).

Table 8-1. TF's distributed training capabilities and their support in the various training APIs

Training API	Mirrored Strategy	TPUStrategy	MultiWorker Mirror Strategy	CentralStorage Strategy	Parameter Server Strategy
Keras Model.fit	Supported	Supported	Supported	Experimental support	Experimental support
Custom training loop	Supported	Supported	Supported	Experimental Support	Experimental Support
Estimator API	Limited support	Not supported	Limited support	Limited support	Limited support

In the remainder of this section, we will take a closer look at each of these strategies in turn, starting with the original approach.

ParameterServerStrategy

The `ParameterServerStrategy` (sometimes referred to as "parameter server and worker") is the oldest approach, which TF has supported from the beginning. Each machine takes on the role of a worker or a parameter server, and TF divides the tasks into worker tasks and parameter server tasks. Worker tasks can be anything from reading input to updating variables, computing forward and backward passes, and sending updates. Parameter server tasks include storing the parameters of the machine learning model during training (i.e., the weights of the neural network), maintaining strong consistency of the parameter values among the servers, and serving information to the workers that process data and compute updates to the parameters upon request.

The rules are simple:

- Variables are stored on parameter servers and are read and updated by workers during each training step.
- Each variable is stored on a single parameter server.
- Workers perform their tasks independently, without communicating with other workers. Workers communicate only with parameter servers.
- Depending on the number of variables, there may be one parameter server or multiple parameter servers.

This model is great when there are many CPUs/GPUs, large matrices of calculations, and sparse lookups. It is considered an *in-between graph strategy*. This is a concept from TensorFlow 1, which means that each worker runs its own function independently, reading the variables, performing the operations, and updating the parameter server. This allows the workers to run asynchronously and makes it easy to recover from failures.

With this strategy, the workers use asynchronous remote procedure calls (RPCs) to communicate with the parameter servers to read and update each variable. This allows the workers to act independently and process input at their own speed.

A potential drawback with this approach is that network bottlenecks can occur at the beginning of each training step, when the workers all attempt to contact the parameter server(s) to read the variables without the runtime providing a specific order. This is often an issue when calculating the first step of the first neural network layer.

---

1 This model separates a remote procedure call from its return value, overcoming some of the shortcomings of the traditional RPC model (where the client is blocked until the call returns).

Figure 8-3 shows a high-level diagram of the architecture of this strategy. The parameter servers themselves can be distributed, depending on the number of parameters, availability requirements, etc. that they need to support. Each worker has a replica of the model and is working on a specific piece of the data (X_1, X_2, X_3, etc.). The arrows in the diagram show the worker–PS communication. Depending on the number and distribution of the parameter servers, there may be a dedicated server manager (the "chief" in Figure 8-2) to manage each set of PSs.

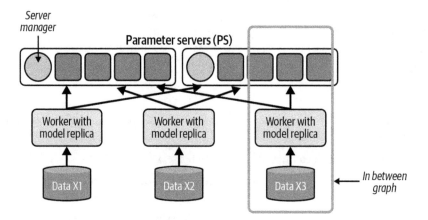

Figure 8-3. ParameterServerStrategy architecture

The `ParameterServerStrategy` is a generic strategy: all functions/operations can run on a worker, so any machine learning algorithm that can be decomposed into a series of independent functions can leverage it. With TensorFlow 2, the strategy evolved, with the introduction of a dedicated *cluster coordinator* (*https://oreil.ly/GLZpk*). The cluster coordinator is responsible for creating the required resources for workers and parameter servers while also coordinating the training itself. This approach helps alleviate the overhead of RPCs in the initial phase.

The following code snippet shows how to define the strategy and the coordinator. Both functions take multiple parameters, such as `cluster_resolver`, which holds the cluster spec:

```
# define the strategy
strategy = tf.distribute.experimental.ParameterServerStrategy(
    tf.distribute.cluster_resolver.TFConfigClusterResolver())
# define the coordinator
coordinator = tf.distribute.experimental.coordinator.ClusterCoordinator(
    strategy)
```

Now that you understand the `ParameterServerStrategy`, let's move on to the next one and learn how the TF strategies evolved to overcome the challenges presented so far.

CentralStorageStrategy: One Machine, Multiple Processors

The CentralStorageStrategy was developed as an early solution to the RPC problem. With this strategy, you have one machine with multiple CPUs and GPUs to compute the in-graph operations:

- The CPUs hold variables (similar to a PS).
- The GPUs execute operations (similar to workers).
- They all communicate synchronously on the same device, which means they work together in lockstep.

Each CPU holds a subset of the variables, which it updates at each step. The variables are not shared across processors; each one performs its updates, then they exchange their information to synchronize the gradients (the model's trained variables) at every step. This can be done easily because the processors are all on the same machine. Each training step involves one full run on the graph (a full epoch). It is all coordinated via a single client, the main thread. This strategy makes training on a single machine more efficient, which is useful in embedded scenarios where there is only one machine available.

You can create a CentralStorageStrategy instance with this code snippet:

```
central_storage_strategy = tf.distribute.experimental.CentralStorageStrategy()
```

While this approach overcomes the problem of networking bottlenecks, it introduces a different difficulty: with one machine, there is only one central storage, and the tasks share the same disk space and RAM. This means that each variable and operation is represented in memory only once; you get a single copy of the variable on the CPU and one replica of the model per process (GPU). It's also important to note that when there's only one processor, there's no acceleration happening.

To work around these issues, TF introduced the MirroredStrategy approach. We'll look at that next.

MirroredStrategy: One Machine, Multiple Processors, Local Copy

Similar to the CentralStorageStrategy, the MirroredStrategy supports multiple CPUs/GPUs on one machine. However, every processor that holds a replica of the training operations' logic also holds its own local copy of every variable. The variables are copied across all the processors and kept in sync (i.e., *mirrored*) by applying identical updates across them, as you can see in Figure 8-4. This approach is different from the ParameterServerStrategy and CentralStorageStrategy because with those each processor/machine holds a subset of the training variables, not the entire set.

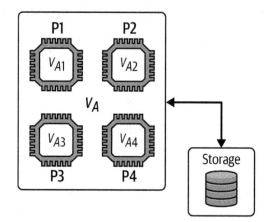

Figure 8-4. MirroredStrategy architecture

To ensure identical updates are made across the processors, this strategy uses an *all-reduce* algorithm, which is common in the computer science world. Each processor communicates with every other processor to exchange updates (the "all" part), and a reduce function is used to aggregate the values, reduce them to a single value, and return that result to all the processors.

Reduce operations are commonly used in parallel programming to reduce each element of an array into a single result. They must be associative operations. In other words, the order in which you act on the data must not matter. An example is the sum operation, where there is no importance to the order of the operands; the result is the same regardless of whether you calculate $a + b$ or $b + a$. The same also holds for max, min, mean, and a number of other operations that enable synchronization between variables.

 An advantage of the all-reduce approach is that it can be optimized in hardware. For example, if your machines use NVIDIA processors, you can configure your cluster to use NVIDIA's all-reduce communication functionality to accelerate the synchronization of variables. I won't discuss specific hardware optimizations here, as those vary by vendor, but it is good to be aware of this and act accordingly.

The following code snippet shows how to create a MirroredStrategy instance—to specify the machines, you can either update the TensorFlow cluster config file (more on that soon!) or pass this information to the function:

```
mirrored_strategy = tf.distribute.MirroredStrategy()
```

While this strategy is great for specific scenarios, such as when working with embedded devices, sometimes we need to train on multiple machines. This capability is provided by the `MultiWorkerMirroredStrategy`, which I'll cover next.

MultiWorkerMirroredStrategy: Multiple Machines, Synchronous

The `MultiWorkerMirroredStrategy` is very similar to the `MirroredStrategy`: it provides an implementation of synchronous training distributed across machines, each of which can have more than one processor. Each variable is replicated and synced across machines and processors. This approach works well when there is good connectivity between machines. Since it relies on an all-reduce algorithm, all of the machines need to communicate in order to synchronize the variables.

So what does synchronous training actually look like in this case? Let's say we have an algorithm that consists of two neural network layers and has two variables to train during the training process. Layers A and B are replicated to the two machines, A and B, as shown in Figure 8-5. You can see that each of those machines has its own copy of all the variables, and each one has its own piece of the data as inputs: input 0 and input 1.

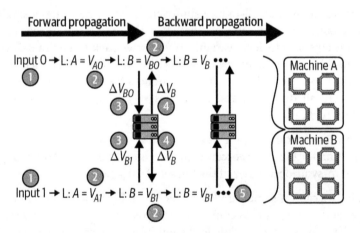

Figure 8-5. Synchronous computation with the `MultiWorkerMirrorStrategy`

Let's take a look at how the synchronization itself works. We have four components:

- Two variable components, because we're keeping separate copies of each of the variables on each of the machines

- Two data components, because each machine operates on its own subset of the training data (input 0 and input 1)

The logic is as follows:

- Each machine takes in its own input (1) and does a forward propagation pass using just its local copies of the variables (2). Machine A computes layer A and layer B using input 0, and machine B computes layer A and layer B using input 1.

- Before beginning the backward pass, we want to optimize the training variables, so we compute the gradients using the local copies of the variables (3). Machine A computes V_{A0} and V_{B0}, and machine B computes V_{A1} and V_{B1}.

- Now we want to aggregate the training variables to make sure they are in sync. We do this using the all-reduce approach: we send the copies of the gradients over the network and aggregate them (4). That is, each machine aggregates V_{A1} and V_{A0} into ΔV_A, and V_{B1} and V_{B0} into ΔV_B. Alternatively, this aggregation may take place on a different machine/processor—for example, an NVIDIA GPU, which is optimized to run reduce operations super fast—which may have this as its sole job. After aggregation, it would broadcast the updated gradients, ΔV_A and ΔV_B, back to the machines.

- Finally, we compute the backward pass (5).

In this process, we used an all-reduce approach that communicates a single aggregated gradient value out to all the machines (V_{A0}, V_{A1}, and so on). Each machine then applies that gradient to its local variable. If you refer back to Figure 8-5, you can see that each machine has four processors, which means that the gradient is replicated locally to four processors. Since all-reduce produces the same value in all the replicas, the updates are all the same, and the values stay in sync across all the different machines and replicas.

Once this process is complete, the next forward pass can begin immediately; there is no delay waiting for the values because, by the end of the step, all of the replicas have updated and in-sync local copies of the full set of variables.

Additionally, we can get some parallelism here by doing an all-reduce of the gradients of one layer at the same time as computing the gradients of other layers (for example, calculating layer B's gradients while exchanging layer A's gradients to sync the replicas. This approach works well when there is a backward pass; with the appropriate synchronization, we can fully utilize our hardware by keeping both the network communication and computation parts busy at the same time. This is great for throughput and performance.

Hierarchical all-reduce is an implementation of the all-reduce process where aggregation and gradient calculation are done within each machine, and this information is communicated across machines later, in a sort of hierarchical way. So if a machine is a worker and each worker has multiple processors, they can run multiple tasks in lockstep while synchronizing the gradients at each step locally. The results can then be synced with those of the rest of the machines in the network later. This approach often performs better and is more scalable. It reduces the dependency on the parameter server, and it allows the next step of training (the second epoch) to begin immediately, without the worker having to wait while its results are synchronized with those of the other workers. Note that instead of having four machines with one processor each, having two machines with two processors each will result in faster execution (since there is less network communication required) while still ensuring cluster fault tolerance.

The MultiWorkerMirroredStrategy also supports the *ring all-reduce* or *ring-reduce* algorithm. The communication approach here is different: instead of all the processors communicating with and receiving messages from all the others, each processor receives information from just one processor, updates it, and sends the information to a different processor. The processors are connected in a circular or ring formation, as shown in Figure 8-6. Ring all-reduce is often more efficient than all-reduce since it sends fewer messages over the network.

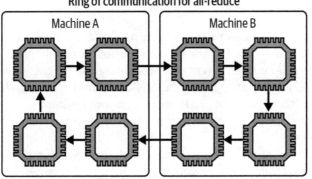

Figure 8-6. Ring all-reduce communication architecture for synchronous gradient computation

Additional variants of the all-reduce communication structure exist, such as tree all-reduce, round-robin all-reduce, and many more. TensorFlow supports various cross-device communication (or *device ops*) implementations out of the box, including `tf.dis tribute.CrossDeviceOps`, `tf.distribute.HierarchicalCopyAll Reduce`, `tf .distribute .Reduction ToOneDevice`, and `tf .distribute .Nccl All Reduce` for NVIDIA processors. When choosing one, always make sure to validate its support in your hardware.

Note that to enable this strategy, you have to make sure you set up the `TF_CONFIG` environment variable to specify the roles of each machine in the TF cluster. Here is an example of what this looks like in a configuration file:

```
os.environ["TF_CONFIG"] = json.dumps({
    "cluster": {
        "worker": ["host1:port", "host2:port", "host3:port"],
        "ps": ["host4:port", "host5:port"]
    },
    "task": {"type": "worker", "index": 1}
})
```

With the `MultiWorkerMirroredStrategy`, there is a designated worker that coordinates the cluster's activities. This worker is responsible for producing a summary file for further logging and checkpoint information for failure recovery, in addition to processing its piece of data. It's called the *chief worker*, and it is the worker at index 0 in the array of cluster workers in `TF_CONFIG` (in our example, the chief worker is *host1*).

The chief worker's most important task is saving checkpoints, which capture the exact values of all parameters used by the model at a particular point in time. They can be used for fast recovery in the event of a machine, network communication, or any other possible cluster failure, making the application resilient and fault-tolerant. Suppose you're in the middle of performing a massive computation to train your machine learning model, which might take days or even weeks. Suddenly, there is a power outage in the data center, and all the machines go down. Restarting the entire training process could delay building the model by weeks or months—but with the checkpoint mechanism, the chief worker is responsible for saving the variables' state and values to the filesystem at set intervals. This means that, given the code and checkpoint data, we can recover the process from the last checkpoint and don't have to start the entire computation from the beginning again. This is a massive time-saver. (As a side note, these scenarios do not happen rarely—they are pretty common in a large cluster with many moving parts.) Both Spark and TensorFlow allow for checkpoints to be saved during computations. TensorFlow persists the state of the model and its data using `tf.train.Checkpoint`. Later, it can be constructed through a high-level API. Spark saves the node metadata together with the state of the data, making it straightforward to load and continue the computation from the checkpoint.

 There is an inherent possibility that every task in a cluster might communicate with tasks on other machines. Be sure to configure your firewall or virtual network security protocols so that all communications between the cluster machines on your defined port will be authorized. To reduce the configuration overhead, it is often more convenient to use the same port for all cluster machines.

TPUStrategy

The final distributed training strategy TensorFlow provides is the `TPUStrategy`, for synchronous training on TPUs and TPU pods. It's similar to the two mirrored strategies, as it supports communication between individual processors within a machine, as well as communication between machines. As mentioned earlier, TPUs were created by Google and can be found in a number of Google platforms. Using the `TPUStrategy` requires access to a dedicated Google platform and hardware, so we're not going to dive deeper into it in this book.

What Things Change When You Switch Strategies?

As mentioned at the beginning of this section, TF provides a modular code approach to switch between strategies. When choosing a training strategy, here are some of the factors you will need to keep in mind:

- Communication style (either synchronous or asynchronous)
- Variable replication (whether local copies of all the variables are kept on each worker)
- How gradient aggregation takes place within and/or across machines and how the results are communicated to the workers
- How backpropagation takes place and when syncing of the variables takes place (during or only after the full process)
- How metrics are accumulated, which is impacted by the all-reduce algorithm and communication approach

Now that you're familiar with the various TF distributed training strategies, next we'll turn our attention to the APIs it provides to train a machine learning model.

Training APIs

Choosing a training strategy is a crucial step, but as we saw in Table 8-1, our choice of strategy can be affected by the training API we want to use. TensorFlow provides three options:

Keras API
> The tf.keras API offers a wide array of built-in algorithms and models that are ready to be used for building machine learning models.

Custom training loop
> We can use the TF Core APIs to build our own training loops, layers, operations, etc.

Estimator API
> The Estimator API uses a similar approach to the Spark MLlib estimators that we discussed in Chapter 6. Estimators enable various graph architectures; they are part of the TensorFlow v1 library and abstract TensorFlow computational APIs. Depending on our needs, we can choose to work with premade estimators or create customized ones to meet our requirements.

Over the next few pages, you will see that these APIs provide varying degrees of flexibility and so require different levels of machine learning expertise. One of the simplest APIs to learn is the Keras API, which is what we will start with.

Keras API

Keras is a high-level deep learning API written in Python that runs on top of Tensor-Flow. The Keras API provides a Pythonic approach to train new machine learning models and work with existing models. Keras provides extensive functionalities and also includes numerous built-in public datasets (*https://oreil.ly/ZGBs0*), such as the Boston housing dataset, MNIST, CIFAR10, and others.

Using a built-in dataset is a fantastic way to get started. If you want to learn how to use the API, you don't need to search for or create a dedicated dataset, as you already have access to several that are ready to use: the datasets are preprocessed and can be ingested into the training APIs immediately.

Keras also provides numerous pretrained models. These are one of the greatest advantages of this training API: since the models themselves are made of layers (as depicted earlier, in Figure 8-1), we can decide whether we want to reuse the existing layers as they are or change them. For example, we can use an existing model as a base model, then add a prediction layer at the end that will be the output layer given the existing data. This saves much of the work involved in training a model from scratch for the task at hand.

Why would that work? Or produce a good model at all? This is a great question. When going through the various scenarios of when we might want to use a neural network, there is often a common baseline, such as classifying images. Much of the training is related to detecting colors, edges, shapes, etc. and is not dependent on the exact data used as input. This means you can use the weights from a pretrained model as a starting point for making predictions on your own data, based on your business requirements.

As mentioned in Chapter 5, this approach is sometimes called *transfer learning*. In transfer learning, knowledge acquired while solving one problem is applied to a different but related problem. The Keras API makes it easy for us to do exactly that—I'll show you how it works using MobileNetV2.

MobileNetV2 transfer learning case study

MobileNetV2 is a deep convolutional neural network composed of 53 layers trained on the ImageNet dataset, which consists of more than a million images in 1,000 different categories (for example, keyboards, mice, pencils, and many kinds of animals). You can load a pretrained version of the network via the tf.keras API.

Let's start by importing it:

```
from tensorflow.keras.applications.mobilenet_v2 import MobileNetV2
```

After importing the neural network, we can access its summary simply by calling the summary function. We can also define how we want to load the model. This is done by specifying the input shape of the data we're working with (as (*height, width, chan nels*)), whether we want to include the top (classification) layer, and the weights to use. It's important to define the weights if we intend to avoid training the whole model from scratch with random weights, which is what will happen if we don't provide a value for this variable or specify None. In our case, we want to leverage the existing weights based on the ImageNet dataset (alternatively, you can pass in the path to a weights file to be loaded). The following code snippet will load the model:

```
# define params
IMG_SHAPE = (224, 224, 3)
# Load the model as base_model
base_model = MobileNetV2(input_shape=IMG_SHAPE, include_top=False,
                         weights='imagenet')
```

Using the model requires an understanding of its layers and their usage. Some layers, for example, are used for feature extraction. If we don't want to extract new features, we can freeze the parameters and define the base_model itself as not trainable. This will enforce the transfer learning effect, and we will only add a new classification layer to classify our images. The next code snippet demonstrates exactly that:

```
# Freeze parameters in the feature extraction layers
base_model.trainable = False
```

```
# Add a new classification layer for transfer learning
global_average_layer = keras.layers.GlobalAveragePooling2D()
prediction_layer = keras.layers.Dense(num_classes)
```

Note that I've also added a `GlobalAveragePooling2D` layer, which is intended for pooling operations for spatial data. In images, pooling relates to the pool of pixels. The goal of this layer is to progressively reduce the spatial size of the representation and the number of parameters and amount of computation in the network. This is a must-have when you want your final model to fit into smaller devices, such as embedded or IoT devices.

 While distributed training is usually done with a dataset that is too large to fit in a single machine's memory, that doesn't necessarily mean that we can't end up with a small model that does. Reducing the size of a neural network or other machine learning model so it can run on a memory- or power-constrained device—including everyday IoT devices such as TVs, refrigerators, cars, etc.—is the main goal of TinyML. If you are interested in learning more about this topic, take a look at *TinyML* (*https://oreil.ly/tinyML*) by Pete Warden and Daniel Situnayake (O'Reilly).

Now that we have the `base_model` and two layers, we want to stack them together into a final model. For that, we use the `Sequential` function, which enables us to specify how the layers will be stacked. The function takes an array of layers, which enables us to arrange the layers in the order in which we want the model to operate, as you can see in the following code snippet:

```
from tensorflow.keras.models import Sequential
model = keras.Sequential([
    base_model,
    global_average_layer,
    prediction_layer
])
```

The outcome of this is a model where the added layers are not trained yet (only the base model has its weights set up), and we need to train them to get the correct weights. To train the last two layers, we ingest the training dataset into the model, making sure to split it into a training set and a validation set (for training purposes, our model needs both):

```
new_model = model.fit(train_dataset,
                      steps_per_epoch=steps_per_epoch,
                      epochs=NUM_EPOCHS,
                      validation_data=val_dataset,
                      validation_steps=validation_steps,
                      verbose=2).model
```

In this code snippet, we call the `model.fit` function on the model with all the input it requires, including the training dataset. This will train the two last layers and produce the fully trained model. You can also configure the number of steps per epoch, number of epochs, and validation steps, to customize what happens while the training is taking place.

Now that we've created the model, we can configure it by adding a loss function, metrics, and/or dedicated Grappler optimizers for the graph. To keep things simple here, I'll keep the model as it is, but in real-world scenarios, you'll likely want to configure it in a way that suits the business problem you are solving. If you do decide to configure the model, use the `model.compile` function before and after `fit`.

Once it's ready, we can use the `model.predict` function to make a prediction with the model:

```
predictions = new_model.predict(val_dataset)
```

This will take a validation dataset item as input, do a forward pass through the neural network, and provide a prediction.

This example illustrated how you can leverage the power of existing models in Keras to solve your business problems by using those models as a foundation. Notice that under the hood, `tf.keras` APIs themselves are distributed-aware. So, based on the strategy you select, they know how to replicate variables and operations. To have them run as part of the strategy's scope, remember to specify the scope with the `strategy.scope` function. Under that scope, you only need to define the model and call `model.compile`. To train the model, we call `model.fit` (which can be called outside of the strategy's scope).

Here's what it looks like all together:

```
strategy = tf.distribute.MultiWorkerMirroredStrategy(...)
with strategy.scope():
    # Model building/compiling must be within strategy.scope()
    Model = tf.keras.Sequential(...)
    model.compile(...)

batch_size = 50  # Must be divisible by the number of replicas
new_model = model.fit(...)
tf.saved_model.save(new_model, some_path)
```

In this code, we create the `MultiWorkerMirroredStrategy` instance that replicates the model across machines and then use its scope to define the model and compile it. Following that, everything related to the model, such as sequential stacking, compiling, fitting, and then saving it, happens within the relevant scope.

The saved model is saved as a regular model (without the training strategy attached), so when you load it, it will run as a regular model on a single device. This flexibility enables us to decide how we want to load the trained model and run predictions with it (more on that in Chapter 10).

Now that you know how to leverage an existing model as a base and add layers to build a solution, let's take a look at how you would build it from scratch with Keras.

Training the Keras MobileNetV2 algorithm from scratch

The main difference between the previous approach and the one we'll take here is the trained weights of the neural network itself. When using an existing deep learning algorithm without the pretrained weights, the layers are already defined, and what changes are the weights connecting the graph layers and the feature extraction process.

To get the neutral network itself without the trained weights, all we need to do is specify `weights='None'` when we create the base model instead of `weights='image net'`, as we did in the previous example. This results in random initialization of the weights, which will be adjusted during training:

```
# Create the base model from the pretrained MobileNetV2 model
base_model = MobileNetV2(input_shape=IMG_SHAPE, include_top=False,
                         weights='None')
```

Then, to enable training new parameters in the model's feature extraction layers, we need to set the `base_model.trainable` parameter to `True` like so:

```
# Enable parameter training in the feature extraction layers
base_model.trainable = True
```

And that's it! The rest of the flow goes just like the previous example. Next, we'll look at a much more low-level solution: building a custom training loop (CTL) from scratch.

Custom Training Loop

TF's custom training loop API provides granular control over training and evaluating loops built from scratch. It allows you to construct training loops step by step and provides access to the framework's low-level APIs. This is fantastic if you want to customize the learning algorithm of a model. Note that with a CTL, we are responsible for distributing the dataset using the strategy instance we create. Here, we'll use the `MultiWorkerMirroredStrategy` as an example:

```
strategy = tf.distribute.MultiWorkerMirroredStrategy()
```

When we write a CTL, we must take care of each step in the training process. This includes the following:

1. Providing the data sources to load the data from (the dataset that is split and shared across replicas, and the variables that the replicas will update during the training procedure)

2. Defining the computations that each replica will run on its piece of the dataset, using its allocated resources

3. Combining the output of the replicas (which reduction operations to apply, e.g., *sum, mean, max,* etc.)

4. Deciding how to use the output from the previous step to update the variables (e.g., all-reduce or, less commonly, concatenation for edge cases)

5. Broadcasting the result to all the replicas, in the case of all-reduce (you can also use MPI or other functions that suit your use case better)

6. Performing the next round of training (up to the specified number of epochs) given the updated variables

This approach exists in TF to allow more complicated algorithms to be developed for research purposes—I'm talking here about scenarios where there is no out-of-the-box premade algorithm available or when the researcher wants to investigate how each layer impacts other layers, take a novel approach to operator usage, and much more. Since this API is more common in research settings, I will not discuss it in detail; I invite you to learn more about it on the Google Brain team's website (*https://oreil.ly/Zgm7y*).

What I will show you now is how to build a custom loop with strategy awareness. As you know already, we have to set up the strategy at the beginning, and as with the Keras API, we can use the scope function:

```
with strategy.scope()
    reader = ...
    dataset = make_petastorm_dataset(reader)
        # provide TF with information on how to split the dataset
        dataset = strategy.experimental_distribute_dataset(dataset)
        ...
        model = create_model()
```

Notice that not all operators need to be inside the scope, but it is much simpler to put everything inside the scope to avoid mistakes. This also makes your code more modular.

We pass the make_petastorm_dataset function a Petastorm reader instance created with the make_batch_reader function, described in "Loading Parquet Data into a TensorFlow Dataset" on page 169. This takes care of reading the data in batches when we provide it with a defined batch_size. After that, the strategy.experimental_distribute_dataset function determines how to split the data based on the batch size. If you wish, you can provide TF with a different split function, such as a function that takes an input context and returns a dataset per replica batch size; however, I don't recommend doing that unless you are experienced in working with distributed data. Finally, we call `create_model` from within the strategy's scope so that any variables will be created using the policy dictated by the strategy.

With a CTL, you can leverage Keras APIs to define optimizers, loss functions, and more—all of which should take place within the scope. Next, we'll take a quick look at the third training API, the TF Estimator API.

Estimator API

 This is an old API that should not be used for new code. I will briefly cover it to help if you are working with legacy code and need to configure the training distributed strategy. If you are developing new code, you should use one of the training APIs discussed in the previous sections.

The Estimator API offers limited support for all distributed training strategies in TF v2. This is because it is an older API (from TF v1) and is in maintenance mode. Similar to the Keras API, it's strategy-aware, which means that after defining the training strategy, all we need to do is create a config instance and pass it to the `Estimator` instance. This is what distributed training with an `Estimator` looks like:

```
strategy = tf.distributed.MirroredStrategy()
run_config = tf.estimator.RunConfig(train_distributed=strategy)

estimator = tf.estimator.Estimator(model_fn=model_function)
estimator.train(input_fn=input_fn_train)
```

First, we create the strategy, then we specify the configuration for an `Estimator` run. `tf.estimator.RunConfig` defines how the `Estimator` will operate, which is why passing the strategy to the constructor with the `train_distributed` parameter is a must.

The third line creates the `Estimator` itself, and the fourth line runs the training as described in `run_config`.

Note that with this code, the `model_function` provided to the `Estimator` is called once per replica. The `Estimator` itself already knows how to merge the results of the model function into a single coherent answer.

How does this code differ from the previous approaches? We don't use the `strategy.scope` function! This makes the whole process of choosing the strategy and executing within it kind of hidden to us.

Now that we have a distributed model, we can save and load it using TensorFlow APIs, similar to how we do with MLlib. Here is an example of how we do this:

```
tf.saved_model.save(model, model_path)
uploaded_model = tf.saved_model.load(model_path)
```

To learn more about how to handle this, including the different variations, programming language support, and so on, see the TensorFlow docs (*https://oreil.ly/MjGCO*). We'll discuss loading and deploying models further in Chapter 10.

Putting It All Together

You now have a good understanding of the various training strategies provided by TF and how things work. Now it's time to use the Caltech 256 image dataset to tie everything together.

In Chapter 5, you learned how to extract features from the Caltech 256 dataset, create grayscale versions of the images, extract the labels, and more. To use this dataset with the Keras MobileNetV2 model, we will need to do some additional data processing. We will use Petastorm for this, and we'll take advantage of TensorFlow's transfer learning capabilities to train only some of the layers.

As a first step, we'll define a supporting function to convert the dataset schema into a schema that can be used with MobileNetV2. Our preprocess function resizes each image using the Pillow API and creates a Keras image array, as shown in the following code snippet:

```
from tensorflow.keras.applications.mobilenet_v2 import MobileNetV2,
    preprocess_input
def preprocess(grayscale_image):
    """
    Preprocess an image file's bytes for MobileNetV2 (ImageNet).
    """
    image = Image.open(io.BytesIO(grayscale_image)).resize([224, 224])
    image_array = keras.preprocessing.image.img_to_array(image)
    return preprocess_input(image_array)
```

To run this function, we need to iterate over our dataset using the pandas DataFrame. As discussed in previous chapters, Spark's support for pandas DataFrames is more optimized than Spark UDFs.

The following supporting function will take a pandas DataFrame as input and return a pandas DataFrame as output:

```
def transform_row(pd_batch):
    """
    The input and output of this function are pandas DataFrames.
    """
    pd_batch['features'] = pd_batch['content'].map(lambda x: preprocess(x))
```

```
pd_batch = pd_batch.drop(labels=['content'], axis=1)
return pd_batch
```

Here, we use the map function to iterate over the content column and execute the preprocess function on it. We save the result in a new column named features; then we remove the original content column with drop(labels=['content'], axis=1), since it is no longer needed. The function returns the updated pd_batch.

transform_row is used with a Petastorm TransformSpec instance. TransformSpec uses this function in the constructor to define how to transform the data from Parquet into the format that fits the algorithm (in our case, MobileNetV2). Transform Spec also takes the optional parameters edit_fields and selected_fields, specifying the fields the transformation is operating on and the fields it needs to produce at the end. The following code snippet shows how to use it:

```
from petastorm import TransformSpec
IMG_SHAPE = (224, 224, 3)

transform_spec_fn = TransformSpec(
    func=transform_row,
    edit_fields=[('features', np.uint8, IMG_SHAPE, False)],
    selected_fields=['features', 'label_index'])
```

Note that we must provide the schema information for every column, represented by a 4-tuple with the following information: (name, numpy_dtype, shape, is_nullable). In our case, we transform only one field, features, which is of type np.uint8. We provide it with the IMG_SHAPE of (224,224,3) and specify False as the field cannot be nullable.

Now that we've defined transform_spec_fn, we need to define the Petastorm converter. We do this (as discussed in Chapter 7) using the make_spark_converter function, which will leverage the Spark cluster to build a converter and convert the data into a TF dataset:

```
# training dataset
converter_train = make_spark_converter(df_train,
                                       parquet_row_group_size_bytes=32000000)
# validation dataset
converter_val = make_spark_converter(df_val,
                                     parquet_row_group_size_bytes=32000000)
```

We use the make_spark_converter function when we already have a materialized Spark DataFrame and want to convert it into a TF dataset. This approach is different from the approach we discussed before, which included writing the data to disk and loading it using Petastorm.

We can now convert the DataFrame with make_tf_dataset, configuring trans
form_spec=transform_spec_fn and batch_size=BATCH_SIZE. Here we create two
TensorFlow datasets, one for training and the other for validation:

```
def within_strategy_scope(...):
    with converter_train.make_tf_dataset(transform_spec=transform_spec_fn,
                                          batch_size=BATCH_SIZE) as train_dataset,
         converter_val.make_tf_dataset(transform_spec=transform_spec_fn,
                                          batch_size=BATCH_SIZE) as val_dataset:

        model = get_model(lr=0.001)
        model.compile(optimizer="SGD",
                      loss=keras.losses.SparseCategoricalCrossentropy(from_logits=True),
                      metrics=["accuracy"])
        # tf.keras only accepts tuples, not namedtuples
        train_dataset = train_dataset.map(lambda x: (x.features, x.label_index))
        steps_per_epoch = len(converter_train) // (BATCH_SIZE)

        val_dataset = val_dataset.map(lambda x: (x.features, x.label_index))
        validation_steps = max(1, len(converter_val)) // (BATCH_SIZE)

    hist = model.fit(train_dataset,
                     steps_per_epoch=steps_per_epoch,
                     epochs=NUM_EPOCHS,
                     validation_data=val_dataset,
                     validation_steps=validation_steps,
                     verbose=2)

strategy = tf.distribute.MultiWorkerMirroredStrategy()
with strategy.scope():
    within_strategy_scope(...)
```

This code example uses the supporting function get_model, which returns the model.
We compile it with the model.compile function, discussed in "MobileNetV2 transfer
learning case study" on page 183, then map the datasets with TF's map function to fit
Keras's input requirements, as it accepts only tuples and not namedtuples.
steps_per_epoch is calculated by dividing the training dataset size by the batch size.
For example, if we have 1 million entries in the training dataset and a batch size of
1,000, steps_per_epoch will be 1,000,000/1,000 = 1,000 (that is, there will be 1,000
steps per epoch). The same goes for validation_steps. Last, we train the model with
the model.fit function. The hist instance returned by this function holds the history of each epoch/iteration over the data. You can examine this information later to
better assess the model's accuracy.

Troubleshooting

Errors can occur during the conversion from Spark to Petastorm to TensorFlow. For
example, you may see an exception such as the following:

```
raise ValueError(f'All dimensions of a shape: {field.shape} in: {field.name}
field must be constant. '
ValueError: All dimensions of a shape: (None, None) in: features field must be
constant. If a dimension is variable, we won't be able to coalesce rows when
preparing a batch.
```

To troubleshoot this, you need to go back to your `transform_spec` definition. Peta-storm translates this spec into the `arrow_reader_worker`, which requires the Tensor-Flow tensor to be of a fixed shape. If you attempt to provide a `None` value to represent the tensor shape, you will encounter this error.

To fix the problem, the `Unischema` variable has to be of a fixed length; otherwise, the data coalesce logic it executes behind the scenes won't work. In other words, when preprocessing the data, you need to make sure your variables have fixed lengths.

On top of that, you'll want to make sure your images are all the same size, or you'll run into the following error message:

```
Input element must have the same batch size in each component.
```

Summary

This chapter introduced several new concepts, focusing on the topic of TF's distribution strategies. We went deep into this framework's approach to distributed machine learning and walked through a full end-to-end example of using it to train a model. You should now understand how TF's strategies work and how they compare to Spark's. As you've seen, although there are many similarities between TF and Apache Spark, there is also some variation in their naming conventions and operations.

It is important to remember that there is no single authoritative approach to building distributed systems but rather many different approaches based on adjacent concepts, structures, and optimizations. The main difference between TF and Spark is that Spark was built as a generic distributed analytics engine, while TF was built as a deep learning engine.

Next, we will explore PyTorch's distributed training approach and how it differs from TensorFlow's.

## CHAPTER 9

PyTorch Distributed
Machine Learning Approach

PyTorch is an open source machine learning library developed by Facebook's AI Research (FAIR) team and later donated to the Linux Foundation. It was designed to simplify the creation of artificial neural networks and enable applications such as computer vision, natural language processing, and more. The primary interface to PyTorch is Python, but it's built on low-level C and C++ code. This is a very different approach from Spark, which uses Scala and Java (JVM-based programming languages) at its core.

In the previous chapters, you've learned about the building blocks of the machine learning workflow. We started with Spark, then expanded to explore TensorFlow's distributed training capabilities. In this chapter, we will turn our attention to PyTorch. The goal is to help you better understand what PyTorch is and how its distributed machine learning training works, from an architectural and conceptual perspective, so you can make better decisions when combining multiple frameworks together in a distributed setting.

We will also go through a step-by-step example of working with distributed PyTorch while leveraging the previous work we did with Spark in Chapters 4 and 5 and Petastorm in Chapter 7.

This chapter covers the following:

- A quick overview of PyTorch basics
- PyTorch distributed strategies for training models
- How to load Parquet data into PyTorch
- Putting it all together—from Petastorm to a model with PyTorch

- Troubleshooting guidance for working with Petastorm and distributed PyTorch
- How PyTorch differs from TensorFlow

 If you're new to PyTorch, I suggest that you first read an introductory text like Joe Papa's *PyTorch Pocket Reference* (*https://oreil.ly/pytorch-pr*) (O'Reilly). This chapter provides a quick overview of the basics; it will mostly focus on the distributed training strategies and how to connect PyTorch with Spark.

A Quick Overview of PyTorch Basics

You've learned about a lot of technological concepts in this book, and it is important that you use the right terminology for the tool at hand and that you understand the differences between the various machine learning frameworks. If you are new to PyTorch and want to familiarize yourself with its terminology, this section is for you. While many naming conventions are the same, some are entirely different. This section will highlight some of the key terms and concepts in PyTorch, starting with its computation graph.

Computation Graph

Like TensorFlow and Spark, PyTorch uses a computation graph. An example is shown in Figure 9-1; as you can see, it emphasizes forward computation through the neural network itself while supporting the backward computation of gradients during the training runs.

In this figure, the circles (*x1*, *x2*, etc.) represent *tensors*, and the rectangles represent the *operations* on the data, like *Log*, *Sin*, and * (used for multiplication). The graph computation starts from the bottom left, by calculating *x1* * *x2*—an operation that generates a tensor, *a*. During this operation, the graph also saves information for the future backward-multiplication gradient operation (called *MultBackward* in Figure 9-1). This information will later support the backward propagation of loss (as a reminder, in a neural network, the algorithm uses this information to calculate the delta over the graph and improve the training process). PyTorch computes the gradients with respect to the inputs by using a process called *automatic differentiation*, and the computation graph is executed by the automatic differentiation engine.

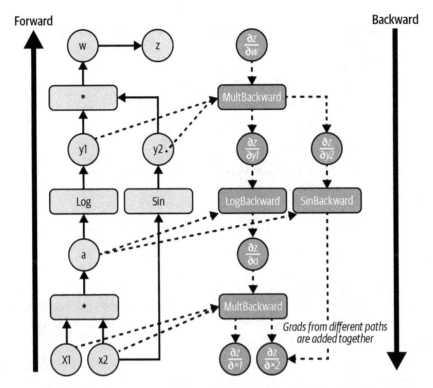

Figure 9-1. Example of a computation graph extended with the backward pass (from the PyTorch blog (https://oreil.ly/9WnNf))

Figure 9-2 shows a subset of the computation graph, focusing on the forward computation alone.

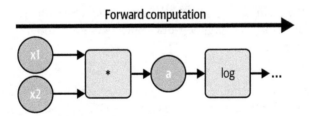

Figure 9-2. Breaking down the forward computation approach

We multiply *x1* and *x2*, which yields the value *a*. We then run another operation on that value (*Log(a)*), and so on. Since this is a subset of the neural network, we know that there will be a backward propagation pass to adjust the values of the weights and train the model. Figure 9-3 shows the mechanism of maintaining the delta value the algorithm needs for backward propagation.

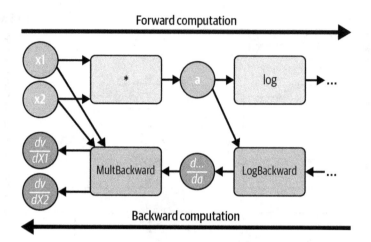

Figure 9-3. The graph supports forward and backward computation

On every forward iteration, there is a process calculating the differentiation for the backward iteration that will come. In other words, PyTorch's automatic differentiation engine calculates the gradients automatically before the backward computation even starts.

Note that in PyTorch, the computation graph is *dynamic*, compared to in TensorFlow, where graph construction is *static*. With the static approach, the program constructs the graph first and executes it only once it is complete. With the dynamic approach, the graph is built at runtime, and execution starts before the graph is completed; the program builds the computation graph on the fly as needed.

PyTorch Mechanics and Concepts

These are the basic concepts that you should be familiar with when working with PyTorch, to understand its neural network implementations and how it interprets the computation graph:

torch.Tensor
    PyTorch tensors are similar to TF tensors; they are multidimensional matrices that contain scalar types such as float, int, etc. The types can be NumPy types, optimized for CPUs or GPUs. Tensors also have a *stride*, which represents the step size in memory the machine needs to reach the next successive array element in the physical memory. Think about a matrix representation in memory; how many bits do we need to read to reach the next value in it? This is the stride. A tensor's stride depends on its physical representation, which is conditioned by the machine's configuration (hardware, memory, etc.—for example, a GPU would behave differently than a CPU).

`torch.autograd`

Autograd is PyTorch's built-in automatic differentiation engine. When you declare tensors with `requires_grad=True`, it collects the input and output gradients of every operation on the tensors. Later, the PyTorch engine uses this information during the automatic calculation of gradients in a backward propagation pass. In other words, the autograd graph is constructed during forward computation and used during backward computation. To understand this better, take a look at the following Python code snippet showing local training before moving to distributed training:

```python
import torch
import torch.nn as nn
import torch.optim as optim

# set up model
net = nn.Linear(10, 10)  ❶

# load input and target
input = torch.randn(20, 10)  ❷
tgt = torch.randn(20, 10)

# forward pass
output = net(input)  ❸

# compute loss using input and target
mselss = nn.MSELoss()  ❹
lss = mselss(output, tgt)

# backward pass
lss.backward()  ❺
```

❶ First, we create a linear layer using the following math equation: $y = x * A^T + b$. The input, (10, 10), means that the layer expects 10 input features and outputs 10 features as well. Internally, there are two functions: the first one is the multiplier ($x * A^T$), and the second one is the bias function ($+ b$).

❷ Next, we generate dummy input and dummy label/target tensors with a given size of 20 by 10.

❸ Now we apply the linear model over the input to generate the output. During its execution, PyTorch builds the autograd graph implicitly. Autograd records the input and the output (y) of the function, which it saves for calculating the gradient. Since the linear model consists of two operations, it will record both. That is, it will create two nodes: one for the multiplier, which will store the input (x) and weight (A^T) of the operation, and one for the bias, which stores the output of the multiplication process ($x * A^T$) and the bias.

❹ We use the MSE (mean squared error) loss function to compute the error and the difference between the output and the expected target label/output.

❺ Finally, we call backward on the loss tensor, which traverses the autograd graph built during the forward pass to compute the gradients for each parameter. After that, all the Parameter instances in the model will have a graph_view parameter that stores the gradients computed during the backward pass. The next layer could be, for example, an optimizer; it will reference the parameters calculated previously and apply the gradients to them. This operation will update the parameters' values to correct them and reduce the loss. (This concept exists in TensorFlow as well, but it's not a main feature of that framework and requires much tweaking.)

AutogradMeta

This is the object that holds the metadata that is generated to support the backward pass through the autograd graph. It is defined in PyTorch C++ source code as follows:

```
struct TORCH_API AutogradMeta : public c10::AutogradMetaInterface {
  std::string name_;

  Variable grad_;
  std::shared_ptr<Node> grad_fn_;
  std::weak_ptr<Node> grad_accumulator_;
  // other fields and methods
  ...
};
```

AutogradMeta holds a C++ shared pointer instance named grad_fn_. This is a function to calculate the actual gradient. There is also a C++ weak pointer instance named grad_accumulator_ that, when available, accumulates gradients.

Variable

A Variable in PyTorch is a wrapper around a tensor that encapsulates additional information, such as the AutogradMeta object, the tensor's value, and the gradient. From a computation graph point of view, Variables are represented as nodes in the graph.

torch.layout

This object represents how the tensor memory is structured, dense or sparse, according to the tensor's requirements.

torch.mm

This is a function that performs a matrix multiplication on two input matrices/tensors.

`torch.utils.data.DataLoader`

A data loader in PyTorch iterates over the dataset and generates batches of data to train the model on one machine. In "Loading Data with PyTorch and Petastorm" on page 221, you will see how Petastorm works with the PyTorch data loader.

`torch.optim.Optimizer`

PyTorch's `torch.optim` package implements several optimization algorithms. The optimizer's goal is similar to that of all algorithms in machine learning: reducing the loss and improving accuracy. In a neural network, this involves adjusting the node weights and learning rate. Every PyTorch optimizer has a `state_dict` method that returns a `dict` containing information about the optimizer's state, including the parameters it needs to optimize and the model's hyperparameters.

 As a quick reminder, model parameters are calculated automatically from training data, while model hyperparameters are set manually and used in the processes of calculating model parameters. Hyperparameters don't change during the training process; parameters do change and are impacted by the algorithm and the hyperparameters.

Autograd collects information about the operations in the graph to optimize the neural network during the backward computation. It doesn't perform the optimizations immediately, during the forward pass; the optimized parameters are synchronized during the loss computation step of a backward pass (see the previous code snippet for details). The reason for this is that backward propagation is more expensive in terms of network communication.

In this step, PyTorch calculates the gradients incrementally, which provides a good opportunity to calculate the parameters as well and, by doing so, avoid another run of expensive communication (more on that in the next section). Later, to update the parameters, we need to explicitly call `step` on the `optimizer`. The following code snippet demonstrates calculating the loss and later running the optimizer step to update the parameters:

```
# compute loss function
loss.backward()
# update the training parameters according to the loss function outcome
optimizer.step()
```

Depending on the type of optimizer you are using, you may need to provide it with other inputs.

The Trade-Offs of Optimizers

The optimizer used to train a neural network can have an effect on the time it takes to train the machine learning algorithm. When choosing the optimizer, consider the size of your data and the available and required memory and computation resources. We will not discuss the algorithmic side of it, as there are many good resources available on that topic (for example, O'Reilly's *Programming PyTorch for Deep Learning* (*https://oreil.ly/pytorch-dl*), by Ian Pointer). However, some examples will give you an idea of the elements to consider here.

The Adam (Adaptive Moment Estimation) optimizer is considered efficient for working with large data since it requires minimum memory space, which is critical when you are dealing with large datasets that can produce lots of information to use for optimization. Remember that some optimizers are more computationally expensive, while others are more memory-intensive. If you are short on memory but can wait longer for the optimizer's function to converge, favor a more computationally expensive one. If that is not the case and you are optimizing for speed, use a more memory-intensive optimizer that converges faster.

Another example is gradient descent, the most basic and commonly used optimizer. PyTorch offers two implementations for this: SGD (which implements stochastic gradient descent) and ASGD (which implements averaged stochastic gradient descent). Backpropagation in neural networks leans on the gradient descent approach; the challenge is the high calculation cost. Optimizing the loss function and finding the local minimum values where loss is the lowest requires calculating the gradient on the whole dataset and keeping the information for calculation. With a large dataset, gradient descent is both computationally heavy and memory heavy, and convergence takes a very long time. The key takeaway is to be wise when picking an optimizer and make sure you understand its trade-offs well.

PyTorch Distributed Strategies for Training Models

The nice thing about PyTorch is that it enables an application to grow gradually from simple to complex, running on one machine when you have a prototype and scaling to multiple machines in the production or staging/development environment as necessary. The torch.distributed package provides a set of PyTorch features that allow training of machine learning models across machines (i.e., distributed data-parallel training).

Let's start with a story. In 2020, Shen Li, a FAIR researcher, decided to investigate how to accelerate data-parallel training with PyTorch. He and his team conducted research (*https://oreil.ly/UjGcR*) to examine multiple configurations, experimenting with optimizers, parameters, etc. This led them to an interesting conclusion—in the distributed data-parallel (DDP) training world, there are no one-size-fits-all solutions:

There are various techniques to improve its speed, creating a complex configuration space. Based on our observations, there is no single configuration that would work for all use cases, as it would highly depend on the model size, model structure, network link bandwidth, etc.

Now that you understand the landscape a little better, this section will provide some guidance that you can use to make decisions and familiarize yourself with different PyTorch abstractions. You will learn about the various distributed strategies from a procedural and process communication standpoint, which will add to your machine learning training toolkit.

Introduction to PyTorch's Distributed Approach

PyTorch's base library for all things distributed is `torch.distributed`. It handles all the aspects of distributed communication from a hardware and networking perspective, such as InfiniBand interconnect for GPUs/CPUs. In any distributed system, hardware is the base, and you should optimize the application to match the hardware. `torch.distributed` allows you to do this regardless of the specifics of the setup you're working with.

We can categorize the features in `torch.distributed` into three main components:

Distributed data-parallel training (DDP)
> PyTorch's `DistributedDataParallel` class implements distributed data parallelism based on the `torch.distributed` package at the module level. How are the two different, and why do we need both? That's a good question. The short answer is that `DistributedDataParallel` handles only the application itself—the training of the algorithms at the application level—while `torch.distributed` handles hardware.
>
> As part of DDP, PyTorch introduces multiple abstractions that will be covered in the following section.

RPC-based distributed training (RPC)
> PyTorch's distributed RPC framework (`torch.distributed.rpc`) supports the training process at a higher level and provides mechanisms to enable remote communication between machines. It enables functionality such as distributed pipeline parallelism, a parameter server paradigm (similar to TensorFlow's, discussed in Chapter 8), and more. It also provides a distributed autograd framework for model-parallel training.

Collective Communication (c10d)
> This library provides additional functionality that expands the communication structure and supports sending tensors across processes within a group. It provides APIs for collective and peer-to-peer communication, such as `all_reduce`,

`all_gather`, `send`, and `isend`. The DDP and RPC frameworks are built on top of it. As developers, we rarely interact with this library, but it is good practice to familiarize yourself with the concepts.

As a last step, after deciding which of these strategies to use and implementing it, you will initialize the distributed environment by calling the initialization method:

```
torch.distributed.init_process_group()
```

We'll take a closer look at each of these approaches in the following sections.

Distributed Data-Parallel Training

As part of DDP, PyTorch introduces multiple abstractions that will be covered throughout this section. We'll start with buckets.

Instead of looking at a specific neural network layer, PyTorch divides the communication into *buckets*. A bucket holds the indices of where each value in the `input` belongs. The bucket boundaries are set by a tensor instance called `boundaries`. As shown in Figure 9-4, buckets can consist of multiple layers or one layer, depending on how we define them with `torch.bucketize`. Buckets are a critical component of the architecture as they define gradient calculating boundaries within the backward propagation pass. That is why *bucket1* is at the bottom of Figure 9-4.

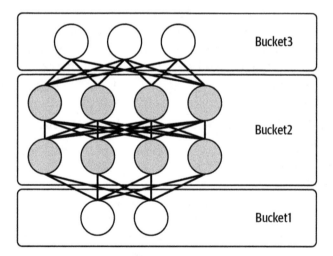

Figure 9-4. PyTorch abstraction of layers in buckets

Depending on the machine's communication strategy, buckets can also assist in defining when to kick-start the next gradient computation pass. When all buckets are done, an all-reduce operation is used to accumulate the values across buckets. The PyTorch engine works in a greedy manner, which means that not all layers and gradients will always fit in the same bucket. This turns the distributed bucket abstraction into a stochastic system, which enables the PyTorch engine to decide at runtime which compute operation is more efficient, given the known information.

DDP takes in a seed value as well to ingest into the model parameters at the beginning. It is important that you provide the seed in a distributed setting. If you don't, each machine will generate its own seed, which will likely differ from those used by the other machines. This will cause the model parameters to be different as well and, as a result, harm the coverage process.

RPC-Based Distributed Training

The remote procedure call procedure enables a program on the local machine to start a program on another machine, as long as they share the same address space. It's as though the resident of apartment A could start the washing machine in apartment B, just by supplying that machine's address. This is the concept behind RPCs.

In PyTorch, the RPC framework allows data scientists to train models across multiple machines using primitives for remote communication and a higher-level API for recognizing models split across machines. What are the main use cases to be aware of? As mentioned previously, PyTorch's RPC framework enables the implementation of the following paradigms:

- A *parameter server* (similar to in TensorFlow), where one or more servers store the parameters and distributed trainers communicate with them to fetch and update the values
- *Model parallelism*, which allows different parts of a large model that cannot fit on a single GPU to be placed on separate GPUs
- *Pipeline parallelism* (an experimental feature), where each input minibatch is split into microbatches that can be executed concurrently on all the GPUs

This is a low-level framework for general distributed training. It makes sense to take advantage of it in scenarios that are not covered by DDP.

The APIs the framework provides can be grouped into four categories based on the features they support:

Remote execution

> You can run arbitrary functions remotely and get a return value back or create a reference to the return value. This is something we can expect from any RPC system.

Remote references (RRefs)

> An RRef is a distributed shared pointer to an object. It allows you to access and reference a value on a remote worker without fetching the actual data from that object. Due to its structure and implementation, it provides automatic reference counting, which can be useful for understanding how often a remote data object is referenced, for example.

Distributed autograd

> The autograd engine runs locally on each worker involved in the forward pass; out of the box, it does not scale. Distributed autograd extends this beyond the boundary of a single machine, stitching together the local autograd engines on all the machines so the backward pass can be run in a distributed fashion.

Distributed optimizer

> The distributed optimizer collects the RRefs of all the parameters to optimize and creates a local optimizer on each of the workers where the parameters live. It then uses RPCs to execute the optimizers locally. Depending on which optimizer is used, it periodically averages the results across workers.

Let's dive into each of these a little more deeply so you can better understand what they look like in code and in execution diagrams.

Remote execution

PyTorch's remote execution APIs allow us to run user functions remotely. The first thing we need to do is initiate the RPC by calling the `init_rpc` function. This function requires three parameters: the name of the machine, its globally unique ID/rank within the group, and an `int` that represents the number of workers in the group (`world_size`). Take a look at the following code snippet:

```
init_rpc("w0", rank=0, world_size=32)
```

The `init_rpc` function does two things here. First, it starts an agent running in the background. When the agent is ready, it can start receiving and processing requests from other peers. Second, it starts rendezvous communication, connecting with peers. At the end of this stage, the agent is aware of all RPC processes that are running and all the peers in this RPC group are aware of each other.

---

1 In PyTorch, *rendezvous* refers to the process of peer machine discovery and distributed primitive synchronization.

Note that there is no client/server architecture here; all communication is peer-to-peer (we will talk more about how this works in "Peer-to-peer communication in PyTorch" on page 219). The default backend leverages the TensorPipe library, which provides a tensor-aware point-to-point communication primitive specially designed for machine learning. To change that, you can provide the function with a dedicated BackendType; this allows you to change certain elements of the configuration, such as timeout for peers to reply and the init_method used. w0 (the name of the machine in this example) stands for worker zero. Starting now, we will use w0, w1, w2, w3, etc. for worker 0, worker 1, worker 2, worker 3, and so on.

Now that the machines are ready, we can start sending remote function calls to peers in the group, as shown in Figure 9-5. For that, there should be a tensor and a remote operation we would like to execute, along with the rest of the arguments that the operation requires.

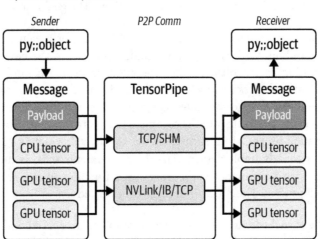

Figure 9-5. PyTorch remote execution diagram

When discussing communication, it's important to distinguish between two key concepts:

- *Communication topology*, which denotes how the machines are organized in the group and who communicates with whom (such as peer-to-peer or client/server)

- *Communication type*, which defines how the machines communicate with one another

PyTorch enables us to choose the exact communication type we want to have between the machines, for each operation. You can choose from three options: rpc_sync, rpc_async, and remote. The following code snippet demonstrates the use of all three:

```
# initialize RPC and a torch
rpc.init_rpc("w0", rank=0, world_size=32)
x = torch.zeros(32) ❶

# synchronous - returns the result
ret = rpc_sync("w1", torch.add, args=(x,1)) ❷

# asynchronous, returns future
fut = rpc_async("w1", torch.add, args=(x,1)) ❸

# asynchronous, returns reference to result
@torch.jit.script ❹
def script_add(x,y):
    return x+y

rref = remote("w1", script_add, args=(x,1))
```

❶ We initialize a torch of size 32 with zeros as values. The goal is to mock a tensor.

❷ We use the synchronous API when we need to wait for a value to be returned before proceeding. With rpc_sync, we cannot proceed to the next step until the communication is established, the operation takes place, and the value is returned. This is a *blocking function*; it blocks the program from continuing until a response is returned to the caller. rpc_sync's first input argument is the name of the process to connect with; the second is the operation that we want to run on the destination process. In this case, we use torch.add, which is a PyTorch function that is already implemented. The third argument, args, is the list of arguments we wish to provide to the torch.add function to use as input on the destination process. The function returns the updated tensor.

❸ We use the asynchronous API when we want to run an operation on the destination process but we don't need the results right away. The rpc_async call here is similar to the previous call to rpc_sync (it takes the same arguments), but in this case the function doesn't block the program from continuing to execute the next command. An async call returns a *future*—an object that acts as a proxy to a result that is unknown at the present time because its computation isn't complete. To retrieve the results when they are needed, we need to call fut.wait and save them into a variable. wait is a blocking function that will block the program until

---

2 In computer science, this is a function that blocks the program from processing the next operation until a response is received. It often involves I/O, communicating with a remote machine, or other processes.

the results are returned. This functionality enables us to execute multiple future operations in parallel. For example, if we want to perform add and max operations on the same worker, we can run them concurrently, then call wait on both and sum up the two torch vectors using the + operator:

```
fut_add = rpc.rpc_async("w1", torch.add, args=(x, 3))
fut_max = rpc.rpc_async("w1", torch.max, args=(x))
result = fut_add.wait() + fut_max.wait()
```

This enables concurrent control over the operations.

❹ The remote function (the third API) doesn't fetch a value; its purpose is to execute a function remotely that creates something. It takes the name of the process to run the function on, the function to run, and if necessary the args or kwargs for the function invocation. You can also provide an optional timeout parameter. In this example, we run an annotated TorchScript function, script_add. TorchScript enables us to compile a program locally and later load it in a process without a Python dependency. We can leverage this functionality for executing the remote function. @torch.jit.script is the Python annotation that defines it; whenever we use this annotation, the Python interpreter, together with PyTorch, inspects the source code and turns it into a TorchScript. The remote function is asynchronous, meaning the program isn't blocked. However, the main difference between the remote and rpc_async APIs is that the remote API returns a remote reference to the value on the other machine (RRefs are discussed in the following section). The return value lives in the destination process and is not fetched back to the original process that triggered it. To summarize this example, the script_add function is sent to w1 with the arguments of x (the torch) and 1, the value that the program adds to the torch's values.

 You can also use the TorchScript approach after training. Let's say we've trained a model with PyTorch in a Python environment. Now, we wish to export the trained model into an environment where using Python programs is disadvantageous due to the lower performance of this language in the multi-threading world. TorchScript creates a standalone C++ program that can run on a different process/machine without a Python environment.

How do you choose between the three available remote execution options? As with everything related to machine learning and building distributed execution graphs, the answer is: it depends. The guidance here is to break down the network layers and consider the functionality of each. Does one operation need to wait for another one to finish? Are they dependent on one another? If so, rpc_sync would be a good approach here. Can we parallelize some operations, making them concurrent? Can we continue with the training without having all the information available? In this case, we can use rpc_async. Do we want to execute a function on a remote server without returning a value back? For example, when we have a topology with a parameter server and trainers, we can create the parameter table on the PS without fetching back the table, since the main program running won't need it. The remote function is the best choice here.

Remote references

During the process of training in a distributed system, it is common to have a driver node that drives the execution of the training loops and worker nodes that operate on the data. So there might be scenarios where we need to create remote references, for example for user-defined functions. In this scenario, the UDF is defined on the driver and shipped to the workers, which each operate on their chunk of data in parallel, without sending the results back to the driver. The workers hold on to the results, and the driver only has references to them. This is similar to the concept of distributed shared pointers in computer science, where the pointer stores the address where the data is stored but not the actual data itself. Any machine with a copy of the reference (called *users*) can request the object from its creator (the *owner*).

Using RRefs to orchestrate distributed algorithms. The remote function, introduced in the previous section, creates an RRef on the designated worker. This function powers PyTorch distributed algorithms by orchestrating the execution of operations and callable functions over the worker processes. Let's take a look at the following code snippet and Figure 9-6 to get a better understanding of how it works:

```
@torch.jit.script
def some_add(rref_x, rref_y)
    return rref_x.to_here() + rref_y.to_here()

# these functions run on worker process "w0"
ra = remote("w1", load_data_a)
rb = remote("w2", load_data_b)
rc = remote("w3", some_add, args=(ra,rb))
rd = remote("w4", {some function that takes rc as input})
```

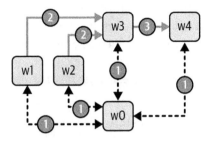

Figure 9-6. Remote orchestration of a simple add function that powers many distributed training algorithms

The code snippet runs on worker w0 and creates four remote references, on workers w1, w2, w3, and w4 (action 1 in Figure 9-6). The remote calls to w1 and w2 ask each of them to load a different chunk of the data and return RRefs to that data. w1 loads data chunk a, and w2 loads data chunk b. In Figure 9-6, init is the action number 1.

w3 is assigned the function of adding the two chunks of data using the some_add function, which takes two RRef objects as input and calls to_here on them. This call starts the fetching of the data, so the results from w1 and w2 are fetched to w3. w3 adds the results locally and returns an RRef to the results to w0 (action 2 in Figure 9-6). w4 can now perform some additional function using the results from w3 (action 3 in Figure 9-6).

Note that since the program's main entry point runs on worker 0, all the communications run through it. However, this communication is relatively lightweight since it contains only the control messages of the remote references themselves. The calls to fetch data from w1 and w2 and are executed only on w3. Here, the remote references help us to achieve two goals:

1. The code stays in one process on our driver, w0, which acts as the main orchestrator.

2. This avoids the price of carrying and moving data from the worker processes to the orchestrator. (In Spark, this is the collect function that we want to avoid at all costs when working with scalable data that cannot fit into one machine's memory.)

The orchestrator is one important aspect of working with RRefs; another is the ability to identify objects by reference.

Identifying objects by reference. As the previous example showed, PyTorch's remote references were also designed to uniquely identify objects in a distributed environment and can later be passed as RPC arguments, avoiding communicating real data.

When w0 calls the `remote` function, a `UserRRef` object is created locally. w0 can send this object as an argument to other workers and, by doing so, enable them to fetch the result or pass the reference along. At the same time, the call to `remote` creates an `OwnerRRef` object instance on the named worker, which contains the actual result of executing the function. In short, w0 created `UserRRefs` owned by w1 and w2 and sent them to w3.

A user machine can get a `UserRRef` in three scenarios:

1. It can receive a `UserRRef` from the owner.
2. It can receive a `UserRRef` from another user.
3. It can create a new `UserRRef` owned by another worker.

The owner keeps track of the number of references in order to better asses when it can delete the data itself during a garbage collection operation. We aren't going to dive into any more detail on that, but if you'd like to learn more about it, check out the RRef design note (*https://oreil.ly/uYzCh*) on GitHub.

The key point to remember about RRefs is that they allow data scientists to design more complicated distributed machine learning algorithms that are not implemented out of the box in PyTorch. This functionality is often used by researchers driving innovation in the machine learning algorithm landscape. It's good to understand it as you dive deeper into PyTorch and distributed machine learning, as well as for troubleshooting.

Distributed autograd

Earlier in the chapter, you got a glimpse into how PyTorch's automatic differentiation engine works locally. Now, we are ready to level up and explore how it works on distributed datasets. In a distributed setting, the model is replicated on multiple machines, with each machine processing one part of the dataset. This means that each machine will calculate its own gradient value based on its input. Although the operations are the same, the input plays a big part here.

PyTorch's RPC-based distributed autograd framework takes advantage of remote execution and remote references, discussed previously, to collect and calculate the gradients during the training. For distributed purposes, the autograd engine is extended using function/operation context—this approach is similar to the one with TensorFlow discussed in Chapter 8. A shared pointer to the context, which has a globally unique identifier, is distributed to each one of the nodes that takes part in the

---

3 In memory management, garbage collection attempts to reclaim memory that was allocated by the program but no longer referenced.

training. Potentially, every worker can retrieve context information (send and recv functions, gradients, etc.).

Moreover, the autograd functions on the different machines are stitched together with every RPC call, which lets us keep track of the changes in gradients in the distributed system. The goal of distributed autograd is to provide a similar experience to running a backward pass on the local machine. That means that for every forward pass, the machine also stores the send and recv information (identifying the sending machine and receiving machine, respectively). This makes sure that there's always a reference to the nodes in the distributed autograd graph and fuels the backward pass.

The following code snippet starts a distributed autograd context:

```
import torch.distributed.autograd
with autograd.context() as ctx:
    # some functionality within the context
```

The distributed optimizer and the calls to start forward and backward passes should all be invoked within this context.

The distributed optimizer

So far, we've seen optimizers used in various frameworks: Spark, TensorFlow, and PyTorch. Why do we need a distributed optimizer with PyTorch? In distributed training, the model parameters are scattered across multiple machines, and we need to optimize all of them. Without a distributed optimizer, data-parallel training would require each machine to collect the parameters from all of the others and then run a local optimizer. This would create a large amount of overhead in terms of communication (many-to-many or *n:n* communications) and computation, as each machine would need to run the optimization function. It would also result in bottlenecks and the risk of discrepancies for optimizations run on machines that missed some messages or weren't able to collect all of the data for some reason.

PyTorch solves these problems by implementing a thin wrapper called Distributed Optimizer. Instead of collecting all the parameters, this wrapper only takes remote references to them. During the initialization of the optimization function, it contacts the owners of these parameters and runs the optimization locally on those machines. With this approach there is still many-to-many communication, but it's lightweight as the data doesn't have to be transferred; it's just a call to the owners to collect, calculate, and optimize the parameters. Later, when we run the step function within the autograd context, this function will reach out to all the participating optimizers to execute step locally.

The following code snippet demonstrates how to use the distributed optimizer:

```
# within the autograd distributed context
dist_optim = DistributedOptimizer(
```

```
    optim.SGD,
    [rref1, rref2],
    lr=0.05
)
```

If you do decide to develop your own distributed training algorithm, pay attention to the optimizers that are supported in `torch.distributed`. Note that not everything is supported there, and you might need to implement some functionality yourself.

TorchServe, a popular tool for serving PyTorch models, also supports gRPC (Google's high-performance RPC framework) as a communication protocol. However, contrary to gRPC, PyTorch's RPC implementation understands tensor objects. If you are trying to hook together a PyTorch training algorithm with gRPC, the third-party library will expect JSON, a string, or another user-defined data type to handle the tensors. This will force you to take care of the serialization work that is already implemented and optimized in the PyTorch RPC library. While this can be and has been done success-fully, it introduces more work—and we all want to make our jobs easier, not harder, right?

Communication Topologies in PyTorch (c10d)

PyTorch supports two types of communication: collective communication and peer-to-peer (also known as point-to-point) communication. Both APIs enable defining and adjusting the topology. Under the hood, DDP uses collective communication, while RPC uses peer-to-peer communication. Both support synchronous and asynchronous operations.

> The peer-to-peer and collective communication APIs are imple-mented in the `torch.distributed.distributed_c10d` library in C ++, for performance reasons. Like the RPC APIs, these are low-level APIs you should know about if you're trying to troubleshoot existing applications or build your own distributed algorithm.

Collective communication in PyTorch

In computer science, *collective communication* is defined as any communication that involves a group of processes/machines. The most used operations are *broadcast, bar-rier synchronization, reduce, gather, scatter, all-to-all complete exchange*, and *scan*. PyTorch's c10d library provides various APIs for collective communication, including `all_reduce` and `all_gather`, as well as peer-to-peer communication APIs (discussed in the following section). It supports sending tensors across machines within a group, which is necessary because many algorithms require those kinds of operations. For example, `reduce` is critical; it reduces the target tensors in all processes to a single tensor and returns the result to all processes.

Figure 9-7 shows how the parameters are saved alongside their gradients (as discussed in "Distributed autograd" on page 210) and an all-reduce operation is used to exchange the information between the processes. Note how the parameters in each process are split into buckets, as described in the section on DDP. The all-reduce operation runs in the bucket index order to maintain the order of execution, which helps us avoid having inconsistent results across processes and machines.

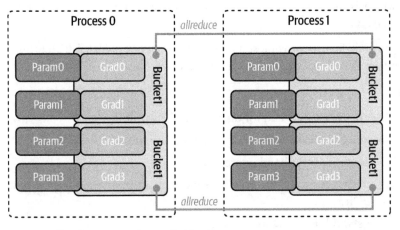

Figure 9-7. An all-reduce operation in PyTorch

The `all_reduce` function collects all the tensors and initiates an operation that reduces them into a single result tensor. After it's done, it returns the result to the individual processes/machines. In PyTorch, `all_reduce` is implemented to support tensors. Under the hood, it supports the use of all three built-in backend protocols (Gloo, MPI, and NCCL) for distributed CPU and/or GPU training. Note that not all backend protocols support all hardware processors, meaning that not all operations support CUDA.

The same goes for `all_gather`, though this is a more expensive function. An example of its use is for assessing the size of a tensor: the PyTorch engine will gather all the tensor sizes and define a default size based on the largest one. You can find multiple uses for this function in the c10d library.

How does collective communication impact our development? When we start writing a distributed application with PyTorch, our first task is to define the environment, spin up the workers, and start the processes. During the initialization process, we need to specify the backend communication protocol. This setup work for the cluster of machines should be done together with a sysadmin or using a coordination tool to avoid mistakes.

Collective communication works for all the processes in a group (a subset of the processes in the cluster). So we first need to start a group. This is how we do that:

```
dist.init_process_group(backend, init_method='tcp://10.0.0.20:23456',
                        world_size=4, rank=args.rank)
```

The first argument to `init_process_group` is the type of backend: one of `mpi`, `gloo`, or `nccl`. The other arguments are optional; they include `init_method`, which specifies how to start the process group (usually this is a URL to a script on a shared filesystem); `world_size`, which is the number of processes/machines in the group; and `rank`, which is the rank of the current process that is running (a number between 0 and `world_size` – 1).

PyTorch's contributors provide some guidance (*https://oreil.ly/EkdQ0*) around which backend we should use, depending on the hardware:

- Rule of thumb
  - Use the NCCL backend for distributed GPU training.
  - Use the Gloo backend for distributed CPU training.
- GPU hosts with InfiniBand interconnect
  - Use NCCL, since it's the only backend that currently supports InfiniBand and GPUDirect.
- GPU hosts with Ethernet interconnect
  - Use NCCL, since it currently provides the best distributed GPU training performance, especially for multiprocess single-node or multi-node distributed training. If you encounter any problem with NCCL, use Gloo as the fallback option. (Note that Gloo currently runs more slowly than NCCL for GPUs.)
- CPU hosts with InfiniBand interconnect
  - If your InfiniBand has enabled IP over IB, use Gloo, otherwise, use MPI instead.
- CPU hosts with Ethernet interconnect
  - Use Gloo, unless you have specific reasons to use MPI.

Take advantage of this guidance and consult with your sysadmin to determine the best backend to work with.

Once you've initialized the process group, you're ready to connect and start the cluster itself. From a main function, we can start an iterative process that goes over all the machines and initializes the process on each one. Let's take a look at the following template code (from the docs (*https://oreil.ly/l4Ia4*)) to better understand how to get started:

```
"""run.py:"""
#!/usr/bin/env python
import os
import torch
```

```
import torch.distributed as dist
import torch.multiprocessing as mp

def run(rank, size):
    """ Distributed function to be implemented later. """
    pass

def init_process(rank, size, fn, backend='gloo'):
    """ Initialize the distributed environment. """
    os.environ['MASTER_ADDR'] = '127.0.0.1'
    os.environ['MASTER_PORT'] = '29500'
    dist.init_process_group(backend, rank=rank, world_size=size)
    fn(rank, size)

if __name__ == "__main__":
    size = 2
    processes = []
    mp.set_start_method("spawn")
    for rank in range(size):
        p = mp.Process(target=init_process, args=(rank, size, run))
        p.start()
        processes.append(p)

    for p in processes:
        p.join()
```

As you can see here, there is a main function with a defined size, which is the number of machines/processes on the machines we want to initialize. The for loop in the main function iterates over the specified range of rank values, starting from 0 and finishing at rank – 1. Recall that rank here refers to the number of the machine we start the process on, which is also its ID in the system. Inside the loop, we call mp.Process, which returns a process instance named p, followed by p.start and processes.append(p). mp is the multiprocessing function available in PyTorch. During the iteration over all the machines, it starts processes on each of them, with the target function being init_process. This is a nonblocking operation that only defines the process itself. Later, the start function starts it. The script also saves these processes in an array, which we have access to for further computations and operations on the cluster.

Inside init_process, the script defines the environment and the group it is part of. The process is aware of the world size, its rank, and the backend it should use for communication. It also receives the run function (in the function signature, this is the fn argument). This function has the implementation of what this process needs to run.

Here's an example of the all-reduce run function from the docs:

```
""" All-Reduce example."""
def run(rank, size):
```

```
""" Simple collective communication. """
group = dist.new_group([0, 1])
tensor = torch.ones(1)
dist.all_reduce(tensor, op=dist.ReduceOp.SUM, group=group)
print('Rank ', rank, ' has data ', tensor[0])
```

This code creates a new group for the all-reduce distributed operation with a list of group members, [0,1]. This means that processes 0 and 1 are now part of the group that will run this operation. It also defines a tensor of size 1 with ones as values. This is a mock tensor for the purposes of the template; you would want to use the real tensor on which you want to run the reduce operation. Finally, it calls dist.all_reduce, passing it the tensor, the reduce operation to run (in the template's case, this is SUM), and the group that will take part in it. The following operations are available out of the box in PyTorch:

```
dist.ReduceOp.SUM
dist.ReduceOp.PRODUCT # stored API in the configuration
dist.ReduceOp.MAX
dist.ReduceOp.MIN
dist.ReduceOp.BAND # Bitwise AND
dist.ReduceOp.BOR  # Bitwise OR
dist.ReduceOp.BXOR # Bitwise XOR
```

PyTorch provides the following collective communication APIs:

scatter
Distributes the list of tensors at the root rank level (rank 0, by default) across all the ranks/processes in the group, as shown in Figure 9-8. In this example, before executing scatter, rank 0 has the list of tensors [t0, t1, t2, t3]; after executing this function, rank 0 has t0, rank 1 has t1, and so on.

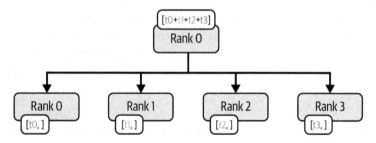

Figure 9-8. Scatter functionality

---

4 BAND, BOR, and BXOR are not supported with the NCCL backend.

5 Figures 9-8 through 9-13 are courtesy of the PyTorch documentation's contributors and can be found at *https://pytorch.org/tutorials/intermediate/dist_tuto.html*.

gather
   The opposite of scatter, this function collects the tensors from the group and
   stores them in rank 0. Rank 1 passes t1, rank 2 passes t2, and so on, as shown in
   Figure 9-9.

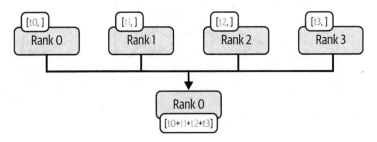

Figure 9-9. Gather functionality

reduce
   This function is similar to gather, but it appends the tensors, ending up with one
   tensor that represents the gathered tensors. In this case, rank 0 would end up
   with T=t0+t1+t2+t3, as shown in Figure 9-10.

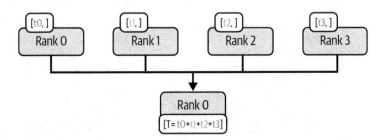

Figure 9-10. Reduce functionality

all_reduce
   With the all_reduce function, every process in the group shares its information
   with and collects information from the rest of the group, as shown in
   Figure 9-11. This is similar to reduce, but all machines take part in sending and
   receiving, and at the end of the process, all the machines will have the same tensor. As discussed before, this can lead to errors if there are any failures in communication over the network.

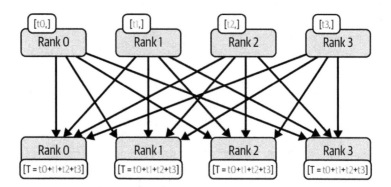

Figure 9-11. All-reduce functionality

all_gather

This is similar to `all_reduce`, only here the processes are all sending and receiving tensors to and from the rest of the group without operating on the received tensors. Instead, the received tensors are saved in an array, as shown in Figure 9-12. As the name suggests, all of the processes perform the gather functionality.

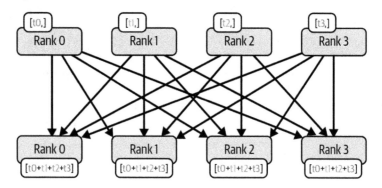

Figure 9-12. All-gather functionality

broadcast

The `broadcast` function duplicates a tensor across machines, as shown in Figure 9-13. This is useful when you have information that can fit into memory and should be utilized by all ranks.

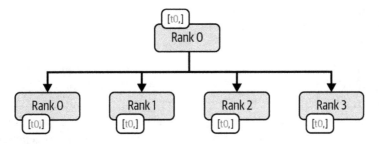

Figure 9-13. Broadcast functionality

Now that you have a better understanding of the collective communication APIs PyTorch provides, it's time to move on to the other communication type, peer-to-peer communication.

Peer-to-peer communication in PyTorch

PyTorch provides four APIs for peer-to-peer (P2P) communication, aka point-to-point communication. These include the send and recv functions mentioned in "Distributed autograd" on page 210, used for synchronous communication, as well as similar functions for sending and receiving tensor data asynchronously: isend and irecv.

We can use the same template code shown in the previous section to distribute the tensors and initialize the cluster; the only thing that changes is the run function. The following code snippet contains a simplified example of how to implement run using the P2P APIs available in torch.distributed:

```
def run(rank, size):
    tensor = torch.zeros(32)
    if rank == 0:
        tensor += 1
        # Send the tensor to process 1
        dist.send(tensor=tensor, dst=1)
    else:
        # Receive tensor from process 0
        dist.recv(tensor=tensor, src=0)
    print('Rank ', rank, ' has data ', tensor[0])
```

This is a classic example of blocking P2P communication. In the run function, we have a tensor of size 32 with zeros as values (this acts as a mock tensor). The if statement checks the rank of the current process. If it is rank 0, we update the tensor and send it to rank 1, as specified by the dst=1 argument to the send function.

If the rank is not 0, as defined by the else clause, the process receives the tensor using the dist.recv function. The print function is used here solely to provide information for debugging the process during troubleshooting. For a real-world application, it is best to leverage the Python logging mechanism; this allows you to categorize the log messages by severity (debug, info, error, etc.) and later search for issues by severity level.

To implement nonblocking (asynchronous) P2P communication, all we need to do is replace the dist.send and dist.recv functions in the definition of the run function with dist.isend and dist.irecv. With asynchronous communication, you will need to call wait on the request object that you received from the action to wait for the execution to finish before proceeding to the next one. If there is no dependent operation, you still have to call wait before the run function finishes.

Figure 9-14 demonstrates P2P communication, where rank 0 sends information to rank 3.

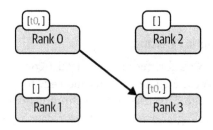

Figure 9-14. P2P communication between rank 0 and rank 3

The discussion of asynchronous and synchronous communication here probably reminds you of the RPC protocol, and for good reason: PyTorch's RPC framework is built on top of the P2P communication APIs, which act as enablers for the remote function. As discussed in "Remote execution" on page 204, this function runs a user function using a background thread on the specified worker process. Instead of returning data over the network, it returns a lightweight reference that acts as a pointer.

What Can We Do with PyTorch's Low-Level APIs?

Research, optimization, and troubleshooting! Working with low-level APIs of a distributed system often requires a profound understanding of the system itself, but they can be helpful, for instance, for troubleshooting high-level APIs in a real-world situation. Let's look at an example. In 2021, Chaoyang He et al. decided to build an automated elastic pipeline for distributing transformers as part of distributed training. They created the PipeTransformer (*https://oreil.ly/MEJfx*), shown in Figure 9-15. The pipeline is transformed according to the number of parameters in the training phase. Remember that in a neural network, the number of parameters can change in each network layer. So it might happen that at the beginning there are billions of parameters, and as the training evolves, so does the number of parameters. You can see that pipeline 0 uses more machines and cores at time step 0 than it does at time step 1.

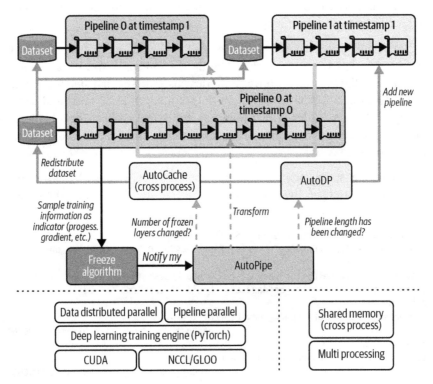

Figure 9-15. Overview of PipeTransformer training system diagram

Here, specifically, the researchers used the freeze algorithm, which can identify and freeze some layers gradually during training, which helps the number of parameters to converge and provides more control over the training. The freeze algorithm notifies the AutoPipe module about changes in the number of parameters, gradients, etc. In turn, the AutoPipe notifies the AutoDP about the pipeline length, notifies the AutoCache about the frozen layers, and also calls `transform` on the pipeline itself to execute it. PyTorch's low-level APIs, coupled with dedicated hardware and a high-level API, enabled the team to build this system and test their research.

Loading Data with PyTorch and Petastorm

In Chapter 7, we discussed bridging between working with Spark into PyTorch. As you know, for most of the data transformations required for machine learning workflows, the software is developed with the Spark framework and saved to Parquet files—but PyTorch doesn't provide an out-of-the-box data loader for the Parquet format, so if you need to use PyTorch APIs, you'll need to introduce dedicated tools to load this data. This book focuses on leveraging Uber's open source project, Petastorm, for this purpose, but you should keep an open mind about other tools and watch for new entries to the market.

As a data scientist, when loading data in PyTorch, you would typically use Data Loader together with the Dataset class. However, with Petastorm you can avoid them entirely and use the Petastorm converter library instead. The first step is to create the converter itself—this is what enables you to take a Spark DataFrame and convert it into a PyTorch data loader with converter_train.make_torch_dataloader. This function will generate the desired DataLoader so you can continue your work with PyTorch distributed APIs.

Let's take a look at some code to better understand the API. As with TensorFlow, the first thing to do is create the converter for the training dataset and the evaluation dataset:

```
# Set a cache directory on DBFS FUSE for intermediate data
spark.conf.set(SparkDatasetConverter.PARENT_CACHE_DIR_URL_CONF,tmp_path)

# TIP: Use a low value for parquet_row_group_bytes. The default of 32 MiB
# can be too high for larger datasets. Use 1 MB instead.
# train
converter_train = make_spark_converter(df_train,
                                        parquet_row_group_size_bytes=32000000)
# test
converter_test = make_spark_converter(df_test,
                                       parquet_row_group_size_bytes=32000000)
```

The make_spark_converter function is a generic function, so it's the same as the one we used for TensorFlow. Once the Petastorm converter is ready, we can leverage it to convert to the loading mechanism we want to use it with.

As you can see in the next code snippet, we make a PyTorch data loader using the converter_train.make_torch_dataloader function. We pass it a transform_spec_fn that details how to process the data. This function offers another opportunity to preprocess the data before training the model itself; for example resizing of the images can be done here:

```
with converter_train.make_torch_dataloader(
        transform_spec=transform_spec_fn) as loader:
    model = train(loader)

with converter_test.make_torch_dataloader(
        transform_spec=transform_spec_fn,num_epochs=1) as loader:
    accuracy = test(model, loader)
    return accuracy
```

The `make_torch_dataloader` function creates a `TorchDatasetContextManager` that manages the creation and termination of a Petastorm reader. Under the hood, the `TorchDatasetContextManager` is leveraging the `make_batch_reader` function to create the reader. You can provide the function with the `petastorm_reader_kwargs` argument, which Petastorm will transfer to `make_batch_reader`.

To summarize its behavior, it does two things:

1. Opens a Petastorm reader on the Parquet file directory URL using the `make_batch_reader` function

2. Creates a PyTorch `DataLoader` based on this reader

The `DataLoader` in Petastorm is a data loader adapter for `torch.utils.data.Data Loader`, which uses PyTorch's collation functionality to combine the data in the batches. By default, it uses `default_collate`, which checks what type of data the `Dataset` returns and tries to combine it.

The reader also enables you to *shuffle* the queue. This randomizes the batch data entirely by adding an instance from a different file to the queue at random on each iteration. If you wish to use this functionality, use the `shuffling_queue_capacity` parameter in the call to `make_torch_dataloader`, passing it the size of the queue you wish to have. Note that this parameter is set to 0 by default, and no shuffling is done in this state. Shuffling the queue is a great feature if your data is sorted, as with a sorted dataset, it's possible that the algorithm will develop a bias toward the first data it encounters (depending, of course, on the algorithm and the statistical behavior of the data).

The whole operation iterates and returns items from the reader in batches. It also promotes and sanitizes multiple Spark types into PyTorch-friendly types, as detailed in Table 9-1.

Table 9-1. Spark types promoted to PyTorch types

Spark types that need to be promoted	PyTorch types to which Petastorm promotes them
`int8`, `uint16`	`int32`
`uint32`	`int64`
`Boolean`	`uint8`
`timestamp`	`float32`, via Petastorm's `decimal.Decimal` type[a]

[a] Here there are two phases to the data type transformation: first the Spark `timestamp` values are converted to the Petastorm `decimal.Decimal` type, and then these values are converted to `float32`.

---

6 PyTorch's supported types are double, float, float16, float32, int64, int32, and uint8.

What are the limitations? Good question. NumPy strings, arrays of strings, object arrays, and object classes are not supported. What about None? PyTorch does not support nullable fields, which means that as part of the filtering process, we must filter out or provide a default value for any feature with a value of None.

When working with unsupported data types, most of the collisions result in the following exception: PyTorch does not support arrays of string or object classes. If you encounter this exception, note that the reason Petastorm cannot fill in the blanks here is because PyTorch itself would have not supported this data type either. So be mindful when designing the process to start with. To get around this, you'll need to change the design of your data or use a workaround. A decent option is to use transform_spec=transform_spec_fn to process the data, as discussed at the end of Chapter 8.

After we have the PyTorch DataLoader ready, the next step is to use it for training, validating, and testing.

 The DataLoader constructor accepts an argument for defining the number of workers to use to load the data. However, there is a problem in its implementation. Under the hood, Petastorm's PyTorch DataLoader implementation uses mp.spawn, which pickles the model and the parameters and saves it to disk. If there are any translation issues along the way, this will crash your program, so you'll need to avoid using this. It can also dramatically slow down the process and create a bottleneck.

Troubleshooting Guidance for Working with Petastorm and Distributed PyTorch

Various challenges can arise when working with multiple computation engines, due to mismatches and bugs like the ones mentioned in the previous section. We'll look at a few here, starting with mismatched data types.

The Enigma of Mismatched Data Types

Types are one of the great mysteries when working with data. Why does every platform decide to introduce and support its own types? I guess we'll never figure that one out!

Existential questions aside, if you remember, Table 2-1 in Chapter 2 showed how data types in Spark are mapped to data types in Python. Since Chapter 2, our data has gone through multiple iterations and formats. A moment's reflection on how the data flowed in our examples shows that the trip was fascinating, with many type changes along the way:

- File → Spark casting → Spark processing → Save to Parquet → Petastorm → PyTorch

It's a good practice for you and your team to keep track of the data versions and changes by using an auditing mechanism. Details on the file format and encoding (such as UTF-8, UTF-18, etc.) can be recorded, together with the library that produced and saved it. Tracking all of this information can provide you with everything you need for a holistic and systematic troubleshooting process.

As an example, there is a known challenge when working with a plain Python list (or any Spark array format, which is translated into a plain Python list in PySpark) and Petastorm. While writing can work with arrays, loading the data in PyTorch will often fail on schema mismatch. One workaround is to take the RDD approach and strip away the Spark DataFrame abstractions. Doing so enables you to make sure you are using data types that fit with Petastorm and later PyTorch.

The following code sample demonstrates forcing Petastorm to convert the data to a specific schema. If you remember from the discussion following Table 9-1, PyTorch does not support arrays of string or object classes. However, you will often need to work with arrays or lists. To get around this issue, you can translate the list/array to a supported type by providing a Unischema definition that takes an array as one of the data types and translates it to an np.array, which is later translated into a PyTorch tensor:

```
Schema = Unischema('Schema', [UnischemaField('id', np.string_, (1, None),
                                    NdarrayCodec(), False),])

def row_to_dict(schema, row):
    def type_check(k,v):
        if isinstance(v, list):
            return np.array([v], dtype=schema._fields[k].numpy_dtype)
        else:
            return v
    return {k:type_check(k,v) for (k,v) in row.asDict().items()}

def generate_dataset(output_url='{path_to_petastorm_data}/petastorm/'):

    with materialize_dataset(spark, output_url, Schema):
        rows_rdd = df.rdd.map(lambda x: row_to_dict(Schema, x))
                    .map(lambda x: dict_to_spark_row(Schema, x))
        spark.createDataFrame(rows_rdd, Schema.as_spark_schema())
                    .write
                    .mode('overwrite')
                    .parquet(output_url)

generate_dataset()
```

In this code, we first define the desired schema: a field named id of type Ndarray Codec. Next, we create a row_to_dict function that does type checks against the defined schema. If it is an instance of a list/array, it will confer to enforce the type and the NumPy value. It iterates over each one of the rows in the Spark DataFrame to make sure it conforms to the schema by calling the _fields[k].numpy_dtype operation.

We then define a generate_dataset function that strips away the Spark DataFrame by using df.rdd. This calls the internal RDD that is part of the DataFrame, and now we can easily execute RDD functionality on it, such as mapping. Notice that here there is a *two map function* approach: one map is used to enforce the type as necessary, and the other one (dict_to_spark_row) is a Petastorm function that is required by the Petastorm API.

Finally, we save the data to a dedicated Petastorm location.

After getting the data into the desired type and state, we can load it from the out put_url with the dedicated Petastorm converter that we defined earlier, in "Loading Data with PyTorch and Petastorm" on page 221. Now let's look at another problem you may need to troubleshoot when working with Petastorm and distributed PyTorch.

The Mystery of Straggling Workers

Straggling workers are workers that are running behind the rest of the cluster. They might have failed and relaunched, or there may have been a network issue that caused them to receive the data late, or some other problem that can arise in a distributed system may have slowed them down. Synchronized training accentuates the problem of straggling workers in a distributed system, as the data they produce becomes stale and irrelevant.

These processes can also create a bottleneck when adding more machines for distributed processing. If 25% of the machines in a system are straggling, as you scale up the number of machines, more and more of them will be affected. This might not seem like such a big deal if you have 4 machines, but if you scale up to have 32 or 128, it won't be a problem you can ignore, and it might require rethinking the structure of operations and communication. Of course, this problem is model-dependent, and it's hard to provide best practices for dealing with it. The best approach is to be vigilant and notice if there are any changes in how long it takes the training to finish when scaling horizontally. The trade-off is often in the model's accuracy—there is no optimal solution to get high-level accuracy using asynchronous communication. Therefore, it is best to keep this in mind and understand which outcome you want to prioritize: better accuracy during model building or faster convergence/training of the model?

How Does PyTorch Differ from TensorFlow?

Now that you have a better understanding of PyTorch and its distributed training mechanism, you're probably asking yourself this question: how does it differ from TensorFlow? We've discussed functionality and terminology already, but from a running and operation perspective, there are a few more things you should know about.

Table 9-2 breaks down the differences between TensorFlow and PyTorch in several key areas.

Table 9-2. PyTorch versus TensorFlow

	PyTorch	TensorFlow
Visualization and debugging	Has fewer tools for visualization and debugging, as it is a relative newcomer in the industry.	Has better tools for visualization for debugging, as it is a more mature tool in the industry.
Computation graph	Construction is dynamic, and it's updated during runtime. The graph consists of tensors, operations, and information required for backward propagation and is executed by the autograd engine. Supports imperative programming using inheritance, etc.	Construction is static. `tf.Graph` data structures contain a set of tensors and `tf.Operation` objects, which represent units of computation. Supports symbolic manipulation; good for algebraic expressions. Also supports imperative programming using inheritance, etc.
Programming limitations	Considered less generic.	Has lots of boilerplate code.
Language support for model loading	Loading models in languages other than Python is considered more complex.	Models can be loaded in other supported languages, such as Java and C++.
Supported deployment options	TorchScript—use a dedicated script and wrap the machine learning model according to the desired pattern (deployment patterns are discussed further in Chapter 10).	TensorFlow Serving (commonly used for small-scale applications), Flask web server, mobile (Android/iOS; the models themselves can be optimized to fit in the memory of a mobile or IoT device).

A general difference between TF and PyTorch's distributed machine learning capabilities is that PyTorch's approach is more specific and is intended to provide fine-grained control for practical machine learning experiments. Your choice of tools will ultimately come down to what your organization really needs and what it can afford. You need to consider what tools are already supported, how the machine learning lifecycle works with those tools, whether they can be replaced easily, etc.

To determine which framework to use to enrich your distributed machine learning capabilities, it is a good idea to examine and assess its ecosystem offerings. While it is a relative newcomer, PyTorch has a growing ecosystem (*https://oreil.ly/cxVeV*) with over 50 libraries and projects. Some are dedicated to specific domains, such as natural language processing or computer vision solutions, while others support the machine learning process itself (such as accelerators) or provide enhanced security and privacy (such as PySyft (*https://oreil.ly/c7Da7*)). For example, suppose you need to train a machine learning model while decoupling the training from private user data. A good place to start would be exploring what exists in each tool's ecosystem to enable this. This understanding will greatly facilitate the decision process. You can choose either to adopt an existing framework or to develop your own.

Summary

In this chapter, you learned about all the main components of distributed PyTorch and took a deep dive into its RPC framework. You also got a better understanding of how PyTorch differs from TensorFlow in its approach to distributed systems and machine learning flow. More often than not, you will need to take into consideration the waiting time aspect. Training a model with one GPU can take four days. If you want to turn that into an hour, you can leverage a machine with 64 GPUs—but what if you don't have access to such a machine, and you want to speed up the training process? Multinode training may be an option: 8 nodes with 8 GPUs each can support the 64 GPU requirement. This is where PyTorch's distributed optimization comes into play, as it provides much more flexibility in how things are distributed than Spark or TensorFlow.

Up to now, we have covered training machine learning models at scale and how to go about optimization and bridging from one framework to another. In the next and final chapter, you will learn about various topics relating to deploying your machine learning model and monitoring it in production, including knowing when to archive it.

## CHAPTER 10

Deployment Patterns for Machine Learning Models

Throughout this book, we've been discussing the machine learning lifecycle. As a quick reminder, at a high level, the lifecycle of a machine learning system is similar to the software development lifecycle. This means it includes multiple stages, which we can summarize as follows:

Development
: Training the model

Validation
: Validating the model

Staging
: Testing the model in a production-like environment

Deployment
: Putting the machine learning system into production

Archiving
: Retiring the model and, if necessary, replacing it with a new version

In the previous chapters, we've covered the first few stages of the lifecycle in depth, including various tools and methods for distributed training. In this final chapter, I will provide guidance on how to think through the deployment process and what considerations you should be aware of. Deployment takes place once you have a model that produces accurate results that you are content with and you're ready to serve it and put it into production. If this is not the case, it's best to continue exploring with additional algorithms and parameters, and perhaps fresh data.

When thinking about deploying a model, we need to define when and where it will be used in the overall production system workflow. It may be part of a bigger data flow, or it may be a standalone application exposing APIs for users to interact with. The model can also be wrapped and served as a UDF as part of a Spark flow (more on that later).

This chapter covers the following:

- Deployment patterns
- Monitoring tactics
- The production feedback loop
- Deploying with MLlib
- Deploying with MLflow
- Iterative development

Deployment Patterns

You have various options for deploying your machine learning models. We'll dig into some of them in this chapter, and I'll provide practical examples as well. Each pattern will require different code and components to keep the model performing well in production. So how do you know which one will work best for your use case?

When considering the best pattern for deploying your model, the focus should be on the business requirements. Will the model be used for batch processing or stream processing? Where will it be used? In the case of a high-level client application that runs locally on the user's machine, for example, the model will typically be loaded into memory so the user can interact with it directly. This is the case with IoT devices like smart cars, for example, where the model is likely deployed to the car to reduce communication and network overhead.

Another thing you will need to consider is whether the production environment differs from your development and testing environment. This is typically the case.

Let's look at a few of the deployment patterns that you might use, depending on your particular business requirements, to give you an idea of the things you will need to keep in mind when evaluating the options.

Pattern 1: Batch Prediction

When using batch prediction, you run the model on new data and cache the results in a database or some other persistent storage. This pattern is useful when you want to generate predictions for a set of observations all at once and the results are not latency-sensitive. It works well if you want to produce, say, one prediction per user per day, running the prediction offline and caching the results.

The pros of this method are straightforward. First, it is easy to implement with Spark: just load the model using the Spark API. Second, it scales easily to large amounts of data, and it's a tried and tested approach. It also provides results to the user quickly, since the predictions have already been made.

What are the cons of this method? For one, it can be harder to scale with complex inputs, which create a large amount of overhead for the batch prediction process as it will need to cover all permutations of the features. As a result, it might not be able to compute all the possible outputs in the time available.

A second issue is that users might get outdated or "stale" predictions—they may still be accurate, but they won't be the most up to date. For example, a movie recommendation system might fail to recommend the latest movies to a customer if they haven't been added to the movie options yet (say, if new movies are released every day but the batch prediction only runs every 48 hours). The model is unaware of the new movies, so it will recommend older ones.

Because it takes time to process and cache the new outputs of the model, it can also be hard to detect problems in the processing pipeline, such as the failure of a batch job. This can result in the model itself becoming stale and irrelevant. We will talk more about this issue in the section on monitoring.

Pattern 2: Model-in-Service

With this pattern, the model is packaged up with the client-facing application and deployed to a web server. As shown in Figure 10-1, the server loads the model and calls it to make predictions in real time, in response to API calls from the client. The model benefits from access to the database as needed.

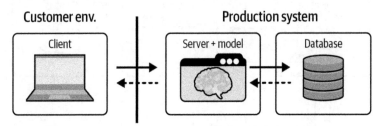

Figure 10-1. A production system with the model deployed to a server and the client interacting with it

While this approach is great for reusing existing production infrastructure, there are many potential problems and compromises you must consider. For example:

- The backend of the web server itself may be written in a different language, such as Java, while your model and libraries are written in Python.

- Having the application and model deployment coupled means they will need to share the same release schedule. Because the model will likely need to be updated much more frequently, managing this process can be challenging and place a burden on the rest of the engineering team.

- If you serve a large model, it may compete for resources with the other functions of the web server. This can slow down the server's response rate and overall throughput.

- Web server hardware is often not optimized for machine learning models. For example, a CPU works just fine for a web server, while a model might need a GPU to quickly process and return a prediction.

- Last, there is the issue of scale. How does your web server scale to answer more API requests? Does that fit with the model's scaling strategy? Conflicts here can limit the performance of the overall system.

Pattern 3: Model-as-a-Service

This is another real-time pattern, where you deploy the model itself as a service (aka a machine learning microservice) to avoid coupling with the backend server hardware and possibly conflicting scaling requirements. That means the list of cons from the last section will almost disappear. With this approach, the model component has its own deployment cycle, code, versions, scaling strategy, etc., and the model is hosted on its own separate server. The backend server interacts with the model by managing prediction requests, as shown in Figure 10-2.

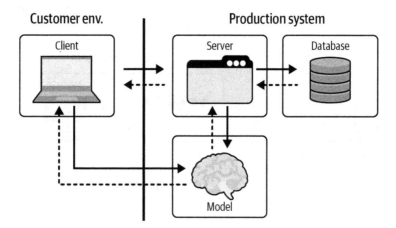

Figure 10-2. Production system with machine learning application and model deployed separately

---

There are great benefits to decoupling the system in this way, such as the following:

Dependability
Bugs in the model are less likely to crash the whole application.

Scalability
You can choose the optimal hardware for your machine learning application, without it being coupled to the scaling strategy for the model itself.

Flexibility
The model can be reused by multiple apps effortlessly; it's a standalone service that can be deployed in other constellations as well.

However, there are also drawbacks to this approach. Notably, the model-as-a-service pattern adds latency to every call since the information must travel across the network to the model service itself, and then the response needs to be sent back. Additionally, from a production infrastructure perspective, this approach adds the complexity of deploying a new service and managing the interactions with it. Finally, from a data science viewpoint, it means that you will need to monitor and manage your machine learning model service, and take responsibility for this component if things stop working.

Determining Which Pattern to Use

The three patterns we just discussed were each designed for different business requirements, which translate into different computing requirements, such as latency, throughput, request size, etc. All of these considerations factor into the decision of which deployment pattern is most suitable for the task at hand.

At a high level, we can distinguish between two types of approach: *real time* and *batch*, with the batch processing method having both the highest throughput and the highest latency (minutes to weeks, depending on the processing schedule), and the real-time methods having the lowest throughput and the lowest latency (milliseconds). The number of concurrent requests, the size of the requests, and the desired solution all impact the choice of which pattern to go with.

With real-time approaches, the exact requirements of the system may vary, permitting more or less tolerance with regard to latency. We can distinguish between three general categories with regard to the level of guarantees that are required about missing the deadline for delivering the results:

---

1 Because the predictions are made ahead of time, a batch processing model can handle a large number of requests quickly by leveraging a caching mechanism and other methods.

Hard

> Missing a deadline is an absolute system failure.

Firm

> It is tolerable to miss deadlines infrequently, but it may degrade the quality of service provided by the system. After the deadline, the result is no longer useful.

Soft

> After its deadline, a result becomes less valuable, degrading the system's quality.

Another categorization you may see, especially if you are working with a data engineer or come from a data engineering background, is *real time* versus *near real time*, where:

- Real-time solutions prioritize latency over throughput and generate results in a few milliseconds.

- Near real-time solutions require rapid inference/prediction, but the results can be delivered with a delay on the order of a hundred milliseconds to a minute. Spark's Structured Streaming engine, for example, operates on microbatches and processes data in near real time; we'll look at this when we discuss deploying with MLlib later in this chapter.

Unfortunately, these terms are not strictly correlated, and machine learning teams may use different terminology to express the same requirements. So it is best to always communicate in terms of latency and throughput when exchanging information within a team or across teams. Figure 10-3 shows the spectrum of latency requirements covered by the different approaches to processing.

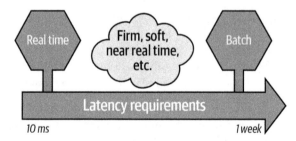

Figure 10-3. The great range of latency requirements of different types of machine learning applications

Production Software Requirements

The main goal of deploying a model is to make it accessible to users, programs, apps, or other models to interact with. However, there's a lot more to it than just putting your model out into the world. Regardless of the pattern you choose for deployment, you will need to establish a framework for the process. To help you with this, here are some of the questions that you should attempt to answer as you prepare to deploy your finished model, organized by topic:

Model application deployment

How will you roll out your machine learning application? How will you manage and update it once it's in production? What will you do in the event of a failure? As with software, you want to be able to turn the model into something that responds to requests. Hard requirements are often set around the deployment process (for example, rolling out gradually, rolling back instantly) and the monitoring process.

Model package deployment

How will you package up the model together with its runtime environment, preprocessing, and postprocessing? What is the deployment cycle, and how will you deal with versioning, archiving, etc.? Today, you can choose from multiple deployment frameworks and solutions—both TensorFlow and PyTorch provide their own deployment options, and there are many other possibilities, such as KFServing. This book won't discuss them further, but knowing they exist is important.

Dependency management

What are the immediate dependencies of the model itself? What does it need to run? What else do you need to run your service or software? The code, model weights, and dependencies all need to be part of the packaged deployment in order for the model to make predictions. But *dependencies cause trouble*. Dependencies in software are hard to maintain consistently; new versions often introduce changes that may break the APIs or logic used to package and build the model. To overcome this, software engineers use two main strategies:

- Limit the dependencies of serving the model
- Use containers to fully control the versions and the runtime environment (discussed next)

Two well-known container technologies are Docker and Linux. The containers hold the executable code and everything needed to run it, including the runtime, tools, libraries, and settings (collectively called an *image*). Various containers might be needed to satisfy all the requirements of a machine learning system: for example, you might have containers for a web server, database, and job queue as well as for the workers themselves.

Model runtime environment

Where and how is the model run? For example, the environment might require a Python installation; in this case, there's also a need for a Python-specific runtime for the model to operate. This is why managing dependencies and runtime environments with containers is a best practice.

REST APIs

REST APIs are commonly used to serve predictions in response to canonically formatted HTTP requests—how do they behave, and how do you design them? How will you package these APIs with your model? Again, the best option today is using containers. You'll also need to think about versioning for these APIs.

 There are alternatives to REST APIs, such as gRPC, that provide a similar experience for receiving and answering requests. There is no unanimous standard for serving machine learning models, so each implementation might be a bit different.

This list provides a starting point for thinking about packaging and deploying your model. Once you've established the framework for this, you'll need to consider the production environment and how you will optimize and scale the deployment. Here are some tips to help you better understand the relationships between these topics and what to look for when you reach the optimization and scaling stage:

Performance optimization

Performance is a critical part of every software solution. Machine learning specifically brings additional requirements and considerations. For example, *to GPU or not to GPU?* There are pros and cons to using GPUs to serve models in production systems. On the plus side, it can result in higher throughput, and this is likely the same hardware that you used to train the model. The drawbacks are that GPUs are more complex to set up and often more expensive than CPUs. Having a GPU run a couple of times for building the model is significantly less costly than having it constantly running in production.

Another aspect of optimization is *concurrency*. This means that we have multiple copies of the model running on different cores of the system, be they GPUs or CPUs. This approach supports a large volume of prediction requests, but it adds the complexity of working with software threads. Working with a pool of threads requires careful attention when tuning them to make predictions. If you need to serve billions of requests daily, it's critical to get this right. If you don't have any experience with threads and concurrency, it is best to consult an expert.

Model distillation/compression

This is related to the packaging of your model and the running environment. It's required when you need your model to have a smaller footprint. After training the model, you save it in a certain file format, at a certain size. This file requires information to be loaded into a machine's RAM and executed. If that information is too big to fit into your machine's memory, you will need to find some creative ways to compress it, or train a smaller model that imitates the larger one. This research domain is driven by deep learning, which tends to result in very large models. A technique you can try out is to train the model again with a smaller numerical representation of the features—for example, you might use int8 instead of float, acknowledging the trade-off in accuracy. This is called *quantization*. Both PyTorch and TensorFlow have quantization built in: the training process is aware of it, and it often results in higher accuracy.

Caching layer

Depending on the model, some inputs might be more common than others. For these cases, instead of calling the model for inference over and over again with the same data, you can build in a caching layer dedicated to storing the results. When a request comes in, you first search for the query in the cache, and then, if there is no previously saved answer, you pass it on to the model to process. The caching approach is very common when working with data and can be a useful approach for machine learning systems.

Horizontal scaling

At some point, all the optimization techniques you implement may prove to not be enough—you may need to serve more frequent API calls and achieve higher throughput. How do you go about it? When you have too much traffic for a single machine to handle, you may need to divide it among multiple machines. For that, you will have to spin up multiple copies of the model service and split the traffic using a load balancer. More often than not, you will leverage a container orchestration tool for this, such as Kubernetes with Docker.

Managed option

You may also want to consider a managed solution to deploy your model as a service without burdening your team with the responsibility for managing it. You may be able to run it as a serverless function on a cloud platform, where the application code and its dependencies are deployed into a container with a well-defined entry point function. The benefit of most cloud solutions here is that you only pay for the compute time. The challenges are the limited deployment package size, lack of access to GPUs, lack of state management for caching, and limited deployment tooling.

It's important to keep all of these topics in mind, as they will guide you in deciding on the best deployment option for your model.

---

2 *Quantization* is the mapping of input values in a large (often continuous) set to output values in a small (often finite) set. It supports producing a compressed model.

Monitoring Machine Learning Models in Production

Your job doesn't end with deploying the model, of course. There are so many things that can go wrong in production! To understand them better, consider the two phases of testing that are part of the machine learning lifecycle: testing the model during development (*validation*) and testing the model during staging, in a production-like environment.

What are the first suspects to look at when our model is not performing as expected? Here are a few examples of problems you may encounter when troubleshooting training before deployment to production:

- Validation loss is below target performance, which means the machine learning model you trained is not performing as well as expected on previously unseen data.
- Test loss is too similar to validation loss (that is, the results are "too good to be true").

Before moving your model from staging to production, be sure to take these actions:

- Verify that your model performs well on critical metrics with both the validation and test sets.
- Validate predictions qualitatively to make sure they make sense.
- Validate that the production model has the same performance characteristics as the development model.
- If you're updating or replacing an existing model, verify that the new model performs better than the previous one. You may want to run several comparison tests to assure confidence in the new model's improvements.

While following these recommendations should help ensure that you get off to a good start, there are, of course, many more things that can go wrong both in testing and after deployment.

It is well known that machine learning models tend to degrade after we deploy them, for various reasons. For example, changes may occur in our data or our business problem; we might encounter the "long tail" problem that occurs when there are many outliers in the data, or we may experience a complete domain shift. Let's take a closer look at some of the problems you may encounter after you deploy your model and how to deal with them.

Data Drift

Model degradation is mainly caused by *data drift*. This means that the data you're feeding to the online algorithm has changed in some way relative to the training data. This is usually statistically tested by comparing the distributions of the production data and the training data.

Modern data architectures enable dynamic changes in the data structure and schema. Data drift can occur any time the data structure, semantics, or infrastructure change unexpectedly. This behavior can break processes and corrupt data. Because data drift relates to changes in the data the application consumes, it can also occur because the full variety of the real-world data wasn't known or captured during training efforts. It can arise from bugs in the upstream data pipelines, too. To avoid this, we would want to look for changes in the data before it is ingested into the model in production—for example, we might suddenly see negative integer values, such as −1 or −5, when we know that integer values need to be positive.

Alternatively, it can also be that a change in the data was caused by a malicious act by one of the system's users, who decided to bombard it with artificial values to affect the balance of the data in the system. It is important to monitor the distribution of our data and its accuracy in order to guard against such attacks. In most cases, you will want to bring in a domain expert for this.

Changes in the distribution of the data can occur naturally as well. Suppose that we add new users with different demographics. Our machine learning model is not aware of the specific characteristics of these users, so to make accurate predictions for them, we will need to retrain the model with training data that reflects these demographics. Data can also be affected by large-scale events, like the global pandemic and financial changes. Depending on the business problem at hand, you may need to give some thought to how to better organize your model's features to cope with such unforeseen events. Again, this typically requires the involvement of a domain expert.

Changes in the model's input data can occur quickly or gradually, over a long period, and they can be permanent or temporary. From a time perspective, we can distinguish between the following categories of data drift:

Instantaneous drift
> With this type of drift, there is an immediate change in the data distribution that is detectable, as shown in Figure 10-4. An example of when this might occur is when deploying a model in a new domain—like deploying a self-driving car in a new city. It can also happen because of bugs in the preprocessing pipeline or major events like a pandemic.

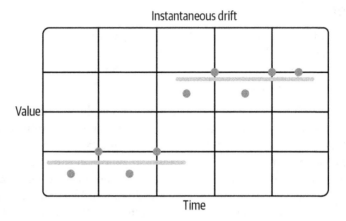

Figure 10-4. Instantaneous data drift

Gradual drift

The values of the features may also change slowly over time, as shown in Figure 10-5. With gradual drift, there is no immediate change in the data distribution that is detectable. For example, user preferences might change as a result of the user population growing older or due to changes in the surrounding culture.

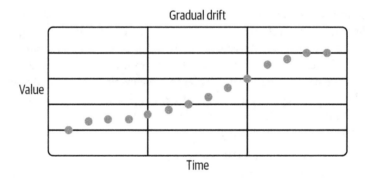

Figure 10-5. Gradual data drift

Periodic drift

This type of drift is less straightforward. As shown in Figure 10-6, changes in the data happen periodically over time, perhaps during the course of a day or even a year. This kind of change may look similar to a directional drift, but after some time there is a correction, and the values go back to what they were before the drift. The changes tend to be cyclical, based on changes in the seasons or during holiday periods, or daytime versus nighttime usage, or when you have users in different time zones.

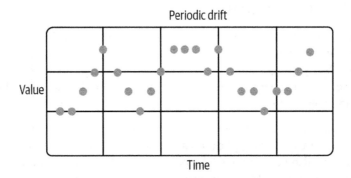

Figure 10-6. Periodic data drift

Temporary drift

Temporary drift is often the most difficult kind to detect. Various events might cause a significant change in the distribution of the data, such as a malicious user attacking the model, or a Black Friday sale, or a new user using the system in an unexpected way that the model wasn't trained to handle. This churn in our data manifests as a temporary drift, as shown in Figure 10-7. Because the distribution of the data returns to normal after some (usually short) period of time, it can be easy to miss this kind of issue.

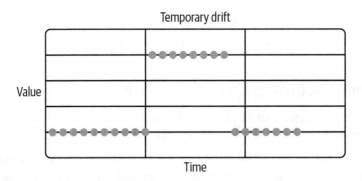

Figure 10-7. Temporary data drift

Detecting all the different ways that data drift can manifest itself revolves around identifying changes in the values of features over time. This is a real-world machine learning problem that is known to have a massive impact in practice. New users receiving stale recommendations, perhaps because of a bug in the retraining pipeline, can lead to large amounts of user churn and potential revenue loss for the organization.

Model Drift, Concept Drift

There are scenarios where our whole model has to change. Changes in real-world environments often result in *model drift*, which diminishes the predictive power of the model. Many things may cause this, ranging from changes in the digital environment (leading to changes in relationships between model variables) to changes in user demographics or behaviors.

Let's say we are tracking user behavior for an online taxi booking service. We've built a model based on use of the application at different times of the day, depending on factors such as availability of public transport and number of cars on the road. However, due to the pandemic, public transportation lines have shut down and people are not commuting to the office anymore. User behavior has changed due to real-world circumstances, so the application concept and the model are not relevant anymore. We'll need to retrain and adjust the model to fit the new realities and keep recalibrating as user preferences continue to evolve. These conditions might also impact the business model as a whole, which will require updates to the system and the model as well.

Another example is a movie recommendation system. Suppose we've built one dedicated to our users, and a new genre that users weren't watching at all when we created the system suddenly becomes popular (say, silent films). The system doesn't cover this genre, but because user preferences have changed, we need to retrain our model to include data on this category.

Detection of model drift is known to be a hard problem and often requires human interaction. It's important to work with users, customers, product managers, and data analysts to better understand the changes that may affect the usefulness of the model.

Distributional Domain Shift (the Long Tail)

It goes without saying that this type of shift is often the hardest to detect. It is also an important one that many organizations aren't aware of.

Domain shift refers to a difference between the distribution in the training dataset and the data the model encounters when deployed—that is, the distribution of the data in production. This can occur because of the approximation functions that machine learning algorithms use, combined with training a model on data sampled from the underlying distribution. There may be artifacts that were introduced by the sampling process, as well as artifacts that were completely missed due to the data distribution having a long tail. This matters when outliers are significant for the model and the business goal. Another way to look at it is to acknowledge that the sampling data may not represent all the parts of the distribution that we care about.

Domain shifts often occur in practical applications of artificial intelligence, and machine learning algorithms often have difficulty adapting to them. A domain shift can happen because of bugs in the training data pipeline or bias in the sampling process. This can happen when certain groups are underrepresented in the training data or when the distribution of the training data does not accurately represent real-world data anymore.

For example, suppose we are building a banking system for predicting loan default, where one of the features is gender. If we train the model using old or insufficient data, that data may be biased toward a specific gender. In real life, our model will need to handle a greater variety of data due to societal changes, and the mismatch between the training data and the production data can result in incorrect outcomes.

To avoid these problems, we need to watch for differences between the training distribution and the production data distribution.

What Metrics Should I Monitor in Production?

Now that you understand the various potential changes that can occur in the data, model, and distribution in production, we can discuss what metrics to monitor to detect these changes.

At a high level, any machine learning system we build has four characteristics that will drive decisions about what to monitor and measure:

Model metrics
> These include accuracy, robustness, and performance. Measuring these metrics is typically harder in production systems than during training, as often we don't have access to all of the required data.

Business metrics
> These show the impact of the machine learning system on the business. For example, for a recommendation system, we would monitor various metrics related to user churn and user engagement: how many people are using the system, how frequently, and for how long in each interaction. We can even split the user base into multiple user groups and run A/B testing of different models in production. Monitoring business metrics is often fairly straightforward, as many organizations already have a business intelligence (BI) or analytics team that measures them. However, there may be conflicting or hidden factors that affect these metrics, so it's best to combine these with other measures.

Model predictions versus actual behavior
> These metrics show how well the model's predictions correlate with actual user or system behavior. Measuring them typically requires some creativity and tailor-made solutions, as it involves capturing real behaviors rather than predicted ones. Often, we will want to create a separate data pipeline to capture and save actual behavior into a dataset. This will tell us how well the model is doing beyond the model metrics that we measure.

Hardware/networking metrics

These show how the system is performing at the hardware/network level. Examples include CPU/GPU utilization, average latency of requests, server response time, server downtime, etc. Keeping track of these metrics is crucial, as it gives us a detailed picture of the impact of the underlying hardware on the system. They are relatively easy to measure since most production systems already have the necessary tools in place, and there are various commercial solutions available for this purpose.

How Do I Measure Changes Using My Monitoring System?

There are multiple strategies for measuring changes in a machine learning system. However, the main approach is similar. We want to be able to detect changes over time, so to begin with, we need a reference to use as a point of comparison.

Define a reference

To build a reference, we look at different time windows of data that we consider good. This will provide us with data points to compare against. Within those time windows, we look for changes in the data and its distribution. As discussed in Chapters 4, 5, and 6, Spark provides us with tools to gather statistics about our data. This is a good place to take advantage of those, to establish a baseline so you can monitor for changes that might indicate drift.

At this point you're probably thinking, "That all sounds great, but how do I pick a reference window?" One option is to start with a fixed window of production data you believe to be healthy—an hour, a day, or whatever makes sense for your business problem. Gather your metrics, and start iterating. Some systems will leverage the sliding window approach, where the time window advances linearly and each (possibly overlapping) segment is compared to the previous one. For example, if I have an array of [1,2,3], a sliding window of size two will yield the following list of arrays: [[1,2], [2,3]]. While this is a great technique for search, it can generate high compute costs and is not very efficient for our current purposes. Consider a timeline of 5 hours with a sliding window of 1 hour and a size of two. You will end up calculating the metrics over four windows of time: [[1,2], [2,3], [3,4], [4,5]].

A better solution—and an industry best practice—is to use the training or validation data and metrics as a reference. This is a more cost-efficient and straightforward practice that is simpler to implement.

Measure the reference against fresh metrics values

After defining a reference and computing the metrics, the next step is choosing a window to measure against the reference. This is very much problem-dependent; it correlates directly to the business goals and is determined by how frequently you want to monitor the machine learning system and potentially replace or retrain it as needed. You might want to monitor your data over a period of an hour, a day, or a month.

To be more pragmatic, choose several window sizes with a reasonable amount of data and compare them. For example, have 1-hour, 12-hour, and 1-day window sizes and slide them over the recent data to monitor the system's behavior. Be aware that depending on the window size, you might miss detecting some outliers. You might want to monitor different window sizes to measure different aspects.

Algorithms to use for measuring

In statistics, you will find multiple algorithms for measuring the difference between two datasets. The classic and best-known ones are the distance metrics. As a data scientist, you might be familiar with these algorithms:

Rule-base distance metrics
> These measure how far the data is from the reference, given a set of rules. They're great for determining the quality of the data. We can compare minimum, maximum, and mean values and check that they are within the acceptable/allowable range. We can also check the number of data points to confirm data isn't missing or being dropped (for example, due to bad preprocessing), check for the presence of null values, and monitor for data drift.

D1 distance
> This is a classic distance metric that calculates the sum of the distances between the fixed data values. It's easy to interpret and simplifies monitoring in general.

Kolmogorov–Smirnov statistic
> This finds the distance between the empirical and cumulative distribution functions. It's a commonly used metric that is relatively easy to interpret and plot on a chart.

Kullback–Leibler divergence
> This measures the difference between two probability distributions over the same variable x. It's a statistical log-based equation that is sensitive to the tails of the distribution. It detects outliers but is a bit difficult to comprehend and interpret. This metric can be useful when you're fully informed about how to use it, but it won't provide much insight in most cases.

There are plenty of others too, but this list is enough to get you started.

What It Looks Like in Production

To monitor drift, the simple tools that already exist in the production system should work. Often, you will need to design a data pipeline with dedicated logic for each of the types of drift you would like to measure. For example, as shown in Figure 10-8, you might develop two data pipelines, each of which returns a metric that signals the presence or absence of drift. The one at the top compares recent data to the reference data, as described earlier. It can be used to detect data drift. The one at the bottom detects drift in the model itself, by comparing the model's predictions with the actual outcomes/results of the system. This will tell us if it's time to retrain the machine learning model. This can be an automated process or one that the team executes manually, following a system alert. This approach is also called the *production feedback loop*; we'll dig into this in more detail in the next section.

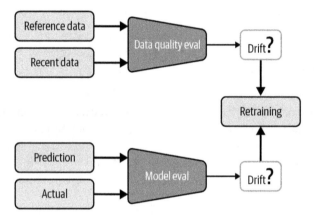

Figure 10-8. Monitoring drift

It's important to keep in mind, of course, that the model you develop will have its own sensitivities, and there is no one-size-fits-all solution.

The Production Feedback Loop

In production, a feedback loop is when the system saves the outputs of the model and the corresponding end user actions as observed data and uses this data to retrain and improve the model over time. The predictions/recommendations themselves are compared against the user's or system's behavior and provide feedback on the model's performance. A well-known case study is Yupeng Fu and Chinmay Soman's "Real-time Data Infrastructure at Uber" (*https://oreil.ly/srOdn*), which lays out how Uber uses real-time production data to improve its machine learning system by implementing two pipelines:

- A pipeline that embeds the machine learning model and is used to predict ride cost
- A pipeline that captures the real outcome

Uber uses this approach to monitor performance over time. The consumers of the real-time data infrastructure, as described in the article, include the system responsible for automated dynamic pricing of rides, dashboards, alerts, analytical apps, and more. As you can see, the machine learning system is only part of the larger story. However, the system does take this information into consideration and updates the features in real time for the next round of predictions. The data feedback loop is a critical system component, as it feeds information back into the production system and triggers alerts.

Bear in mind that while this approach works wonderfully for Uber's use case, it may not be applicable in other organizations. Designing a feedback loop that is based on real outcomes will require you to think outside the box to understand how it can be integrated with the larger system and what it makes sense to measure.

Now that you have a better understanding of the theory—deployment patterns, monitoring, feedback loops, and more—it's time to get more practical with some hands-on examples.

Deploying with MLlib

Chapter 6 covered how to leverage Spark's machine learning library, MLlib. You learned about its various capabilities, including training, evaluating, and tuning your model; building a pipeline; and saving the model to disk so it's ready for deployment.

MLlib's model format is a dedicated format that holds metadata as well as the actual data of the model. The metadata can comprise different elements, depending on the machine learning algorithm.

For example, when working with MLlib's RandomForestClassifier, the data will include information about the weights, number of partitions, etc., for each tree in the random forest (identified by a treeID parameter). The metadata, on the other hand, will hold information about the model's creation, such as:

```
("timestamp" -> System.currentTimeMillis())
("sparkVersion" -> sc.version)
("uid" -> uid)
("paramMap" -> jsonParams)
("defaultParamMap" -> jsonDefaultParams)
```

And the model itself:

```
"numFeatures"
"numClasses"
"numTrees"
```

This information helps you load the model in a different environment. This is helpful for deployment, since we can wrap the MLlib load function with the rest of the application logic as part of the Spark workflow. The data to be loaded and processed can come in two shapes: batch or streaming. In the next section, we'll walk through an example of building a pipeline for deploying a model with streaming data.

 Don't forget to use the exact class that you used to save (and often train) the model to load it afterward. Otherwise, with the highly coupled MLlib format, it simply won't work.

Production Machine Learning Pipelines with Structured Streaming

Before we dive right in, a quick reminder: with Structured Streaming, the schema of the data does not change as it's read in. This simplifies our work, as schema detection takes place earlier, well before the stream of data gets to the model.

To set up the pipeline, you'll need to provide the following items:

Schema
> The specification of the columns in the stream data.

Stream reader
> The specification of the source of the streaming data. For testing, this can also be a static dataset.

Machine learning model
> The model you wish to train.

The following code snippet demonstrates:

```
schema = StructType([ StructField('id', IntegerType(), True),
                        StructField(....) ]

streaming_data = spark.readStream.schema(schema)
                                .option("maxFilesPerTrigger", 1)
                                .parquet(some_path)

streaming_prediction = pipelinesModel.transform(streaming_data)
                                    .groupBy('label') \
                                    .agg(some_aggregations)

# do something with the streaming prediction data
```

The streaming predictions can be used for aggregation, decision making, automation, or whatever business task the machine learning model was designed for.

Let's assume this model was designed to predict click rates. It captures user impressions of a website and tries to predict if a user will click on a specific link. For this particular use case, we can capture the user's actual behavior—whether they clicked or not—to compare the predicted versus actual results. Since it is feasible to save the data and process it as a batch, it's up to us to decide whether to go with a batch or streaming approach.

Using streaming data is always a more complicated solution. However, for a website that runs A/B testing and needs to be updated on the fly, this might yield better results.

With a streaming solution, it is possible to capture both clicks and predictions using two data streams and run a *stream–stream join*. This functionality, added in Spark 2.3, allows us to join two streaming DataFrames. The downside of this approach is that the table's view will always be incomplete for both sides of the join, which might make matches harder.

Stream–stream joins are considered hard to do in an efficient manner in the world of data processing, as they often require shuffling the data over the network during real-time processing. Imagine you have an endless stream of data coming into the system and you need to do a join with another endless stream of data. How do you ensure the streams align correctly? To solve this problem, you can think of it as performing a series of microbatch joins. Because the data may arrive out of order, when performing a stream–stream join with Spark, you should make sure to define the watermark delay (the maximum delay between event time and processing time). This lets the engine know how late data can be and when it's safe to process each microbatch—that is, it defines the time range to wait until the shuffling and join operations can start processing a given microbatch. It can be capped by a timestamp or microbatch size (i.e., the number of rows in the batch).

To read about how to work with the Structured Streaming and batch APIs, stream-stream joins, and more, visit the Spark docs (*https://oreil.ly/_MdEz*).

Deploying with MLflow

We discussed MLflow in Chapter 3. As a reminder, MLflow is a platform for managing the machine learning lifecycle that enables logging and inspecting the results of your machine learning experiments. It has components for tracking the experiments, packaging up the project code, and packaging and deploying models, as well as a model registry.

MLflow provides two different deployment options:

- As a microservice
- As a UDF in a Spark flow

Deploying a machine learning model with MLflow requires you to create an MLflow wrapper. We'll look at that next, then dive into the two deployment options.

Defining an MLflow Wrapper

An MLflow wrapper—an instance of `mlflow.pyfunc.PyFuncModel`—wraps the model and its metadata (the *MLmodel* file), making it easy to ship them together. Here is a reminder of the structure of the model directory created by MLflow:

```
--- 58dc6db17fb5471a9a46d87506da983f
------- artifacts
----------- model
----------- MLmodel
------------- conda.yaml
------------- input_example.json
------------- model.pkl
------- meta.yaml
------- metrics
----------- training_score
------- params
----------- A
------------- ...
------- tags
----------- mlflow.source.type
----------- mlflow.user
```

Because this machine learning model was created in an Anaconda environment, the *MLmodel* folder holds the *conda.yaml* file alongside the *model.pkl* file.

The wrapper itself is a class that we save together with the model, which lets the program that loads the model afterwards know how to load it and use it for prediction. To connect training, deploying, and using the model, you have to define the wrapper class and log it with MLflow's `log_model` function before saving the model. The following code snippet shows how:

```
model_path = "..../mlruns/{experiment_id}/{run_id}/artifacts/models"
wrappedModel = {some_class}(model_path)
mlflow.pyfunc.log_model("pyfunc_model_v2", python_model=wrappedModel)
```

Notice that you need to provide the `model_path` itself, including the `experiment_id` and `run_id`, when you create an instance of your class, then log the model and the wrapper instance together. This provides the connecting tissue between the two.

Let's break it down a bit further. Your wrapper class needs to implement Python Model. This enables you to create MLflow models with the `python_function` (pyfunc) model flavor, which can leverage custom inference logic and artifact dependencies that MLflow manages for you. The interface has three functions: `__init__`, `load_context`, and `predict`. To take advantage of it, your microservice must implement the `predict` function; however, it can override the first two functions as necessary. Let's take a look at what each of them does:

`__init__`

This is a Python private function responsible for setting global parameters. It is called "init" because it performs the required initialization of the service to be used later. This is the first function that MLflow calls when you call the load_model function, used to load a model stored in pyfunc format. It takes as input a PythonModelContext containing artifacts that can be used for making predictions, which MLflow manages for you behind the scenes. The PythonModel Context is available later as well, but for efficiency, it is best to load the context and artifacts into memory as a global parameter that is part of the service you are implementing.

`load_context`

This function is responsible for loading artifacts from the PythonModelContext. MLflow calls it as soon as the PythonModel is constructed when loading a model with load_model.

`predict`

MLflow invokes this function to get a prediction from the model. It takes a PythonModelContext instance and a pyfunc-compatible input to evaluate and returns a pyfunc-compatible output. Be aware that the model may take a long time to return a result; you should be prepared for this, and you may want to handle errors here too. You should also keep logs for alerting and for auditing purposes in the future.

Let's examine some sample code for a model built with TensorFlow. For this exercise, our class is called KerasCNNModelWrapper. It wraps a KerasCNN TensorFlow model that has been trained and tested by our data scientists.

First, we need to ensure we save the model_path parameter to memory:

```
def __init__(self, model_path):
    self.model_path = model_path
```

Note that we aren't required to implement __init__, but for the sake of the exercise, we will implement all of the functions.

Next, let's implement the load_context function. Here, we'll load the model from a Keras-native representation and save it to memory:

```
def load_context(self, context):
    log(self.model_path)
    self.model = mlflow.keras.load_model(model_uri=self.model_path)
```

Loading the model using `mlflow.keras.load_model` is possible only if you've trained and saved the model using MLflow. The `load_model` function takes care of loading artifacts for prediction and everything that we need to run the model in its desired environment.

Finally, we'll implement `predict`. As mentioned previously, you must implement this function every time you use MLflow. The `predict` function is responsible for enriching the input data and preprocessing it to fit the model's expected format, as discussed in Chapter 4. Since in this exercise we're classifying images, preprocessing the data involves resizing and reshaping the images to fit the model's expected dimensions. The input is a pandas DataFrame, which can be of size 1 to N. `class_def` is a Python dictionary of the classification options we have for the model. Our model classifies images according to what appears in the image: a teapot, tweezers, spaghetti, or a yo-yo. The `for` loop iterates over all the input, preprocesses the data, and runs the `predict` function itself, which provides a probability for each of the class options.

The function implementation is provided in the following code sample:

```
def predict(self, context, model_input):
    import tensorflow as tf
    import json

    class_def = {
        0: '212.teapot',
        1: '234.tweezer',
        2: '196.spaghetti',
        3: '249.yo-yo',
    }

    rtn_df = model_input.iloc[:,0:1]
    rtn_df['prediction'] = None
    rtn_df['probabilities'] = None

    for index, row in model_input.iterrows():
        # resize and reshape the image
        image = np.round(np.array(Image.open(row['origin']).resize((224,224)),
                                  dtype=np.float32))
        img = tf.reshape(image, shape=[-1, 224, 224, 3])

        # predict
        class_probs = self.model.predict(img)

        # take the class with the highest probability
        classes = np.argmax(class_probs, axis=1)
        class_prob_dict = dict()

        # calculate probability for each class option:
        for key, val in class_def.items():
```

```
            class_prob_dict[val] = np.round(np.float(class_probs[0][int(key)]),
                                            3).tolist()

    rtn_df.loc[index,'prediction'] = classes[0]
    rtn_df.loc[index,'probabilities'] = json.dumps(class_prob_dict)

    return rtn_df[['prediction', 'probabilities']].values.tolist()
```

In the end, the function returns a Python list containing the prediction for each input together with a JSON object representing the probabilities for all of the classes as a dictionary.

To connect everything together, we have to define the wrapper class and log the model (as shown in the code snippet earlier in this section) before saving it. Here's how we do this for this model:

```
model_path = ".../mlruns/{experiment_id}/{run_id}/artifacts/models"
wrappedModel = KerasCNNModelWrapper(model_path)
mlflow.pyfunc.log_model("pyfunc_model_v2", python_model=wrappedModel)
```

Deploying the Model as a Microservice

In this section, we'll explore how to implement the Model-as-a-Service pattern discussed at the beginning of this chapter. MLflow provides a generic class called `mlflow.deployments.BaseDeploymentClient` that exposes APIs that enable deployment to custom serving tools. All you need to do is wrap your function with a microservice that serves the function through an API of your choice. APIs define how computer programs communicate with each other. Here we are entering the world of managing and versioning APIs.

To simplify things, as discussed in the previous section, MLflow developed a base class named `PythonModel` that represents a generic Python model that evaluates inputs and produces API-compatible outputs. All you need to do is leverage this class and the model that you've already logged using the wrapper class and the artifact path and load it again. You provide the `load_model` function with the `model_path` itself, specifying the correct `experiment_id` and `run_id`:

```
model_path = ".../mlruns/{experiment_id}/{run_id}/artifacts/models"
model = mlflow.pyfunc.load_model(model_path)
model.predict(model_input)
```

There are many ways to run a server; I won't explore that topic in this book since it depends on your cloud provider, production environment, risk assessment, skill set, and more.

Loading the Model as a Spark UDF

As discussed previously, MLflow enables us to train and load a model and manage the artifacts in production. In the previous section, you learned how to load a model as a standalone service. In this section, you will see how to load a model as a Spark UDF, following the Batch Prediction and Model-in-Service patterns from earlier in this chapter.

From a coding perspective, ingesting data into Spark in a stream or in a batch comes down to how we load the DataFrame. For batch data, we use the read function, and for streaming data, we use readStream. A Spark application that uses readStream will potentially never finish. It will listen to a specific channel and will keep pulling new data from it. A batch job, in contrast, has a start and end time; the job finishes at some point and is shut down.

So how do you turn your model into a UDF with MLflow? This is straightforward, using the spark_udf function that MLflow provides out of the box:

```
# Load model as a Spark UDF
loaded_model = mlflow.pyfunc.spark_udf(spark, mlflow_model_path,
                             result_type=ArrayType(StringType()))
```

To combine the UDF with the Spark DataFrame you are working with, all you need to do is call loaded_model:

```
# Predict on a Spark DataFrame
scored_df = (images_df
             .withColumn('origin', col("content"))
             .withColumn('my_predictions', loaded_model(struct("origin")))
             .drop("origin"))
```

This creates a new Spark DataFrame called images_df with two new columns: the first, origin, contains the original content of the images, and the second, my_predic tions, contains the model's predictions. We specify struct("origin") to ensure the data in this column is of the type that pyfunc is looking for in the input. That's it. Later, scored_df can be used downstream to check the predictions themselves or take actions based on them. We drop the origin field at the end since there is no need for it in the new scored_df; this reduces the memory footprint.

How to Develop Your System Iteratively

As you most likely understand by now, you'll want to trigger a new deployment any time a new model is available that is more suitable for your needs or is superior in some way to the current model running in production.

So how do you know when to replace an existing model? There are multiple ways to go about it. The most common one is setting thresholds on test values. Let's say we aim for 80% accuracy on cost prediction for housing properties. Comparing the actual data to our predictions, we determine that our model is performing at a 75% accuracy rate. Should we take action? Probably, as this is below our target accuracy threshold.

Can we produce a better model? This is a tricky question to answer. How do we know for sure that a new model is going to perform better than the existing model? We don't. So we need to be able to track and monitor its performance and revert to the previous version if necessary.

Of course, replacing the model is not the only possible solution. There are multiple actions we can take when we determine that a model is underperforming, including debugging the production system itself. The action you choose to take will depend on your business goals.

This section presents a strategy that you can apply to get the production system up and running from scratch, and to develop it iteratively (in phases) afterward. This framework, known as the Crawl, Walk, Run, Fly approach, can also enable you to better evaluate your work and the expectations of the team you are working with, as well as the state of your production system.

At the beginning, you will *Crawl*—deployment operations will be manual, and you will evaluate and check everything together with your team every time you make a change or an error occurs.

As you gain more knowledge about the system and its requirements, you will move to the *Walk* stage. At this point, you will add automated testing and other automations to your system. The goal here is to develop more confidence and start progressing toward a potentially fully automated system.

Once you are happy with the manual deployment and automated testing procedures, you will start creating scripts to connect the two. This is when you enter the *Run* stage. You'll add more testing for your model in production, fine-tune the alerts, capture any changes in the data flowing into your machine learning model, and monitor throughput and results.

Finally, you will reach the *Fly* stage, where you will have such high confidence in your system, code, scripts, and testing that you will be able to connect the feedback loop of alerts and capturing data drift and changes in production together with triggering a new training process. The Fly state is the holy grail for many teams building and using machine learning systems. However, it is important to take it one step at a time, making sure to stay agile. You have to Crawl before you can Walk or Run, starting out by putting the model into production and monitoring its behavior manually, but eventually you will Fly: your system will be running comfortably on autopilot, and you will only need to fix bugs and introduce new features. At this point, you will be fully connected to the deployment system in your organization.

Summary

In this final chapter, we've looked at the last part of the machine learning lifecycle: deployment, monitoring, and retirement of existing models. Throughout the book, you've learned about various strategies involved in the machine learning workflow, from ingesting data into the system, to cleaning and organizing it, to extracting features, to building models and iterating on them by leveraging Spark together with PyTorch and TensorFlow. This book also discussed in depth some of the issues you may encounter while building machine learning systems. While there is still more to cover in the ever-evolving machine learning world, such as securing systems, feature stores, more sophisticated caching techniques, observability, and more, I hope this book has achieved its main goal of helping you to develop a better understanding of the Spark ecosystem, as well as how it can be integrated with other frameworks and leveraged for distributed training purposes.

Index

R

RandomForest, 16
RandomForestClassifier, 16, 118, 122, 124, 247
RankingEvaluator, 133
RankingMetrics, 133
RAPIDS Accelerator, 160
RAPIDS libraries, 22
rasterization, 63
raw feature, 92
RDDs (resilient distributed datasets), 34, 37, 38, 158, 159
Read–Eval–Print Loop (REPL), 41
real-time deployment approaches, 231-234
receiver operating characteristic (ROC) curve, 132
recommendation systems, 67, 126
reduce function, 217
reduce operations
    all-reduce, 176, 178-180, 213, 215, 217
    MapReduce, 8, 144, 158
reference window, defining to measure ML system changes, 244
RegexTokenizer, 71
regression analysis, 122-127
    and classification, 118, 120, 125
    linear regression, 15, 83, 165
    logistic regression, 117, 120, 125
    multiple regression, 122
    multivariate regression, 122-124
    predictions, 121-126
    simple regression, 122
RegressionEvaluator, 133
remote API, PyTorch, 207
remote execution, PyTorch, 204, 204-208
remote procedure calls (RPCs), 173
    (see also RPC-based distributed training)
remote references (RRefs), PyTorch, 204, 208-210, 211
repartition function, 80
REPL (Read–Eval–Print Loop), 41
reproducibility, ML lifecycle, 46, 52
resilient distributed datasets (RDDs), 34, 37, 38, 158, 159
resource management, 21
REST API, 47, 236
RFormula selector, 97
ring all-reduce algorithm, 179
ring-reduce algorithm, 179
RobustScaler, 76

ROC (receiver operating characteristic) curve, 132
row filtering, 149, 150
RPC-based distributed training, 201, 203-212
    distributed optimizer, 204, 211
    remote execution, 204, 204-208
    RRefs, 204, 208-210
rpc_async, 206
rpc_sync, 206
RRefs (remote references), PyTorch, 204, 208-210, 211
rule-based distance metrics, 245
runs, recording with MLflow Tracking, 50, 51-52
runtime environment, deployment consideration, 235

S

Scala, 80
SCALAR PandasUDFType, 105
SCALAR_ITER PandasUDFType, 105
scatter functionality, 216
schemas, 34
    (see also preprocessing data)
    availability as dependent on file formats, 62
    creating Spark custom, 35-37
    extracted, 63
    handling mismatched data, 225
    inferred, 62
    Petastorm store, 157
    saving, 35
scikit-learn (sklearn) versus MLlib, 42
SDLC (software development lifecycle), 46
selector APIs, MLlib, 70, 97
semi-structured data, 62, 68
sequential computation, in deep learning, 21
Sequential function, 184
serialization of data, 103
setMaxIter function, 125
SGD (stochastic gradient descent), 200
shared memory model, 10
shared pointers, distributed, 208
shell commands, Spark support for, 41
shuffling data, 13, 108, 223
simple regression, 122
skewness in datasets, 85, 108
sliding window approach, testing data references, 244
small files problem, avoiding, 80

About the Author

Adi Polak is an open-source technologist who believes in communities and education and their ability to positively impact the world around us. She is passionate about building a better world through open collaboration and technological innovation. As a seasoned engineer and vice president of developer experience at Treeverse, Adi shapes the future of data and machine learning technologies for hands-on builders. She serves on multiple program committees and acts as an advisor for conferences like Data & AI Summit by Databricks, Current by Confluent, and Scale by the Bay, among others. Adi previously served as a senior manager for Azure at Microsoft, where she helped build advanced analytics systems and modern data architectures. Adi gained experience in machine learning by conducting research for IBM, Deutsche Telekom, and other Fortune 500 companies.

Colophon

The animal on the cover of *Scaling Machine Learning with Spark* is a South American electric eel (genus *Electrophorus*). There are three species in this genus, *E. voltai*, *E. varii*, and *E. electricus*, the best known of the three. Despite the name, they are not closely related to true eels but are rather in the same family as the knifefishes. They are all similar in body shape and color, with rounded heads and dark grayish-brown skin. They continue to grow throughout their lives, adding more vertebrae as they do, and they can reach lengths of six feet or more.

Electric eels inhabit rivers of the Amazon basin and the Guiana and Brazilian highlands. They live primarily in muddy river bottoms or swamps, and since these waters tend to be low in oxygen, electric eels have adapted to breathe air. They must surface to breathe roughly every 10 minutes, absorbing oxygen through special folds in their mouths, and they obtain almost 80 percent of their oxygen this way.

They have three specialized electric organs making up the majority of their bodies, and the cells that produce electric charges are modified from muscle cells. Electric eels can generate both weak and strong electric charges, which they use to deter predators and to locate and stun prey. The maximum discharge from the main electric organ varies from 600 volts to over 800 volts, with the total current reaching about 1 ampere.

Electric eels are considered species of least concern. Many of the animals on O'Reilly covers are endangered; all of them are important to the world.

The cover illustration is by Karen Montgomery, based on a black and white engraving from a loose plate, source unknown. The cover fonts are Gilroy Semibold and Guardian Sans. The text font is Adobe Minion Pro; the heading font is Adobe Myriad Condensed; and the code font is Dalton Maag's Ubuntu Mono.